T0013378

Praise for
Jesus, Day by Day

"*Jesus, Day by Day* is one of those devotionals that tempt one to read, in one sitting, not just today's devotion but tomorrow's and the next day's as well, in part because it provides fascinating insights into daily life in the ancient world. Kaselonis meditates deeply on seemingly minor details of biblical stories and opens our eyes to new ways in which we might apply the experiences of those who lived in the distant past to our own complicated, modern lives."

—Anne Morse, author of the novel *Bedford Falls*
and coauthor of several books with Chuck Colson

"God bless Sharon Kaselonis for her desire to encourage others to dig deeper into the Bible. If you are seeking to grow in your Christian walk, you will love *Jesus, Day by Day.*"

—Ray Comfort, author of *Jesus in Red*

"I believe the most important thing a Christian can do before the day gets started is spend time with our Savior. This book by Sharon Kaselonis is an excellent resource to help you do just that, as she walks you through the entire Bible in one year."

—Eddie Carswell, musical artist with NewSong Ministries
and cofounder of Winter Jam

"If you've longed to switch places with one of the disciples who walked with the resurrected Jesus on the road to Emmaus as 'he explained to them what was said in all the Scriptures concerning himself,' reading *Jesus, Day by Day* comes remarkably close. With seamless conversational engagement, Sharon Kaselonis presents truth after picture after prophecy of Jesus Christ found throughout the Old and New Testaments. While I treasure this book as an invaluable Bible study resource, each devotional entry is an encouragement and a delight to read and carry into the day. *Jesus, Day by Day* will enrich both mind and heart."

—Lori Benton, author of *Burning Sky, The King's Mercy,*
and other historical novels

Jesus, Day by Day

A One-Year, Through-the-Bible Devotional to Help You See Him on Every Page

SHARON KASELONIS

MULTNOMAH

Jesus, Day by Day

All Scripture quotations, unless otherwise indicated, are taken from the King James Version. Scripture quotations marked (ASV) are taken from the American Standard Version. Scripture quotations marked (AMP) are taken from the Amplified Bible. Copyright © 2015 by the Lockman Foundation. Used by permission. (www.Lockman.org). Scripture quotations marked (AMPC) are taken from the Amplified Bible Classic Edition. Copyright © 1954, 1958, 1962, 1964, 1965, 1987 by the Lockman Foundation. Used by permission. (www.Lockman.org). Scripture quotations marked (CSB) are taken from the Christian Standard Bible. Copyright © 2017 by Holman Bible Publishers. Used by permission. Christian Standard Bible®, and CSB® are federally registered trademarks of Holman Bible Publishers, all rights reserved. Scripture quotations marked (ESV) are taken from Holy Bible, English Standard Version, ESV® Text Edition® (2016), copyright © 2001 by Crossway Bibles, a publishing ministry of Good News Publishers. All rights reserved. Scripture quotations marked (NASB) are taken from the New American Standard Bible®. Copyright © 1960, 1962, 1963, 1968, 1971, 1972, 1973, 1975, 1977, 1995 by the Lockman Foundation. Used by permission. (www.Lockman.org). Scripture quotations marked (NET) are taken from the NET Bible®, copyright © 1996–2006 by Biblical Studies Press LLC, http://netbible.com. Used by permission. All rights reserved. Scriptures quotations marked (NIV) are taken from the Holy Bible, New International Version®, NIV®. Copyright © 1973, 1978, 1984 by Biblica Inc.® Used by permission. All rights reserved worldwide. Scripture quotations marked (NKJV) are taken from the New King James Version®. Copyright © 1982 by Thomas Nelson Inc. Used by permission. All rights reserved. Scripture quotations marked (NLT) are taken from the Holy Bible, New Living Translation, copyright © 1996, 2004, 2007, 2013, 2015 by Tyndale House Foundation. Used by permission of Tyndale House Publishers Inc., Carol Stream, Illinois 60188. All rights reserved. Scripture quotations marked (RSV) are taken from the Revised Standard Version of the Bible, copyright © 1952 [2nd edition, 1971] by the Division of Christian Education of the National Council of the Churches of Christ in the United States of America. Used by permission. All rights reserved. Scripture quotations marked (WBT) are taken from the Webster's Bible Translation, containing the Old and New Testaments, in the Common Version, with Amendments of the Language by Noah Webster, LLD, public domain, 1833. Scripture quotations marked (WEB) are taken from the World English Bible.

Hardcover ISBN 978-0-7352-9168-3
eBook ISBN 978-0-7352-9169-0

Cover design by Kelly L. Howard

Published in the United States by Multnomah, an imprint of Random House, a division of Penguin Random House LLC.

Multnomah® and its mountain colophon are registered trademarks of Penguin Random House LLC.

Library of Congress Cataloging-in-Publication Data
Names: Kaselonis, Sharon, author.
Title: Jesus, day by day : a one-year, through-the-Bible devotional to help you see Him on every page / Sharon Kaselonis.
Description: First Edition. | Colorado Springs : Multnomah, 2019.
Identifiers: LCCN 2018059364 | ISBN 9780735291683 (hardcover) | ISBN 9780735291690 (electronic)
Subjects: LCSH: Bible—Reading. | Bible—Meditations. | Devotional calendars.
Classification: LCC BS617 .K37 2019 | DDC 242/.2—dc23
LC record available at https://lccn.loc.gov/2018059364

Printed in the United States of America
2019—First Edition

10 9 8 7 6 5 4 3 2 1

To my three treasures:

Ray, my husband and joy of my life
Raymond, my wise son
Emily, my kind daughter and constant encouragement

I love you.

Beginning at Moses and all the prophets, he expounded unto them in all the scriptures the things concerning himself.

—*Luke 24:27*

Come and See Jesus

I remember it like it was yesterday. I sat on my bed, a typical 1980s teenager, my Bible laid out in front of me. An industrious kid with a hint of mischievousness, I wasn't older than eight when I started a "private school" for the neighborhood kids one summer. I even charged tuition! But there was a problem. I could barely read and hated trying. I'd been diagnosed with a plethora of learning disabilities, and my reading comprehension was dismal. I'd recently become aware of another big problem: my heart was full of sin.

I sat there on my bed that day with a decision to make: whether I would give my life fully to Christ or live for myself. I had one request and prayed, *Lord, I'll follow You. Just please let me read Your Word and understand it.* I opened up my Bible, and for the first time I understood what I was reading! Even more miraculous was the fact that I loved it.

Over time God began to transform my mind. Through Bible college, undergraduate school, law school, and into my law career, I considered God's Word my anchor, but I often meandered through devotions, wondering where to read. Then in 2001 I was introduced to the *One Year Chronological Bible.* This reading plan went through the entire Bible in one year and put the Scriptures in the order the events occurred. My devotions were revolutionized. I no longer wondered what to read; it was mapped out. I no longer got lost in the order of events; they were organized. I no longer left parts of God's Word unread; they were all part of the reading plan. Even if I skipped days or weeks, I could jump right back in and know where to pick up. And I was reading through the Bible each year! A glorious accomplishment.

What truly transformed my relationship with God's Word, however, was learning to read it not as a collection of stories or principles but as a single narrative focused on one vital truth. In Bible college I learned theology. In law school I learned to look at things analytically. Both are useful in life as well as when approaching the Scriptures. But what you and I need most of all is Jesus! If we approach life without Him, we will be lost. If we approach His Word without looking for Him, we will miss the point. Jesus said to the Pharisees, "You search the Scriptures because you think that in them you have eternal life; it is these that testify about Me" (John 5:39, NASB).

Jesus is the very essence of the Scriptures. The Old Testament points to Him, and the New Testament reveals Him. If we look for Him, we will find Him on every page and in every story. After all, He is the Word made flesh (John 1:14). As we approach His Word looking for Him, we find purpose to even those "boring" chapters in Leviticus. Seeing Jesus gives meaning to the Old Testament sacrifices, purpose in the rejection and heartache of Joseph, hope pictured in the sweet love story of Ruth and Boaz, and a reason for even the deepest sorrows in Job. Truly, Jesus Christ is the focal point of the Bible from the beginning to the end. He is our beloved hope.

The power of reading with this one vital truth in mind is what I'm excited to share with you in the pages that follow.

Let's Begin

This devotional follows a chronological reading plan, which means the Scripture readings are organized into the order that the events historically took place. If you read each of the assignments in these daily devotionals, in one year you will have read through the entire Bible!

These 365 daily readings are designed to help you

- create a pattern of looking for Jesus throughout the Scriptures
- develop a love for the Bible as you study the purpose of the Old Testament and how it correlates with the New Testament
- maintain interest throughout the year by highlighting prophecies of Jesus's birth, death, resurrection, and return

- grow in your love for Jesus as you read the testimonies of His saints and understand how God used their lives to foreshadow Christ

Your journey through the Bible will lead you from the perfect creation in Genesis to the perfect restoration in Revelation as you learn to recognize Jesus on every page.

Having read through the Bible using this format for nearly two decades, my love for Jesus Christ has deepened beyond words and my appreciation for His Word has grown exponentially. My desire is to share that with you. So let's begin!

In the Beginning

January 1

TODAY'S READING: Genesis 1–2

In the beginning God created. . . . And God said . . .
Genesis 1:1, 3

For those with eyes to see, Jesus's first appearance in the Bible is right here, at the very beginning. In the beginning God created. He created simply by speaking. God spoke and it was. In creation He revealed to us the power of His word and introduced us to His Son!

God said, "Let us make man in our image" (Gen. 1:26). Here we find the first reference to the Holy Trinity. Jesus is here in the "us." Jesus, God the Son, who holds the creator rights, has been from the beginning (Prov. 8:22–23; Isa. 43:13; Col. 1:17).

We can liken the Old Testament to a picture book that sketches out sweet shadows and presents powerful portraits of our Prince of Peace. We find Jesus revealed in its pages as the "wisdom of God" (1 Cor. 1:24), the "redeemer" (Job 19:25), "Immanuel" (Isa. 7:14), the "righteous Branch" of David (Jer. 23:5–6), and the "Prince of Peace" (Isa. 9:6). But the New Testament reveals the image of the invisible God who became flesh and lived among us:

> In the beginning was the Word, and the Word was with God, and the Word was God. . . . All things were made by him; and without him was not any thing made that was made. . . . And the Word was made flesh, and dwelt among us, (and we beheld his glory, the glory as of the only begotten of the Father,) full of grace and truth. (John 1:1, 3, 14)

Jesus—the Word made flesh, the creator, our lord and savior—is here in Genesis. He is here from the very beginning!

January
2

God's Remedy

TODAY'S READING: Genesis 3

> I will put enmity between thee and the woman, and between thy seed and her seed; it shall bruise thy head, and thou shalt bruise his heel. *Genesis 3:15*

Adam and Eve had everything anyone could ever dream of, but then they sinned. They rebelled against God. The Bible says that because of Adam's sin, all mankind was born into sin (Rom. 5:12). But God, who is rich in mercy, provided a remedy in the form of a redeemer who would take the punishment for sin—the sin of the whole world. That redeemer is promised right here in Genesis 3:15.

Jesus Christ is the seed of Eve, the one who would crush the head of the serpent. Because of Christ's atoning work through His death and resurrection, we are no longer under the curse of sin but are instead children of God. We are joint heirs with Christ, and our Enemy has been defeated!

God saw Adam and Eve in their exposed state of sin and divinely provided them coverings from a sacrifice (Gen. 3:21). Those animal skins pointed to God's ultimate sacrifice, His promised remedy—Jesus Christ.

God's grace covered Adam and Eve. This is good news for us, friend, because that same grace covers you and me. The blood of Jesus washes us clean. He covers our every sin, and we are clothed in Christ's righteousness (Rev. 19:8). So as you start a new day, no matter your situation, remember that God keeps His promises. He provided a redeemer who crushed the head of Satan, and that redeemer—your redeemer—lives! He is God's promised remedy.

His Story Written in History

January 3

TODAY'S READING: Genesis 4–5

This is the document containing the family records of Adam.
Genesis 5:1, CSB

We serve a God who breathes life into the mundane. Today's reading is a great example. In Genesis 5 we find the first genealogy, listing the descendants of Adam. What appears to be an insignificant list of names becomes a masterpiece of intent and design when read through the lens of the gospel. Consider the Hebrew meaning of the names listed in Genesis 5:3–29.

Name	Hebrew Meaning
Adam	Man[1]
Seth	Appointed[2]
Enos	Mortal[3]
Cainan	Possession or possesses[4]
Mahalaleel	Praise of God[5]
Jared	Descend or come down[6]
Enoch	Dedicated or to train[7]
Methuselah	Men or friends[8]
Lamech	Powerful[9]
Noah	Rest[10]

And so it reads . . .

Man, although *appointed mortal,* through God's grace *possesses the praise of God,* who is His Son, Jesus Christ (2 Pet. 1:17; Col. 2:9; Matt. 3:17; Heb. 1:3; 2:9; John 14:7–9; 17:24), who *descended* and *came down.* He was *dedicated to teach men* (Luke 4:23; Matt. 7:29; John 7:16), His *friends* (John 15:13–15), *powerful rest.*

You see, God is a God of details, and right here in the middle of a genealogy, He omnisciently orchestrates a glimpse of His plan of redemptive hope. God was writing a story throughout the generations that pointed to His Son.

Keep reading: 1 Chronicles 1:1–4

The Master Carpenter

TODAY'S READING: **Genesis 6–9**

> Come thou and all thy house into the ark; for thee have I seen righteous before me. *Genesis 7:1*

What a powerful picture of our salvation we find in the story of Noah's ark! God extended glorious grace to Noah by giving him a way to escape His righteous judgment on a wicked world. Noah, however, first had to pick up his hammer and do the job God called him to do.

> Noah did according unto all that the Lord commanded him. (Gen. 7:5)

Later in the Bible we read of another carpenter who finished the work God gave Him to do. Our precious Jesus is the master carpenter who took the nails meant for us and built a bridge to redemption.

> Having canceled out the certificate of debt consisting of decrees against us, which was hostile to us . . . He has taken it out of the way, having nailed it to the cross. (Col. 2:14, NASB)

By obeying God's plan and finishing the work God gave him, Noah escaped the judgment of the flood and was kept safe through the storm. Through Christ's obedience in finishing the work God gave Him, we, too, have escaped judgment.

> So by the obedience of one shall many be made righteous. (Rom. 5:19)

Dear reader, as you pick up whatever "hammer" or tool the Lord has put in your hand today, be faithful and obedient to do the work God has called you to for His glory. But remember, Christ has finished the ultimate work—the work of redemption. It is finished!

On Christ the Solid Rock I Stand

January 5

TODAY'S READING: Genesis 10:1–11:26

They said, Come, let us build us a city, and a tower, whose top may reach unto heaven, and let us make us a name; lest we be scattered abroad upon the face of the whole earth.
Genesis 11:4, ASV

In the Bible stones often signify God's unchanging truth (1 Cor. 10:4; Isa. 8:13–14; Rom. 9:33; Matt. 7:24), whereas bricks often represent human effort.[11] Bricks are crafted to replicate, replace, or provide an alternative to God's provision of stone, and therefore bricks represent a counterfeit.

The Tower of Babel provides a poignant look into our human nature and our propensity to build our own kingdoms using our own wisdom, ideas, and efforts, resulting in a false religion.[12] We humans tend to prefer to chart our own course and map our own way, but if our plans are not God's plans, then we're building with bricks instead of stone.

Humanity's stubborn determination to do our own thing apart from God's will always leads to confusion, or as we see in today's reading, babbling. These people in Genesis 11 started out with what seemed to be a reasonable plan. But they ended up confused and scattered. Sin nearly always looks like a great idea at first, but it inevitably leads to a mess of confusion.

There is a way that seems right to a man, but its end is the way of death. (Prov. 16:25, NKJV)

You and I are God's workmanship, living stones He is building up (1 Pet. 2:5). Rather than building with our own bricks for our own glory, let's determine today to yield to the work of the Holy Spirit, follow His plans, and walk in obedience to His Word. May our lives echo that old hymn: "On Christ, the solid Rock I stand"![13]

Keep reading: 1 Chronicles 1:5–27

January 6

Blameless

TODAY'S READING: Job 1–4

> Have you considered my servant Job? There is no one on earth like him; he is blameless and upright, a man who fears God and shuns evil. *Job 1:8,* NIV

Since we're reading through the Bible in chronological order (the order in which the events happened), we're leaving Genesis to spend several days in Job, one of the most ancient books of the Bible.[14] Biblical scholars believe that Job lived during the time of the patriarchs, specifically Isaac.[15]

Job is presented as a man of outstanding character, a prominent figure renowned for his wisdom and wealth, blessed by God. But Job's world was undone in a moment's time. He lost his family, his health, and his wealth, and he was shunned by his friends before God stepped in and restored his life. Some would say the main lesson of Job is that God can bring good out of the worst of situations (Rom. 8:28).

But even sweeter than when pain turns to profit, burdens to blessings, or a trial to a testimony is when Jesus is revealed in the midst of the difficulties. That is the treasure found in the book of Job. This book holds profound revelations and shadows of Jesus.

In the first chapter, for example, God refers to Job as "blameless and upright" (v. 1, NKJV). Yet we know that none are righteous, that "all have sinned and fall short of the glory of God" (Rom. 3:10, 23, NKJV). Herein lies the glorious grace and mercy of our Lord. Just as He declared His servant Job blameless and upright, so, too, He declares that over you.

You can stand before God in full confidence that your sins are forgiven, you are clothed in Christ's righteousness, and the blood of Jesus cleanses every spot and blemish (1 John 1:9; Eph. 5:27). Like Job, you have found favor with God. He declares you blameless and upright—all because of Jesus (Rom. 5:1).

What a Miracle

January 7

TODAY'S READING: **Job 5–9**

> He performs wonders that cannot be fathomed, miracles that cannot be counted. *Job 9:10,* NIV

Although Job did not know the name of Jesus, he *did* know of a promised redeemer (Job 19:25) and, inspired by the Holy Spirit, spoke of things to come. Job could look at creation and see that God performed wonders. But he could not fully understand how God would use his words to point to Jesus Christ (7:17–21; 9:2, 30–31). Job spoke without knowing that God Himself would become a man and fulfill what Job had written (9:8–10, 33–34).

The conversation between Job and his somewhat misguided friends is full of pictures that point to Jesus. Let's look at just a few.

> He sets on high those who are lowly, and those who mourn are lifted to safety. (Job 5:11, NKJV)

Only Jesus can set the lowly sinner on high (Luke 19:10). He comforts those who mourn (Matt. 5:4), and we are safe under the tender care of our Good Shepherd (John 10:14, 28–29).

> He bruises, but He binds up; He wounds, but His hands make whole. (Job 5:18, NKJV)

Jesus bruised that serpent Satan's head as He took our sins upon Himself (Gen. 3:15; Col. 2:15). He was willingly "wounded for our transgressions" and "bruised for our iniquities" (Isa. 53:5). His hands brought healing to the sick (Luke 4:18), and He makes us whole (Col. 2:10).

> Why then do You not pardon my transgression, and take away my iniquity? (Job 7:21, NKJV)

Indeed, Jesus has pardoned our transgressions, removed our iniquity, and declared us righteous (John 1:29; Rom. 3:24–26). Even in the midst of Job-like trials, Jesus shows you His love by His wounds. He laid down His life, forgiving all your sins and making you whole. What a miracle!

See and Hear

TODAY'S READING: Job 10–14

Lo, mine eye hath seen all this, mine ear hath heard and understood it. *Job 13:1*

Jesus came to bind up the brokenhearted, to give us joy for our sadness, to bear our iniquities, and to carry our sin. So it makes perfect sense that, here in the book of Job, in the midst of great loss, heartache, and suffering, we find hope and reassurance of redemption—a foreshadowing of our Savior.

Job's eyes had not seen exactly how God would keep His promises, and he had not heard all the details of how it would be accomplished, but in his heart he understood it (Job 13:1). Here are just a few of Job's observations that point to Jesus:

Who can bring a clean thing out of an unclean? (14:4)

Jesus literally made the unclean clean. He touched the leper and said, "Be thou clean" (Matt. 8:3). And He cleansed each of us from sin (Eph. 2:1–6).

Surely then you will count my steps but not keep track of my sin. (Job 14:16, NIV)

Jesus destroyed the record of our sins and remembers them no more (Col. 2:14; Heb. 10:17; 1 John 1:9).

My transgression would be sealed up in a bag, and you would cover over my iniquity. (Job 14:17, ESV)

Jesus bore our iniquities. His forgiveness covers our sins (Rom. 4:7).

Your eyes may not yet see how God intends to keep His promises, and your ears may not have heard the details yet, but, like Job, you can let the longings of your heart point you to Jesus Christ. When your heart longs for forgiveness, look to Jesus. He forgives. When you need a fresh start, look to Jesus. He offers new beginnings. Open your eyes to see Jesus, open your ears to hear His Word, and open your heart to trust His goodness.

Jesus, Your Advocate and Friend

January 9

TODAY'S READING: **Job 15–18**

My witness is in heaven, and my record is on high. *Job 16:19*

Truly, we do have a witness in heaven! Jesus Christ, our great high priest, stands on high as our defender, friend, and advocate (Heb. 7:25; 1 John 2:1). Just as Job spoke of, our witness in heaven has blotted out every transgression recorded against us and has written our name in the Lamb's Book of Life.

As we've seen in our Bible readings over the past few days, the book of Job is packed with pictures and prophecies, types and shadows of Jesus. Job's sufferings foreshadowed those of Christ. In chapter 16 we find Job in the depths of despair, grappling with his circumstances and God's purposes for his suffering. In comparison, we look to the Gospels and see Jesus shouldering our deepest despair and bearing the suffering for our sin (Phil. 2:6–11).

We see Job buffeted and ridiculed by his friends. In the Gospels we see Jesus betrayed by His disciple Judas, denied by His friend Peter, and ridiculed and mocked by those nailing Him to the cross.

We also find Job pleading for an advocate. In the Gospels we find our advocate, Jesus Christ, who even now is at the right hand of God making intercession for you and me.

> It is Christ that died, yea rather, that is risen again, who is even at the right hand of God, who also maketh intercession for us. (Rom. 8:34)

Without Christ shouldering our burden, we would be hopeless in this fallen world—but instead, we have all the hope in the world. Whatever your trial, big or small, you have an advocate, a defender, who can relate to your every need. He has offered to carry your burdens, to bear your sin, and to be your friend.

January 10 Knowledge That Leads to Hope

TODAY'S READING: Job 19–21

I know that my Redeemer lives,
and that in the end he will stand upon the earth. . . .
yet in my flesh I will see God;
I myself will see him
with my own eyes. *Job 19:25–27,* NIV

Our redeemer lives, and in the end we will see Him. What hope we find in Job's declaration! It's interesting to note that leading up to those confident words, Job described his trouble as a path shrouded in darkness with no escape or alternate way around (19:8–9). Have you ever felt trapped, with trouble on every side? Job expressed the depth of his heartache and confusion at the injustice he faced. Yet he ended his questions and complaints with a faith-filled declaration that captures the theme of the entire Bible: the hope of redemption through Jesus.

Job was basically saying, "None of this makes sense. This is utterly unfair and unjust. But I know this story has a happy ending—in the end I will see Him face to face."

The redemption Job anticipated foreshadowed the very real hope to come through Jesus Christ.

Regardless of today's circumstances, we, like Job, know how our story ends. Our redeemer promises to see us through! He has promised to take us from glory to greater glory (2 Cor. 3:16–18) and to present us faultless before the presence of His glory with great joy (Jude 24–25).

Whatever trial you face today, God's plans are good and His promises are steadfast. He is weaving His story into every situation you face. He promises to save, and, as for Job, your deliverance draws nigh. Lift your eyes and look to Jesus. Your redeemer lives and in the end you will see Him! This is our everlasting hope. You see, hope has a name and His name is Jesus. He lives, and knowing Him leads to great hope.

Be Still

TODAY'S READING: **Job 22–26**

He stirs up the sea with His power, and by His understanding
He breaks up the storm. *Job 26:12,* NKJV

When confusion rages and difficult situations batter our lives, it is His understanding that breaks up the storms. To look into God's Word, to see Jesus and gain understanding, is to experience what the disciples did when Jesus calmed the wind and the waves by simply speaking, "Peace, be still" (Mark 4:35–41).

The entire Bible, including the book of Job, points our eyes toward Jesus Christ. Through Him we have been given all things (2 Pet. 1:3; Col. 2:10), and in Him dwells the fullness of God (Col. 2:9). Jesus is mightier than the storms we face. Only in Him do we find understanding and peace.

The LORD on high is mightier than the noise of many waters,
yea, than the mighty waves of the sea. (Ps. 93:4)

Job knew God was faithful, but he did not know how his personal story would end. He knew God promised salvation through a redeemer, but he could not see how exactly the Lord would accomplish such a thing. As New Testament believers, we have the privilege of looking back and seeing how God's plan unfolded.

Job longed to see his redeemer, to know His name and to experience fellowship with Him (Job 23:3). You already know His name, the name above all names—Jesus. He lives in you and fellowships with you. You have access into His presence at any moment you choose (Heb. 4:16).

This is the understanding that will break up your storms and bring calm in the midst of a raging sea. Remember, He can calm your storms by simply saying, "Be still." But even if He doesn't, keep your eyes on Him. That's how you will find understanding and purpose in your storms.

January 12

Wisdom's Wealth

TODAY'S READING: Job 27–29

> Where shall wisdom be found? . . . The gold and the crystal cannot equal it. *Job 28:12, 17*

The mining business has been around since the time of Job (Job 28:1–6). It takes great determination to uncover the earth's treasures, and to do so is risky. But for many, the hazards of tunneling through mountains is worth the lure of wealth.

Job reminds us of wealth far more valuable than anything the earth contains (28:17). That wealth is wisdom. And we know wisdom, God's wisdom, has a name—His name is Jesus (1 Cor. 1:24). Jesus is the Word of God; He is wisdom personified (John 1:14).

Jesus is the wisdom Job spoke of.

> He looked at wisdom and appraised it; he confirmed it and tested it. (28:27, NIV)

Indeed, the wisdom of God, Jesus Christ, was confirmed by the Father (Matt. 3:17; 17:5); He was tested (Matt. 4:1–11; Luke 22:42) and found to be perfect.

> Though he were a Son, yet learned he obedience by the things which he suffered; and being made perfect, he became the author of eternal salvation unto all them that obey him. (Heb. 5:8–9)

The worth of God's wisdom is incomprehensible, for Wisdom Himself redeemed us with a price more costly than gold (1 Pet. 1:18–20). As Matthew Henry noted, "There is more true knowledge, satisfaction, and happiness, in sound divinity, which shows us the way to the joys of heaven."[16]

Jesus is wisdom—and the wealth He gives has great worth!

The One Who Answers

January 13

TODAY'S READING: Job 30–31

Oh that one would hear me! behold, my desire is, that the Almighty would answer me, and that mine adversary had written a book. Surely I would take it upon my shoulder, and bind it as a crown to me. *Job 31:35–36*

Perhaps you can relate to Job's bewilderment. He didn't understand why God would allow such dread to fall upon him, and he was frustrated at the injustice of his situation. What Job could not see, however, was God weaving a masterpiece of divine revelation through his desperate plea. Job's heart cry was describing what Jesus would do for us.

Job longed for the One who would hear and answer. Jesus hears our every cry and answers when we call (Heb. 4:16; 13:5).

Job spoke of a written account of his shortcomings, but God's Word tells us that the record detailing our faults was nailed to the cross at Calvary (Col. 2:14) and our Adversary, who brings accusations against us, has been defeated (Rev. 12:10).

In essence, Job shamelessly declared, "I could shoulder any allegation and hold my head high." Unlike Job, we know we cannot shoulder our shame. But we have a Savior who carries the weight of the world on His shoulders. He bore our iniquities as He carried the cross. The crown of thorns placed on His head lifts our heads from shame. The weight of our sin rests on Him. He is our defense.

The longings expressed by Job remind us that God has given us an answer. That answer is the one who shouldered our guilt, the one who wore a crown of thorns, the one who lifts our heads: Jesus.

January 14

Your Ransom Is Paid

TODAY'S READING: Job 32–34

> He is gracious unto him, and saith, Deliver him from going down to the pit: I have found a ransom. *Job 33:24*

In addition to Job's three friends Eliphaz, Bildad, and Zophar (Job 2:11), a fourth companion was a young man named Elihu who had kept quiet due to his age (32:4–7). However, now he offered his elders some wisdom he felt they lacked (32:3; 33:6).

Even so, God in His abundant grace used imperfect, arrogant Elihu to powerfully prophesy of the coming redeemer (33:24), the one who would deliver us from the pit and provide our ransom—Jesus.

Hundreds of years later, the psalmist would echo this same sentiment as he declared,

> The redemption of their souls is costly, . . . that he should continue to live eternally, and not see the Pit. (49:8–9, NKJV)

The debt for sin was too great for us to pay. But God, who loves us, sent His only Son to bear the full cost. Christ paid the price with His own blood. Truly, as Elihu foretold, He is gracious and has delivered us.

> You were not redeemed with corruptible things, like silver or gold . . . but with the precious blood of Christ, as of a lamb without blemish and without spot. (1 Pet. 1:18–19, NKJV)

We live in a fallen world, where seasons of suffering are a result of the curse. But even when our days seem dim, we have the assurance that we've been saved from going down into the pit. Because Jesus graciously paid the ransom to rescue us from sin and eternal death (Matt. 20:28; Rom. 3:24), we are on our way to live with Him in glory!

Where Is God My Maker?

January 15

TODAY'S READING: Job 35–37

None saith, Where is God my maker . . . *Job 35:10*

In his bold discourse, when Elihu pointed out that no one asks where God is, he meant everyone complains about troubles but no one repents of sin. Perhaps this is true in part. We find a similar statement in Romans:

> There is none righteous. . . . There is none that seeketh after God. (3:10–11)

Regardless of Elihu's faulty conclusions, his statement here deserves consideration. Many of us may have asked, "Lord, where are You?" Such a reasonable question. To seek the Lord amid hardship is to seek hope. And that hope has a name. His name is Jesus.

You see, when you find yourself asking where God is, you are looking for Jesus! In his questions Elihu unknowingly spoke of Jesus as he asked, "Who teaches more to us . . . and makes us wiser?" (Job 35:11, NIV). Jesus is the master teacher, and in Him are hidden "the treasures of wisdom and knowledge" (Col. 2:3).

Elihu exclaimed that God reveals man's transgressions to him and commands him to "return from iniquity" (Job 36:9–10, 12). Jesus declared that He came to call sinners to salvation through repentance (Matt. 4:17; 12:41). Elihu described the roaring power of the voice of the Almighty (Job 37:3–5). John the Revelator tells us repeatedly that Jesus's voice is like the sound "of many waters" (Rev. 1:15; 14:2; 19:6).

Let's never forget that Jesus and the Father are one. So when you wonder where your Maker is, just open your Bible and you'll find Him—even here in Elihu's lecture to Job.

January 16 The Gates of Hell

TODAY'S READING: Job 38–39

Have the gates of death been opened unto thee? *Job 38:17*

We've reached the end of the conversation between Job and his friends, the point at which God responds to Job's questions. God's answer turns Job's attention directly away from his situation and toward God's character: His omniscience, His majesty, His power, and His tender mercies.

> Who hath put wisdom in the inward parts? or who hath given understanding to the heart? . . . Who provideth for the raven his food? when his young ones cry unto God . . . (38:36, 41)

But God's greatest answer to Job is found in God's greatest gift: His Son, Jesus.

> Have the gates of death been opened unto thee? or hast thou seen the doors of the shadow of death? (v. 17)

In God's rhetorical question we recognize Jesus as the only one of whom this could truly be said. Jesus died on the cross, tasting death for us (John 19:30; Heb. 2:9), He descended into "the deep" or "lower parts of the earth" (Rom. 10:7; Eph. 4:9), where He preached to those held captive (1 Pet. 3:19), and as He ascended into heaven as a triumphant conqueror, He "led captivity captive" (Eph. 4:8; Ps. 68:18).

Indeed we see Jesus in Job 38. He is the one who has had the gates of death opened unto Him and yet returned to life, the one who has seen the doors of the shadow of death—and destroyed its power! For Jesus Himself declared,

> I am he that liveth, and was dead; and, behold, I am alive for evermore . . . and have the keys of hell and of death. (Rev. 1:18)

Because of His victory, you and I can now boldly proclaim, "O death, where is thy sting? O grave, where is thy victory?" (1 Cor. 15:55).

Beauty for Ashes

TODAY'S READING: Job 40–42

He had also . . . three daughters. *Job 42:13*

At the end of Job's suffering, God gave him three daughters, in whom we find a tender portrait of Jesus, reminding us of His caring provision and sweet restoration. In a description that could be taken from a fairy tale, we're told that "in all the land there were no women so beautiful as Job's daughters" (42:15, ESV). God gave Job beauty out of ashes (Isa. 61:3). We don't know much about these women, but in their names we find a picture of Jesus that rivals their physical beauty.[17]

Jemima means "daylight."[18] Her name reminds us that through the restorative work of Christ we see the light (Matt. 4:16). Jesus is the light of the world, the "bright and morning star" (John 8:12; Rev. 22:16).

Kezia means "cassia," which was a sweet spice.[19] In the New Testament we find three women who came to anoint Jesus's body with sweet spices but found the tomb empty (Mark 16:1). Both in Kezia's life and in Jesus's resurrection, we are reminded of who holds the power of life and death.

Then there was Kerenhappuch, whose name means "horn of beauty."[20] Our hearts echo Psalm 27 as we desire to "gaze upon the beauty of the LORD" (v. 4, NIV). Truly, Jesus is the most beautiful Lord of lords and the "horn of salvation for us" (Luke 1:69).

Whatever difficulties we face today, let's remember the treasure found in the book of Job, a sweet picture of Jesus, our bright and morning star, our risen Lord who makes the bitter sweet, our beautiful restorer of life—our salvation.

January 18

Our Great High Priest

TODAY'S READING: Genesis 11:27–14:24

Melchizedek king of Salem brought forth bread and wine: and he was the priest of the most high God. *Genesis 14:18*

Yesterday we finished reading through Job, so now we are back in Genesis, where we first meet Abram, later called Abraham. In Genesis 14, on his way home from war, Abram meets the priest Melchizedek. Bible scholars have debated for centuries the identity of this mysterious priest. But since we know that Jesus is the very essence of the Scriptures, we can be certain that the priest Melchizedek points to our great high priest, Jesus. Let's look at a few notable connections between the two.

- Melchizedek was both a king and priest (14:18). Jesus is the King of kings and our great high priest (Heb. 10:12–14).
- Melchizedek was king of Salem, which translates as "peace."[21] Jesus is the prince of peace (Isa. 9:6; Eph. 2:13–18).
- Melchizedek was without father or mother, "having neither beginning of days, nor end of life" (Heb. 7:3). Jesus, born of a virgin, is God made flesh. He reigns eternal and His kingdom has no end (Matt. 1:18–25; Luke 1:33).
- Melchizedek, as "priest of the most high God," met Abram after battle, giving him bread and drink to refresh him and a blessing to reassure him (Gen. 14:18–19). Jesus, our great high priest, has offered us His body as the bread of life and His blood as the cup of the new covenant that brings the everlasting blessing of eternal life (Luke 22:19).
- Melchizedek proclaimed Abram victorious (Gen. 14:19–20). Jesus declares us victorious because of the Cross (1 Cor. 15:57).

After a careful comparison it's hard to conclude that Melchizedek was any other than Jesus Himself. Such an appearance in the Old Testament is called a Christophany, and in this Christophany we see Jesus, our great high priest, who blesses us, provides refreshment, and is worthy of our praise and honor. As we return home from our daily battles in this world, may we, like Abram, be refreshed by our great high priest.

Sealed in Blood

TODAY'S READING: **Genesis 15–18**

The LORD made a covenant with Abram. *Genesis 15:18*

God established His covenant with Abram and promised to bless him and give him a son, by whom "all the families of the earth shall be blessed" (Gen. 12:3, NKJV). Sometime later, God confirmed His covenant and reassured Abram (13:14–18). But here in Genesis 15, utilizing a ritual Abram was accustomed to, God physically demonstrated His promise. Each aspect of this holy moment between God and Abram pointed to the very purpose of God's covenant—Jesus Himself.

God told Abram to "take" certain animals. Abram, knowing what to do, split the sacrificial animals, took the parts, and created an aisle, a walkway between them (vv. 9–10).

Jesus, the lamb of God, was sacrificed for the sins of the world. Through the blood of Jesus, a way has been made to the Father (Heb. 9:13–10:18). Fulfilling the Old Testament, Jesus established the New Covenant when He broke the bread and said, "This is my body which is given for you" (Luke 22:19).

This covenant with Abram represented the deadly consequences of breaking the commitment. But God's covenant with Abram was not a mutually binding agreement. This covenant would rely solely on God's faithfulness, not Abram's. Hence, God caused "a deep sleep" to fall upon Abram, after which God and God alone passed through the binding aisle of agreement (Gen. 15:12–17).

God kept His covenant, and He blessed all the families of the earth when Jesus, the seed of Abraham, was sent to shed His blood for the remission of sin (Gal. 3:16). Through the New Covenant we are sealed in the blood of Jesus, God's perfect fulfillment of all He has promised.

January 20

A Merciful Rescue

TODAY'S READING: Genesis 19–21

> The LORD being merciful unto him . . . brought him forth, and set him without the city. *Genesis 19:16*

Today's reading is full of examples of God's goodness, justice, and faithfulness despite our lack of all those things. In the account of Sodom and Gomorrah, we see God's righteous wrath against sin and are reminded to heed His call to run from it and not look back. Abraham's interaction with Abimelech gives us insight into how his lack of trust in God led to manipulation and deceitfulness. Doesn't this remind you of Abraham's "helping God out" with Hagar? How often do we, like Abraham, lose sight of God's promises and question His goodness? The result is a convoluted plan full of our own messy efforts and unfortunate, unnecessary consequences.

However, these chapters full of human failure culminate in a crescendo of praise as the long-awaited child of promise is born! What a wonderful picture of God's own promised Son, Jesus. God promised Abraham a son, by whom He would bring forth a nation, and God promised all mankind His Son, by whom He would redeem the world.

> God sent forth his Son, made of a woman, made under the law, to redeem them that were under the law. (Gal. 4:4–5)

God never leaves His creation without hope! Regardless of past wrongs, failures, or shortcomings, your sins are forgiven through the precious blood of Christ. Truly, glory to God for His faithful, loving provision!

Keep reading: Genesis 25:12–18; 1 Chronicles 1:28–31

Behold the Lamb

January 21

TODAY'S READING: Genesis 22–24

My son, God will provide himself a lamb. *Genesis 22:8*

We've seen Jesus revealed in Scripture from the beginning—God's Word spoken in Genesis 1:1, the promise of a redeemer in Genesis 3:15, and throughout the book of Job. One of the most powerful foreshadowings of the Savior is found in Genesis 22. Here we see Abraham willing to offer Isaac, his son, as a sacrifice. What a precious picture of God, our heavenly Father, willingly offering Jesus Christ, His Son, on the cross.

God had no intention of allowing Abraham to sacrifice Isaac (Deut. 12:31; 18:10), but He used Abraham's obedience to paint a portrait of the ultimate sacrifice.

God told Abraham to take Isaac up to a mountain to be offered to God. Jesus was later offered on Calvary as the perfect sacrifice (Luke 23:33). Isaac carried the wood for the sacrifice. Jesus carried His cross to Golgotha, where He would be sacrificed (John 19:17). Isaac was obedient to the point of death. Jesus was obedient as He died for the sins of the world (Phil. 2:8). Isaac was spared as God provided a ram in the thicket. Jesus spared us as He wore a crown of thorns (John 19:2). Isaac returned home alive and unharmed. Jesus rose victorious from the grave and is coming again to take us to our heavenly home (1 Thess. 4:14–16).

Just as Abraham declared in faith, "God will provide himself a lamb," God has provided Jesus, the perfect sacrifice. Behold the Lamb, God's Son, who takes away our sin.

January 22

I Will Bless Thee

TODAY'S READING: Genesis 25–26

> I am the God of Abraham thy father: fear not, for I am with thee, and will bless thee. *Genesis 26:24*

We belong to a God who hears prayers, gives gifts, opens the barren womb, tells of things to come, instructs, guides, intervenes, frustrates the ways of the wicked, delivers His people from trouble, blesses despite our failures, gives water in the desert and favor to the righteous, reassures the doubting heart, and gives visions and dreams in the night—and all these are demonstrated in today's reading!

As Isaac contemplated his options for dealing with the threat of famine, God met him.

> The LORD appeared unto him, and said, Go not down into Egypt; dwell in the land which I shall tell thee of . . . and I will be with thee, and will bless thee. (Gen. 26:2–3)

In the Scriptures Egypt is often a picture of the world and/or "worldliness"[22] (Gen. 12:10; Num. 11:5; 14:3; Isa. 31:1)—its ways, ideas, opinions, economy, and culture. God essentially told Isaac, "Don't go there to satisfy your hunger, your flesh" (Gen. 26:2). God gives us the same instructions.

> All that is in the world, the lust of the flesh, and the lust of the eyes, and the pride of life, is not of the Father, but is of the world. (1 John 2:16)

Like Isaac, if you find yourself facing famine and are hungry and thirsty, listen to what Jesus says to you:

> I am the bread of life: he that cometh to me shall never hunger; and he that believeth on me shall never thirst. (John 6:35)

Only Jesus can satisfy what your hungry heart and thirsty soul are craving. Only in Him can you find life-sustaining, soul-satisfying truth.

Keep reading: 1 Chronicles 1:32–34

A Treasured Inheritance

January 23

TODAY'S READING: Genesis 27:1–28:9

Your brother came with deceit and has taken away your blessing. *Genesis 27:35*, NKJV

Although Jacob's deception seems to be the focal point in Genesis 27, Esau's role in these scenes offers a great lesson to be gleaned. The Bible tells us that Esau despised his birthright and traded it for a bowl of soup (Gen. 25:34). Although Jacob certainly schemed and used his trickery here, Esau's attitude from the beginning paved the way to his demise.

I find this vignette of Esau fascinating because it gives us a pattern, a poignant picture of the flesh to be wary of in our own lives (Heb. 12:16–17). Esau's carnal outlook began with the condition of his heart. He was regretful rather than repentant. He didn't treasure his birthright, the status and position he held as the firstborn son, but traded it for temporary, fleshly satisfaction.

As believers in Jesus Christ, we have a status to be treasured, held dear, and esteemed. Through the blood of Jesus, we who were once far off have been born again and brought into God's family (1 Pet. 1:23; Eph. 2:13; Titus 3:7) and have been given an inheritance that is everlasting, incorruptible, and doesn't fade away (1 Pet. 1:4). This is a position to be treasured.

Dear Christian, don't despise the gift of new life (2 Cor. 5:17), a clean record (Col. 2:14), the miracle of being born again. Don't set aside the blessing in exchange for temporary, fleshly satisfaction!

Proverbs 4:23 tells us, "Keep your heart with all diligence, for out of it spring the issues of life" (NKJV). Let's remain watchful so we won't follow Esau's tragic example. Instead, let's obey Jesus and store up our treasures in heaven so our hearts will be there also (Matt. 6:19–21). Treasure your new life in Christ, your birthright, and your inheritance as a child of the King.

Keep reading: Genesis 36:1–43; 1 Chronicles 1:35–54

January 24

Stairway to Heaven

TODAY'S READING: Genesis 28:10–30:43

Behold, I am with you and will keep you wherever you go . . . for I will not leave you until I have done what I have spoken to you. *Genesis 28:15,* NKJV

What a wonder it is that God Most High, our creator, meets with us! It's true that He answers when we call, but what amazes me is that He pursues us and initiates a relationship before we even recognize Him as God.

> God commendeth his love toward us, in that, while we were yet sinners, Christ died for us. (Rom. 5:8)

Jacob was fleeing a precarious situation he had created for himself by stealing his brother's blessing and inheritance. Jacob found himself traveling through an unfamiliar land and sleeping with a rock as a pillow. What a helpful reminder that our own self-willed, manipulative efforts lead us to uncomfortable situations, strained relationships, and sleepless nights.

But here is where we can give all glory to God because He is the great deliverer. He calls us and leads us in the way of life (Prov. 12:28). God saw Jacob in his distress and gave him a dream. Jacob saw a stairway to heaven and heard God's promises of blessing.

We were on a dangerous journey (Eph. 2:2), on a path of destruction (Matt. 7:13), but God called us by name and revealed a way to heaven through the Cross of Jesus Christ (Col. 1:20), "whereby are given unto us exceeding great and precious promises" (2 Pet. 1:4).

Jesus is the fulfillment of the ladder that Jacob saw in his dream (John 1:51). Through the blood of Christ, we have access to the very presence of God (Heb. 10:12–19). Before, we had no way of measuring up, but—praise the Lord—Jesus has lifted us up.

If today, like Jacob, you find yourself running from a situation and enduring sleepless nights, consider the Cross. It's your stairway to heaven, the sign of God's love for you and His presence with you.

Battle of Wills

January 25

TODAY'S READING: Genesis 31–32

There wrestled a man with him until the breaking of the day.
Genesis 32:24

God had given Jacob a dream (Gen. 28:12) and confirmed that His covenant with Abraham applied to Jacob (vv. 13–15). God promised to bless Jacob, to multiply his descendants, to give him a vast land, to be with him, and to never leave him. Jacob vowed that if God would help him and fix his family's conflict, then the Lord would be his God (vv. 20–21). God did help Jacob. God blessed the work of his hands and prospered Jacob. But it wasn't until some twenty years later that Jacob wrestled with God, the preincarnate Lord Jesus Himself, and finally submitted to His lordship.[23]

Prior to this, Jacob always referred to the Lord as the "God of my father" (32:9), indicating a distant relationship. Afterward, for the first time, Jacob called God his God (33:20; 35:3), revealing a personal experience and relationship. This was a battle of the wills. After wrestling with God all night, the "crooked heel-catcher" Jacob was given a new name—Israel, signifying "one who has power with God" (32:28).[24] God's touch changed the way Jacob walked (vv. 31–32), and here, in this battle of wills, "God claimed his life."[25]

This scene previews the believer's rebirth and sanctification in Christ. Jesus will give us a new name (Rev. 2:17; 3:12). Because of Jesus we have power, or favor, with God. Like Jacob, we are given great and precious promises. But Jesus desires to touch us and, like Jacob, change our walk. Have you encountered Jesus in a wrestling match over your will? Through the wrestling and submission, you will experience consecration and sanctification—and fully embrace His lordship.

January 26 Go to Bethel

TODAY'S READING: Genesis 33–36

Arise, go up to Bethel. *Genesis 35:1*

Jacob found himself battered by life's circumstances. He faced conflict with his brother Esau, encountered trouble with his children, and found himself at odds with neighboring nations. But God, who is rich in mercy, gave Jacob direction in the midst of life's difficulties.

> Arise, go up to Bethel and dwell there. Make an altar there to the God who appeared to you when you fled from your brother Esau. (Gen. 35:1, ESV)

The name Bethel means "house of God."[26] God told Jacob to return to Bethel, where he first encountered God, and worship. It was at Bethel where God had given Jacob a dream of angels ascending and descending a ladder. Centuries later in a conversation with Nathanael, Jesus referred back to Jacob's dream.

> He saith unto him, Verily, verily, I say unto you, Hereafter ye shall see heaven open, and the angels of God ascending and descending upon the Son of man. (John 1:51)

Nathanael was among the witnesses to Jesus's atoning sacrifice through which He connected heaven to earth (Eph. 2:18).

> Brothers, . . . we have confidence to enter the holy places by the blood of Jesus, by the new and living way that he opened for us through the curtain, that is, through his flesh. (Heb. 10:19–20, ESV)

When discouragement threatens to dim the truth of God's goodness, follow Jacob in returning to a place of worship. Set your eyes on Jesus. He is the proof of God's love and our way to the Father. Through His blood, we can enter God's presence, worship Him, and be refreshed.

Keep reading: 1 Chronicles 2:1–2

Portrait of Redemption

January 27

TODAY'S READING: Genesis 37–39

The patriarchs, moved with envy, sold Joseph into Egypt: but God was with him. *Acts 7:9*

It has been said that Joseph is "the most perfect type of Christ in the Old Testament"[27]—each chapter of his life reflected God's story of redemption, His plan to redeem the hardships Joseph faced by giving them a purpose beyond Joseph's wildest imagination. Like a skilled artist, God chose His instrument and painted a detailed picture of His beloved Son who would come centuries later.

Consider just a few of the details of Genesis 37:

- Joseph was his father's beloved son (v. 3). Jesus was God's beloved Son (Matt. 3:17; John 3:16).
- Joseph's father sent him to Shechem (which means "shoulder"),[28] a place of toil and trouble (Gen. 37:14). Jesus was sent to this world, a place of toil and trouble, to shoulder our sin (John 1:14).
- Joseph went to his own family (his brothers), and they did not receive him (Gen. 37:19–20). Jesus was sent to His own, and they did not receive Him (John 1:10–11).
- Joseph's brothers were jealous and conspired against him (Gen. 37:20). The Pharisees were jealous of Jesus and conspired against Him (Matt. 12:14).
- Joseph was thrown into a well and later lifted out (Gen. 37:22, 28). Jesus was thrown into a grave but rose again (1 Cor. 15:3–4).
- Joseph was sold for silver (Gen. 37:28). Jesus was sold for silver (Matt. 26:14–15).
- Joseph's coat was ruined, soaked in blood (Gen. 37:31). They cast lots for Jesus's garment as He was crucified (Matt. 27:35).

While Joseph had no way of knowing how his circumstances reflected a greater story, we have the privilege of an eternal perspective that shows his life was and is all about Jesus!

January 28

Fruitful Affliction

TODAY'S READING: Genesis 40–41

God hath caused me to be fruitful in the land of my affliction.
Genesis 41:52

Joseph's choice of words here challenges my thinking: "God hath caused me to be fruitful in the land of my affliction" (Gen. 41:52). Joseph did not praise the Lord for delivering him from the land of affliction but for the fruit that came from it. In the midst of many difficult seasons, he remained convinced that God's plans were being accomplished.

We often ask the Lord to deliver us from hardship and disappointment, but are we watching for the fruit God desires to bring out of those very situations?

Consider how Jesus Himself prayed as He faced the Cross: "Father, if thou be willing, remove this cup from me: nevertheless not my will, but thine, be done" (Luke 22:42). He asked God to change His situation, yet He surrendered in view of the fruit His suffering would bring.

> Looking unto Jesus the author and finisher of our faith; who for the joy that was set before him endured the cross, despising the shame. (Heb. 12:2)

We can look at the Cross and Jesus's willingness to endure it and know that God's plans are good, despite any temporal circumstances. Jesus endured the ultimate affliction as He bore the sins of the world.

> Being confident of this very thing, that he which hath begun a good work in you will perform it until the day of Jesus Christ. (Phil. 1:6)

God is working for us, in us, and—by His grace—through us. God used Joseph's life and hardships to point to Jesus, and He wants to do the same in your life. Will you let the Lord redeem the details of your story to give His story the glory? Through Jesus's blood we can be fruitful, even in the land of our affliction.

The Unrecognized Savior

January 29

TODAY'S READING: Genesis 42–44

Joseph knew his brethren, but they knew not him.
Genesis 42:8

After years in prison Joseph again found favor with Pharaoh and was promoted to second in command of Egypt. He finally began to see how God might use his circumstances to save his entire family. He must have been comforted at the realization of good coming from his bad experiences. But can you imagine his joy if Joseph had known how God would use his life to point to His own Son, Jesus?

When famine drove Joseph's brothers to Egypt in search of food, they stood before the very brother they had betrayed—but they didn't recognize him. Joseph had the power to save them, yet they failed to see him as their brother.

So, too, Jesus came to His own, but His own did not receive Him (John 1:11; 19:15). They failed to recognize Jesus as the savior and promised redeemer.

Imagine Joseph's gamut of emotions as he heard his brothers express their regret over selling their young brother so many years before. Joseph left the room and wept (Gen. 42:21–24).

Jesus also wept over His beloved people, who did not recognize Him.

> When he drew near and saw the city, he wept over it, saying, "Would that you, even you, had known on this day the things that make for peace! But now they are hidden from your eyes." (Luke 19:41–42, ESV)

May we recognize Jesus and see Him today in each situation we face—and especially in the scriptures we digest. Let your prayer echo those in the Gospels who came hoping for a personal encounter with the Christ: "Sir, we wish to see Jesus" (John 12:21, ESV).

January 30

Reconciled

TODAY'S READING: Genesis 45:1–46:12

It was not you who sent me here, but God. *Genesis 45:8,* NKJV

Joseph had been ridiculed and betrayed by his brothers, sold into slavery, falsely accused by Potiphar's wife, and unjustly imprisoned. For most of us this would be cause for discouragement and bitterness! But Joseph chose to trust in God and to praise Him for His sovereignty. He recognized that, out of the injustice he suffered, God saved a nation.

> Do not be grieved or angry with yourselves, because you sold me here, for God sent me before you to preserve life. (Gen. 45:5, NASB)

Just as Joseph's rejection and persecution turned to victory, so did Christ's. It is through Jesus's death that we find life.

God allowed Joseph to be betrayed by his brothers and sent to Egypt in order to save a nation. And God sent His own Son, Jesus, to be betrayed and crucified in order to save the world.

> If, when we were enemies, we were reconciled to God by the death of his Son, much more, being reconciled, we shall be saved by his life. (Rom. 5:10)

Picturing Jesus's grace, Joseph stood before his guilty brothers and forgave them, reassured them, and abundantly provided for them (Gen. 45:11). Joseph's brothers were indeed guilty and deserved Joseph's wrath. He would have been justified if he condemned them. In the same way, we were indeed guilty, deserving God's wrath (Eph. 2:3), but Jesus, who is rich in mercy, has reconciled us to Himself (Col. 1:20), embraced us (Luke 15:20), and sets us at His banqueting table. His banner over you is love (Song of Sol. 2:4).

Keep reading: 1 Chronicles 2:18–55; 5:1–6

Blessed in Egypt

January 31

TODAY'S READING: Genesis 46:13–47:12

Have your father and brothers dwell in the best of the land.
Genesis 47:6, NKJV

When Jacob and his family arrived in Egypt, God provided them with the best land. They came during a drought and famine, yet God blessed them abundantly. Here we see a profound example of God's grace and mercy. Jacob's family was broken, and Jacob himself longed to see his lost son, who was in Egypt. We know that God's perfect will was for His chosen people to inherit the Promised Land of Canaan (Gen. 26:1–5). Yet here, God gives Jacob permission to go to Egypt along with a promise to bless his family there.

What a wonderful picture of our life in Christ! We may be broken, traveling through this fallen world, but through Jesus Christ we have abundant life and the promise of blessings.

> My God shall supply all your need according to his riches in glory by Christ Jesus. (Phil. 4:19)

God provided for the people of Israel abundantly while they were in Egypt. We are told that Joseph settled his family in the best part of the land and provided for them straight from Pharaoh's warehouses (Gen. 47:11).

So, too, Jesus has provided for us. Jesus came to give us new life (2 Cor. 5:17), abundant life (John 10:10), and everything pertaining to life (2 Pet. 1:3). He has planted us in His vineyard, grafted us into His family, and made us coheirs with Christ (Rom. 8:17). He has provided for our every need straight from the King's treasures.

This is your inheritance. You are blessed!

Keep reading: 1 Chronicles 4:1–23; 7:1–13, 30–40

February 1

Abundant Forgiveness

TODAY'S READING: Genesis 47:13–50:26

As for you, ye thought evil against me; but God meant it unto good. *Genesis 50:20*

Today we're finishing the glorious book of beginnings, Genesis. We've seen Jesus in God's promise of a redeemer in Genesis 3:15, and we've noted that He is powerfully portrayed in prophecies, types, symbols, and through the lives of key individuals.

Today's reading paints a wonderful picture of God's grace and Jesus's abundant forgiveness. Think back to Genesis 37, where we discovered how Joseph's life so effectively points to Christ. That pattern continues here in these last few chapters of Genesis.

Once their father Jacob had died, Joseph's brothers were concerned that Joseph would take revenge on them for what they had done to him as a boy (50:15). When Joseph heard this, the Bible tells us that he "wept" (v. 17). He must have been thinking, *I've already flooded them with forgiveness and poured out provision, but they continue to doubt.*

What a poignant picture of our own inclination to doubt the extent of Christ's forgiveness, to wonder how He really feels toward us.

Thankfully, God is greater than our mistrusting hearts (1 John 3:20)! He does not hold a record of our wrongs (Ps. 103:12; Isa. 43:25; Acts 3:19; Col. 2:14), and "we have peace with God through our Lord Jesus Christ" (Rom. 5:1).

If, like Joseph's brothers, you find yourself doubting your Savior's forgiveness and love, let your weary heart rest! There is only forgiveness, mercy, and provision in Christ. He's not waiting to take revenge. Instead, He's waiting to embrace you with wide open arms of forgiveness.

Deliverance

TODAY'S READING: Exodus 1:1–4:17

God heard their groaning, and God remembered his covenant. *Exodus 2:24*

The word *exodus* literally means "departure," which is exactly what this book is about—the Israelites departing the land of Egypt after four hundred years of slavery there. If I absolutely had to choose, I'd list Exodus as my favorite book in the entire Bible. Why? Because it's all about redemption, and it's rich with pictures of Christ empowering you and me to walk through the wilderness of this world with Him rather than on our own.

Genesis began beautifully with God's perfect creation, but it ended with Joseph in a coffin and God's people in Egypt. That pretty much sums up the history of humanity: God creates, man messes it up and finds himself dead in his trespasses, in need of a divine revival. Despite that sorry story of ours, God's goodness is grand indeed. He finds us in our state of slavery and provides us that much-needed exodus to freedom!

Remember, the Old Testament is one big picture book, and in the Scriptures, Egypt represents the world. The book of Exodus reveals the tender mercies of God as He hears His people's cry for help and sends them a deliverer.

Like the Israelites, we, too, were once slaves, captive to the world and in bondage to sin. God heard our cry for help and sent His Son, our deliverer (Eph. 2:1–5).

Today, if you find yourself oppressed by your circumstances or your past choices, know that you have access to the Great Deliverer. He hears your cries for relief and remembers every promise He has made to you. Most important, He is faithful to keep His word—just as He did right here in the beautiful book of Exodus.

February 3

An Outstretched Arm

TODAY'S READING: Exodus 4:18–7:13

> I am the LORD, and I will bring you out . . . and I will rid you out of their bondage, and I will redeem you with a stretched out arm, and with great judgments. *Exodus 6:6*

God promised that He would deliver His people from Egypt, that the Israelites would be freed from their bondage, and that He would redeem them with His mighty arm. Indeed, God did deliver His people, demonstrating His mighty power and utterly conquering the Egyptians.

Today we see Jesus foreshadowed in the strength of God's outstretched arm. Consider with me, dear Christian: The same mighty hand that delivered Israel from the bondage of Egypt also bore the nails that set you and me free from our bondage to sin. In His lovingkindness, Jesus stretched out His arms, died on the cross, and rose again in order to completely conquer the power of sin and death.

> . . . blotting out the handwriting of ordinances that was against us, which was contrary to us, and took it out of the way, nailing it to his cross. (Col. 2:14)

We were in slavery to the sin of the world, just as Israel was in slavery to Egypt. As Israel needed to be redeemed, or bought back, from slavery, we needed to be redeemed from sin. Praise be to God, who remains the same yesterday, today, and forever. God was faithful to deliver Israel with a mighty outstretched arm, and He has done the same for us.

> If the Son therefore shall make you free, ye shall be free indeed. (John 8:36)

Keep reading: 1 Chronicles 6:1–4

Set Apart

February 4

TODAY'S READING: Exodus 7:14–9:35

> I will set apart the land of Goshen, in which My people dwell. . . . I will make a difference between My people and your people. *Exodus 8:22–23,* NKJV

God had a plan and a purpose for the Israelites. They were His people and because of that, even as God's judgment rained down on Egypt, the Israelites were protected in the land of Goshen. That's the mercy and grace of God, who cares for His people and works all things for our ultimate good even in the midst of perilous times.

This doesn't mean everything was hunky-dory for the Israelites. Not at all! The Bible tells us that as a result of God sending the plagues, Pharaoh increased the suffering of the Israelites (Exod. 5:6–9). However, herein lies a great truth: although the Israelites experienced Pharaoh's wrath, they were sheltered from God's wrath, set apart in Goshen from the epicenter of the plagues.

Just as God sheltered Israel from His judgment, so you and I are set apart in Christ. We will not come under His judgment, but instead we have passed from death to life.

> Most assuredly, I say to you, he who hears My word and believes in Him who sent Me has everlasting life, and shall not come into judgment, but has passed from death into life. (John 5:24, NKJV)

Today, know that you are not under the wrath or judgment of God (John 3:18, 36; 16:33; 1 Pet. 1:5; 1 Thess. 5:9). Jesus bore that for you. You are His, and He has set you apart!

February 5

A Sheltered Feast

TODAY'S READING: Exodus 10–12

> When I see the blood, I will pass over you, and the plague shall not be upon you. *Exodus 12:13*

God's plan to redeem the world through Jesus is almost impossible to miss in today's passage. Moses, at God's command, instructed the entire nation of Israel to apply the blood of a lamb to the doorposts of their homes. When the angel of death came, he would pass over the homes that were covered in the blood. Just as the people of Israel escaped death because in faith they marked their doorposts with the blood of the lamb, we also are spared eternal death because the doors of our hearts are covered with the blood of Jesus, the spotless lamb.

> Ye know that ye were not redeemed with corruptible things . . .
> but with the precious blood of Christ, as of a lamb without
> blemish and without spot. (1 Pet. 1:18–19)

Jesus was the perfect lamb of God (John 1:29), sacrificed for the sins of the world. He was the fulfillment of Passover, and His blood covers our sins and completely sets us free.

What an eerie scene it must have been—except for those in the camp of God's people in the land of Goshen! On that first Passover night, while the rest of Egypt was covered in darkness and experiencing death, Israel remained safe and secure behind the doors where the blood of a lamb had been applied. They were supernaturally protected as they feasted with family and prepared for their long-awaited and much-anticipated freedom.

Because the blood of Jesus covers us, we are sheltered, death has passed over, and we can eat at the Lord's table, celebrating our freedom from sin and anticipating our exodus from this world to be with Him forever.

Faithful

TODAY'S READING: **Exodus 13–15**

> In your unfailing love you will lead
> the people you have redeemed.
> In your strength you will guide them
> to your holy dwelling. *Exodus 15:13,* NIV

If we're looking, we can find many parallels between God's love and care for ancient Israel and His love and care for us today.

Just as God delivered Israel from slavery in Egypt, Jesus has delivered us from the bondage of sin (Exod. 13:9).

> Being then made free from sin, ye became the servants of righteousness. (Rom. 6:18)

Just as God gave Israel the Passover feast to remind them of His love, protection, and provision, so Jesus has given us the communion feast whereby we see and remember the same.

> When he had given thanks, he brake it, and said, Take, eat: this is my body, which is broken for you: this do in remembrance of me. (1 Cor. 11:24)

Just as God led Israel along the way (Exod. 13:17–18), so Jesus leads you and me today.

> My sheep hear My voice, and I know them, and they follow Me. And I give them eternal life, and they shall never perish; neither shall anyone snatch them out of My hand. (John 10:27–28, NKJV)

Just as God lovingly led Israel, so He lovingly sent His one and only Son (3:16) to lead us to freedom. As you journey through the wilderness seasons of this life, consider how God delivered His people from Pharaoh and cared for them every step of the way—all the while giving us a future glimpse of His coming Son, Jesus, who has delivered you and is caring for you each step of the way.

February 7

Water from the Rock

TODAY'S READING: Exodus 16–18

Thou shalt smite the rock, and there shall come water out of it, that the people may drink. *Exodus 17:6*

It had only been a few weeks since God miraculously delivered the Israelites from Egypt, promising to lead them, provide for them, and fight their battles. But the reality of life in the desert was beginning to set in. The people grew thirsty, and instead of trusting, they began to complain and grumble.

It's easy to read this story and shake our heads at the Israelites: *Don't you remember what God just did for you? How can you forget so fast?* But how often could the same be said of you and me? We should ask ourselves those same questions every single time we face a challenge and find ourselves complaining or wondering how God will meet our needs.

God's provision for us is as sure as His provision for the Israelites. In fact, the apostle Paul tells us in 1 Corinthians that Jesus was the rock that provided water to quench their thirst.

They drank from the supernatural Rock which followed them, and the Rock was Christ. (10:4, RSV)

What a wonderful revelation! "What the smitten rock was to Israel, Christ's crucifixion is to us."[29] The smiting of the rock was God's plan (Exod. 17:5), just as Christ's crucifixion was God's plan (Rev. 13:8). The smitten rock's water offered life (Exod. 17:6), just as Christ's crucifixion extends salvation to anyone who comes to Him (John 4:14; 7:37–38).

Whatever your need is today, be encouraged that God provides us living water from the Rock of Ages. May you drink from Him today and never thirst again.

Treasured

TODAY'S READING: **Exodus 19–21**

> You will be my treasured possession. Although the whole earth is mine, you will be for me a kingdom of priests and a holy nation. *Exodus 19:5–6,* NIV

God revealed His character as He chose, delivered, and led Israel. If we have eyes of faith, we can see throughout Exodus how He works in and through us too.

> All these things happened to them as examples, and they were written for our admonition. (1 Cor. 10:11, NKJV)

God led Israel out of Egypt, just as He leads us out of sin. He chose Israel to be His people and treasured them, just as He's called us and declares us to be His treasure. God set Israel apart to be His special people and a kingdom of priests, just as He has called us to be a royal priesthood, a holy people.

> You are a chosen generation, a royal priesthood, a holy nation, His own special people, that you may proclaim the praises of Him who called you out of darkness into His marvelous light. (1 Pet. 2:9, NKJV)

Although the whole earth is His, He has set His affection on you and desires to work in and through your life (Eph. 2:10).

God declared that Israel was His treasured possession—for out of Israel He would bring a redeemer, His own Son, who would offer deliverance to all humanity and restore our fellowship with God.

God calls His own, individually and personally! You are His treasure, holy because of Jesus's blood, redeemed to be a royal priesthood, and deeply loved.

Jesus in the Law

TODAY'S READING: Exodus 22–24

> They said, All that the LORD hath said will we do, and be obedient. *Exodus 24:7*

These chapters in Exodus hold powerful insights into God's character. I encourage you not to skim over the law, for its high and holy standard reveals those things that God esteems as true, just, and right. Most of all, in it we see the perfection of God's standard that was completely fulfilled in Jesus.

> Do not think that I came to destroy the Law or the Prophets. I did not come to destroy but to fulfill. (Matt. 5:17, NKJV)

The Mosaic law can be broken down into three categories:

1. the moral law consisting of the Ten Commandments (Exod. 20:3–17), which revealed God's holy standard (James 2:10)
2. the spiritual law regarding the feasts, offerings, and sacrifices (Exod. 35–40), which foreshadowed Christ and salvation (Heb. 10:1)
3. the social law, which consisted of relational duties and conduct (Exod. 21–23) and detailed Israel's new way of living[30]

What a glorious revelation of our perfect triune God! The Ten Commandments revealed the Father's holy standard and exposed our desperate need for Christ (Gal. 3:24). The feasts and sacrifices practically demonstrated what Jesus would do for us as He died and took our sin upon Himself (Heb. 7:27). And the social law gave practical standards of conduct, just as the Holy Spirit teaches us to walk in a way that reflects Jesus (John 14:26; 15:26; Gal. 5:22–23).

Truly God's law is perfect and perfectly fulfilled in Jesus! As you read today's chapters, which focus on the social law, consider also Galatians 5 and the fruit of the Spirit. In both you'll find a reflection of Jesus.

Details

TODAY'S READING: **Exodus 25–27**

Have them make a sanctuary for me, and I will dwell among them. *Exodus 25:8,* NIV

Our God cares about details. He gave specific instructions to Israel regarding how to build His sanctuary, the place where His presence would dwell.

> Make this tabernacle and all its furnishings exactly like the pattern I will show you. (Exod. 25:9, NIV)

God provided a complete, detailed record of how He wanted the tabernacle to be built. Israel could have looked at those instructions and found them to be far too rigid, leaving little to no room for personal style or creative expression. But thankfully, they didn't take artistic license, because every aspect of the design of God's house purposefully pointed to Jesus Christ, as we will see later.

For today, let's simply focus on the beautiful truth that, as New Testament Christians, God dwells in our hearts. We (yes, you and I) are His temple, His house, the place wherein He dwells.

> Do you not know that your body is the temple of the Holy Spirit who is in you, whom you have from God, and you are not your own? (1 Cor. 6:19, NKJV)

God had a purpose for every detail in the Old Testament, and He cares about the intricacies and details of your life here and now. Like Israel, we have received His instructions regarding His home in our hearts and how they are to be sanctified and prepared to be a proper dwelling place for His Spirit. We don't get to choose the terms of our relationship any more than they chose the details of the temple, but because of Jesus, who serves in the true heavenly tabernacle, we get to live in daily fellowship with God (Heb. 8:2–5).

Truly, the Lord cares about every detail of His home in your heart.

Your Name on His Heart

TODAY'S READING: Exodus 28–29

Aaron shall bear the names of the children of Israel in the breastplate of judgment upon his heart, when he goeth in unto the holy place. *Exodus 28:29*

God appointed Aaron as Israel's high priest, consecrated to the Lord for the sole purpose of being a mediator between God and Israel. The intricacies of Aaron's high priestly ministry paint a beautiful portrait of our great high priest, Jesus, the final and ultimate mediator between God and man.

There is one God, and one mediator between God and men, the man Christ Jesus. (1 Tim. 2:5)

In Exodus 28 God gave Moses instructions regarding the breastplate that Aaron was to wear. The names of the twelve tribes of Israel were engraved on this breastplate, so that every time Aaron went into the holy place, he wore those names on his heart and brought them into the very presence of the Lord.

Jesus, our great high priest, now stands in the holy place, in the presence of God Almighty as our mediator. He continually intercedes on our behalf (Heb. 7:25), and as He does, He bears our names.

Behold, I have graven thee upon the palms of my hands. (Isa. 49:16)

Jesus has written your name on His hands, and you are on His heart, my friend. You are the joy that caused Him to endure the Cross (Heb. 12:2). Just as the high priest Aaron continually interceded for Israel before Christ came, Jesus, the great high priest, now lives to ever make intercession for us. What an awesome Savior we serve!

Ransomed and Saved

February 12

TODAY'S READING: **Exodus 30:1–33:6**

Each one must pay the LORD a ransom for his life. *Exodus 30:12,* NIV

Under the law of Moses, God required a payment for sin—and He still requires a payment for sin. What may seem harsh as we read the Old Testament was, in fact, painting a picture of the greatest demonstration of grace the world would ever know.

Here in Exodus we read that those who owed a price, or had a levy against them, were to produce the ransom price in order to be set free. I bet you can see the parallel already!

You and I owed a debt as a result of our sin. That debt is payable only by death—physical, emotional, relational, spiritual, and (ultimately) eternal death.

> The wages of sin is death; but the gift of God is eternal life through Jesus Christ our Lord. (Rom. 6:23)

You and I cannot set ourselves free from the debt we owe. So Jesus Himself paid our debt, dying in our place, and in so doing He bought us back. He produced the ransom price with His very life.

If you accept His payment for your sin, then you stand justified and forgiven because of Him. You were bought with the precious blood of Christ.

> There is one God, and one mediator between God and men, the man Christ Jesus; who gave himself a ransom for all, to be testified in due time. (1 Tim. 2:5–6)

Your salvation is free, but it cost Jesus everything. He laid down His life in exchange for yours. He ransomed you. He saved you. He loves you!

February 13

Rest in His Presence

TODAY'S READING: Exodus 33:7–35:35

> My Presence will go with you, and I will give you rest.
> *Exodus 33:14,* NIV

The old cliché is true: "Where God guides, He provides." Case in point, when He led Israel out of Egypt and through the wilderness, He provided not only food and water but also His presence and peace.

God's promise to Israel sounds like a promise Jesus has given you. Just as God went with Israel, Jesus sent His Spirit to live in you, and His presence indwells your heart.

> He shall give you another Comforter, that he may abide with you for ever; . . . I will not leave you comfortless: I will come to you. (John 14:16, 18)

And just as God gave Israel rest, so Jesus brings rest to your weary soul.

> Take my yoke upon you, and learn of me; for I am meek and lowly in heart: and ye shall find rest unto your souls. (Matt. 11:29)

Jesus in His mercy leads you and walks with you through this life, which can sometimes feel like a wilderness. But just as God the Father cared for and provided for Israel, the Son cares and provides for you.

> Grace and peace be multiplied to you in the knowledge of God and of Jesus our Lord, as His divine power has given to us all things that pertain to life and godliness. (2 Pet. 1:2–3, NKJV)

Just as God's presence went with Israel throughout their journey, He promises to be with you always.

> I will never leave thee, nor forsake thee. (Heb. 13:5)

As you read of Israel's journey, remember Jesus is with you. His presence lives in you. He is providing for you, protecting you, and offering you rest.

God's Workmanship

TODAY'S READING: Exodus 36–38

> [In] every wise hearted man . . . the LORD put wisdom and understanding to know how to work . . . for the service of the sanctuary. *Exodus 36:1*

Once again we see that God cared about specificity and detail in the tabernacle. He had a vision with great purpose: the tabernacle was to be a picture of our relationship with Him and a shadow of what Jesus would accomplish thousands of years later.

Today we are His sanctuary. We are living temples that He is building according to His perfect design and purpose (2 Cor. 6:16).

> You also, as living stones, are being built up a spiritual house, a holy priesthood, to offer up spiritual sacrifices acceptable to God through Jesus Christ. (1 Pet. 2:5, NKJV)

We are told that God filled the workmen in Israel with wisdom and understanding pertaining to all the service of the Lord. Similarly, you are created to walk in service to the Lord.

> We are his workmanship, created in Christ Jesus unto good works, which God hath before ordained that we should walk in them. (Eph. 2:10)

In the Old Testament God had His people build His temple. Today Jesus Himself is building His church (Matt. 16:18). In the Old Testament God's Spirit dwelled in the temple. Today Jesus lives and abides in us (John 15:7–11). The Old Testament temple was a foreshadowing of Christ's work in you!

Dear servant of the Lord, be certain today that He is faithful to equip you for whatever service He has called you to. He will fill you with wisdom, understanding, and skill as you take in His Word cover to cover. Keep reading the Scriptures, my friend, and watch Him do the equipping supernaturally!

February 15

Wait, Watch, and Follow

TODAY'S READING: Exodus 39–40

Throughout all their journeys . . . *Exodus 40:36,* NASB

Did you know that God's presence did not follow Israel through the wilderness? It's true. Rather, Israel followed God's presence. What a picture of how our walk with Christ should be!

In today's reading we find the tabernacle being set up, Aaron being anointed as a high priest, God taking possession of the tabernacle through His presence, and Israel following where God leads.

We've already considered how Exodus is a picture of our Christian walk, and I hope my life will conclude the same way this book does:

> In all the travels of the Israelites, whenever the cloud lifted from above the tabernacle, they would set out; but if the cloud did not lift, they did not set out. (40:36–37, NIV)

Have you ever considered the practical benefits of how God led the Israelites? He gave them shade from the hot desert sun with a cloud during the day, and as the temperatures tumbled at night, He provided a pillar of fire for warmth. So as the Israelites traveled, they simply stayed where it was cool during the day and warm at night. So sweet, so simple!

In a similar way, as you and I follow Jesus, our good shepherd, He leads us beside still waters and has given us all things pertaining to life and godliness (John 10:27–30; 2 Pet. 1:3). Just as Israel followed the cloud, we follow the Spirit (Gal. 5:16–25).

The Israelites' journey was not self-directed or strategized. They simply waited. They watched. They followed. May you, in all your life's travels, simply watch and go where God is clearly leading you.

The Light of Leviticus

February 16

TODAY'S READING: Leviticus 1–4

The priest shall make atonement for him in regard to his sin.
Leviticus 4:35, NASB

A close look at Leviticus reveals a supernatural shadow of Jesus Christ on every single page. In the New Testament Paul explains that the law, as seen in Leviticus, was given to reveal God's standard for holiness and our inability to meet it (Gal. 3:24). Paul says in Romans 7:12 that the law is holy and just and good. We, however, in our carnality, are simply unable to keep all the rules and regulations of the law (James 3:2).

But where we fall short of the law, Jesus triumphs! What the blood of bulls and goats could not do, the perfect Lamb of God accomplished once and for all (Heb. 10:4, 12). Jesus was the final, perfect sacrifice, the fulfillment of every aspect of the law.

In Leviticus 1 God details His standard for an acceptable walk, worship, and service. In the Gospels we see Jesus shouldering the consequences of our failure to meet that standard (Phil. 2:6–11).

In Leviticus 2–4 we find the high priest offering the required sacrifices. In the Gospels we see Jesus, our great high priest, offering Himself as the fulfillment of the Levitical sacrifices.

Jesus fulfilled every aspect of the law that we will read about in Leviticus. He is our great high priest who stands ever making intercession for us. He is our peace offering, cleansing our consciences of past sin. He is our atonement, covering our transgressions. He is the sweet-smelling sacrifice that, as hard as we may try, our dead works cannot produce. He is our fellowship offering, opening the holy of holies and making a way for us to fellowship with God. He is the fulfillment of Leviticus, the light behind the law.

February 17

A Clean Conscience

TODAY'S READING: Leviticus 5–7

It is a guilt offering. *Leviticus 5:15,* NIV

Need a clean conscience? We all do! Sin brings guilt, and guilt causes a sickly soul, a heavy heart, and a mental mess. The only remedy is atonement.

In the Old Testament God instructed Israel to offer sin and guilt sacrifices in the form of bulls and goats. These sacrifices, however, simply foreshadowed Jesus Christ, the sacrificial lamb of God. Israel had to offer their sacrifices year after year, day after day. But Jesus was the ultimate sacrifice, the absolute fulfillment of all the types and shadows that came before Him. He finished the work they could never accomplish, and His blood cleanses us completely.

> The law, having a shadow of the good things to come . . . can never with these same sacrifices, which they offer continually year by year, make those who approach perfect. . . . But in those sacrifices there is a reminder of sins every year. For it is not possible that the blood of bulls and goats could take away sins. . . . For by one offering He has perfected forever those who are being sanctified. (Heb. 10:1, 3–4, 14, NKJV)

In Leviticus God provided His people a guilt-free conscience through the doctrine of atonement. The word *atonement* means exactly what its syllables spell out: "at-one-ment." Sin separates us from God, but through atonement we are brought back into fellowship and are able to be "at one" with Him. For the ancient Israelites, "at-one-ment" came by sacrifice. The same is true for us!

> Not only so, but we also joy in God through our Lord Jesus Christ, by whom we have now received the atonement. (Rom. 5:11)

Through Christ's atoning sacrifice you are forgiven (3:24–26). Rejoice today, knowing that you can live guilt-free and in perfect peace.

A Better Way

TODAY'S READING: Leviticus 8–10

This is the thing which the Lord commanded that ye should do: and the glory of the Lord shall appear unto you. *Leviticus 9:6*

God's Word is full of treasure. Especially here in Leviticus! Because Jesus is the perfect fulfillment of all we find here in the law. The rules, the regulations, and the sacrifices—they all point to Jesus.

The priest's job was to offer sacrifices for the people's sin, according to the law. Aaron, as the high priest, received the sacrifices, applied the blood, and blessed the people—all according to the law.

The book of Hebrews tells us Jesus is better than the law because He fulfilled the law.

> The law made nothing perfect, but the bringing in of a better hope did; by the which we draw nigh unto God. . . . By so much was Jesus made a surety of a better testament. (7:19, 22)

Jesus is better than Moses. Moses gave the law, but Jesus freed us from the law. Jesus is better than Joshua and Aaron. They led Israel into the Promised Land, but Jesus leads us into eternal life. Jesus is better than the priests and the sacrifices. He is our great high priest and the perfect lamb of God. Jesus is better than the Mosaic covenant. He brought us the New Covenant based on grace and His work alone!

> [We have] therefore, brethren, boldness to enter into the holiest by the blood of Jesus, by a new and living way. (10:19–20)

Today consider what was required under the law and how Jesus perfectly fulfilled every requirement so that you can enter into God's presence and have fellowship with Him!

Obedience Saves Lives

TODAY'S READING: Leviticus 11:1–13:46

Do not make yourselves unclean. *Leviticus 11:43,* NIV

Long before germs were discovered, our omniscient Creator knew the importance of cleanliness and instructed His people accordingly. Consider Israel's perspective on these laws; without any scientific background or knowledge, the Israelites must have found them arduous, imposing, and restrictive. Now, of course, we understand the importance of good hygiene. But it's likely the people of ancient Israel simply viewed these as burdensome laws to obey without understanding exactly why.

We know, however, that none of God's laws are given in vain. The Bible says Scripture is "profitable" (2 Tim. 3:16). Out of obedience Israel implemented these laws, and hundreds of thousands of lives were saved. Throughout the course of history, the Jewish people have been spared from deadly diseases of global proportions. The plague that swept through Europe in 1346 did not reach the Jews. In 1505 most of Italy was afflicted with typhus, but the Jews were spared. In 1691 the Jews found themselves immune to Rome's devastating plague. And in 1736 dysentery swept through Norway, but again the Jews escaped.[31]

> The law of the LORD is perfect and preserves one's life. (Ps. 19:7, NET)

As New Testament believers, we also have instructions to follow that may not make sense to us or to society around us, but we can be sure that obedience saves lives! That salvation may, in fact, be physical, but through Christ it is absolutely the escape from spiritual death unto life everlasting.

You see, Jesus Christ perfectly and completely satisfied God's law, fulfilling every aspect that it pointed to.

> Being found in appearance as a man, He humbled Himself and became obedient to the point of death, even the death of the cross. (Phil. 2:8, NKJV)

Through Christ's obedience our lives were saved. Who knows how many may be drawn to Jesus and salvation through our obedience?

Dressed for Success

February 20

TODAY'S READING: **Leviticus 13:47–15:33**

If any clothing is contaminated . . . *Leviticus 13:47,* NIV

The law of Leviticus told the Israelites precisely how to live so that a holy God could dwell among a sinful people. In the midst of this unattainable, black-and-white standard, we see the greatest hope of all, Jesus Christ. In Jesus the Levitical shadows, illustrations, and types are all fully satisfied and perfectly fulfilled.

For example, God provided specific instructions regarding clothes that were contaminated with mold or mildew or that had been exposed to leprosy (Lev. 13:47, 52). Mold, mildew, and leprosy can permeate fabric, spread to people, and cause sickness. God told Israel to destroy infected garments in order to eliminate such sickness and stop the spread of damaging bacteria. In a similar way, He has provided warnings in His Word that instruct us to stay away from things that contaminate and show us the way to purity when we come into contact with such things.

We were all wearing "contaminated" clothing before we came to Christ. But God took our sin and self-righteousness, which the Bible calls "filthy rags" (Isa. 64:6), and robed us in Jesus's righteousness.

> My soul shall be joyful in my God; for he hath clothed me with the garments of salvation, he hath covered me with the robe of righteousness. (61:10)

You are washed and cleansed by the blood of Jesus Christ. He has made you white as snow, forgiven your iniquities, and clothed you in new garments.

> To her was granted that she should be arrayed in fine linen, clean and white: for the fine linen is the righteousness of saints. (Rev. 19:8)

You are clothed in His righteousness and dressed for success, all because of Jesus!

A Scapegoat

TODAY'S READING: Leviticus 16–18

The life of the flesh is in the blood. *Leviticus 17:11*

In Leviticus 16 we find a tale of two goats. Verses 7–10 tell us that the high priest was to cast lots (kind of like drawing straws) to select one of the two goats. The goat that drew the short straw was sacrificed for the sins of the people, and its blood was sprinkled on the mercy seat in the holy of holies. The other one became the scapegoat and was set free outside the city wall to symbolically carry away the sins of the people.

As we've seen before, God has a purpose in every detail, even when it comes to two goats! Notice how the blood of the goat was sprinkled on the mercy seat, the lid that covered the ark of the covenant. The ark carried the Ten Commandments—the law—which we cannot keep. But God "covers" the law by His mercy, through the shed blood of Jesus. What an awesome picture He was painting with these two goats: the blood of the one goat covered the sins of the people, and the other goat carried them far away. And that's exactly what Jesus has done for us. He shed His blood to mercifully cover our failure to keep the law, taking our sins far from us (Mic. 7:19; Ps. 103:12).

To be sure we understand the illustration, Leviticus 17:11 declares, "The life of the flesh is in the blood." In those ten little words are the clearest explanation for a critical question about Christianity: "Why is it so bloody?" Simple, because *life* is in the blood. In other words, if you have blood, you have life. On the contrary, if you have no blood, you have death. And Romans 6:23 tells us that the wages of sin is death. We all know we're sinners (3:23), so what did God do? He died in our place, giving His life blood for ours. And that, my friend, is the gospel, pictured as powerfully and potently here in Leviticus as anywhere else in the Old Testament.

Citizens of Heaven

TODAY'S READING: Leviticus 19–21

I am the LORD your God. *Leviticus 19:3*

The children of Israel were in Egypt for four hundred years. I would guess that during that time they picked up a little bit of the Egyptian culture. In today's reading we see God calling the Israelites to a unique way of life.

> Do not act like the people in Egypt, where you used to live, or like the people of Canaan, where I am taking you. You must not imitate their way of life. . . . I am the LORD your God. (Lev. 18:3–4, NLT)

Just as God delivered Israel from Egypt, He has delivered us from the bondage of the sin of this world. That deliverance comes with a call to live differently.

You and I are followers of Jesus Christ. We were spiritually dead and full of sin, but we've been "born again" (John 3:3). We are new creations in Christ. Old things have passed away, and all things are made new (2 Cor. 5:17). We now are citizens of heaven, and like the people of Israel, we're on our way to a new home, which God Himself is preparing.

> Our citizenship is in heaven, from which we also eagerly wait for the Savior, the Lord Jesus Christ. (Phil. 3:20, NKJV)

God has called us to live as people of His kingdom, to leave behind the ways of the world and to follow His Son (Rom. 12:2).

> Be imitators of God as dear children. . . . For you were once darkness, but now you are light in the Lord. Walk as children of light. . . . And have no fellowship with the unfruitful works of darkness, but rather expose them. (Eph. 5:1, 8–11, NKJV)

Today, my fellow sojourner, be an imitator of Christ. Be obedient to walk in His marvelous light, and, in so doing, light up the dark world around you.

February 23

Let's Feast

TODAY'S READING: Leviticus 22–23

Concerning the feasts of the LORD, which ye shall proclaim to be holy convocations, even these are my feasts. *Leviticus 23:2*

One of the literal meanings of the Hebrew word translated as "feasts" (*mow`ed*) is "appointed times."[32] God works in, with, and through "appointed times," as is clearly seen throughout the Scriptures. Here in Leviticus 23 God appointed seven feasts, or holidays, for Israel to celebrate at specific times.

The first four feasts took place during the spring: Passover, Unleavened Bread, First Fruits, and Weeks (or Pentecost). Most theologians agree that these feasts pointed to future events that were later fulfilled through the birth, death, and resurrection of Jesus Christ:

1. Passover: pointed to the Messiah as our Passover lamb (1 Cor. 5:7)
2. Unleavened Bread: pointed to Jesus's sinless life as well as how His body would not be left in the grave (Matt. 16:6; Mark 8:15; Acts 2:27; Ps. 16:10)
3. First Fruits: pointed to Jesus's resurrection (1 Cor. 15:20)
4. Weeks: pointed to the great harvest of souls fulfilled on the actual day of Pentecost (Acts 2)

The final three feasts God instituted were Trumpets, the Day of Atonement, and Tabernacles. These are most often referred to as the "fall feasts" because of when they occur in the Jewish calendar. Many commentators believe these feasts have yet to be fulfilled, since they point to the rapture of the church and Christ's second coming. These are our "blessed hope" (Titus 2:13).

Just as the four Old Testament spring feasts were fulfilled in the New Testament literally and precisely as those feasts were being celebrated,[33] we can be confident that these three fall feasts will likewise be fulfilled literally and precisely in connection with the Lord's second coming.

Let's keep reading God's Word as we eagerly anticipate their fulfillment. Soon and very soon we will feast with Him in heaven.

The Oil

TODAY'S READING: Leviticus 24–25

. . . so that the lamps may be kept burning continually.
Leviticus 24:2, NIV

God provided precise instructions for the priests to follow in the tabernacle. All the particulars were given for what, when, where, and how they were to go about their duties. This level of detail likely prompts you to wonder why all this is so important. The answer is simple: each aspect is a symbol pointing to the perfect work of Jesus Christ.

Consider the oil lamps, which were to be filled with pure olive oil and placed outside "the veil of testimony in the tent of meeting" (Lev. 24:3, NASB). They were to be tended constantly, never allowed to burn out.

Oil in Bible typology often represents the Holy Spirit. Throughout the Scriptures oil was used in the lives of kings, priests, and prophets as a symbol of their consecrated lives, to denote the fact that they were set apart, called, and covered uniquely and specifically by God's Spirit.[34] The prophet Zechariah, for example, was given a vision of a golden lampstand with two olive trees on each side. As the trees dripped oil into the lampstand, God spoke to Zechariah, saying,

> Not by might, nor by power, but by my spirit, saith the LORD of hosts. (Zech. 4:6)

As Christians, Jesus tells us we are lights set on a hill (Matt. 5:14) and without Him we can do nothing (John 15:5). Paul further teaches us we can do all things through Christ who strengthens us (Phil. 4:13). Truly the oil that lights the lamp of our lives is His Holy Spirit, by which we can do all He has called us to do. Our lives are to be fueled by the Spirit (Eph. 5:18). But like the lamps in the tabernacle, our lights must be continually tended, constantly filled and refilled so they don't go out. How do we do that? Consider where these golden lampstands were placed. *In the tent of meeting.* Today meet with your Savior, take in His Word, and be filled so that His light shines in and through you!

February 25

Heads Held High

TODAY'S READING: Leviticus 26–27

> I will walk among you and be your God, and you will be my people. . . . I broke the bars of your yoke and enabled you to walk with heads held high. *Leviticus 26:12–13,* NIV

Leave it to God to take an entire nation out of slavery and turn it into a powerful people. Because of God's work in them, the people of Israel no longer hung their heads in the shame of slavery. Rather, they were well on their way to becoming a mighty nation.

> I will give peace in the land, and ye shall lie down, and none shall make you afraid. . . . And ye shall chase your enemies, and they shall fall before you. . . . For I will have respect unto you, and make you fruitful, and multiply you, and establish my covenant with you. (Lev. 26:6–7, 9)

Just as God delivered Israel from physical slavery in Egypt, He has set us free from spiritual slavery. The Bible tells us that we were slaves to sin but Christ came to deliver us (Rom. 6:20; John 8:36).

Because of God's favor and mighty outstretched arm, the people of Israel were able to walk with their heads held high.

> Thou, O LORD, art a shield for me; my glory, and the lifter up of mine head. (Ps. 3:3)

Because of Jesus Christ we no longer have to hang our heads in the shame of our sin. Dear Christian, are you being held captive by a particular sin? If so, know this: Jesus wore a crown of thorns and hung His head as He died on the cross of Calvary so He could lift your head high above the grip of sin. Confess your sin today, my friend. The Bible tells us He's "faithful and just to forgive" it (1 John 1:9). And then walk with your chin up and your eyes lifted, focusing your gaze on Jesus, knowing that in Him you are already victorious and by His Spirit you have the power to overcome.

A Path in the Wilderness

February 26

TODAY'S READING: Numbers 1–2

Take a census of . . . Israel, by their families . . . according to the number of names. *Numbers 1:2,* NASB

If you happen to have a math phobia like me, the mere name of the book of Numbers may discourage you. But unlike my answers on math tests, all God's numbers are accounted for, line up nicely, and add up perfectly. Not one is missing. That's our great God! The Creator of the universe is able to breathe life even into numbers. We read in Matthew 10:30 that He has numbered every hair on your head. Clearly, our Lord is into numbers. And our Lord is in the book of Numbers, so let's dive in.

First, I hope you'll notice how God points to His Son, Jesus, even in the overarching themes of His books:

- Genesis: the book of creation and fall
- Exodus: the book of redemption
- Leviticus: the book of worship and fellowship with God
- Numbers: the book of service and sanctification

What a wonderful picture of our salvation through Christ and the Christian life that follows. God created perfectly, man sinned rebelliously, God redeemed mercifully, and now He teaches us worship, fellowship, service, and sanctification graciously.

The book of Numbers describes Israel's forty years in the wilderness and details a pattern of submission and obedience that inevitably leads to deliverance. The story of Israel's sojourn, or pilgrimage, accurately pictures our Christian walk and the life of our Lord Jesus. Christ overcame in the wilderness (Matt. 4:1–11). He came to serve (Matt. 20:28; John 6:38), and He clearly lived a life of pilgrimage (Luke 9:58). As you read through Numbers, may you find victory in the wilderness as you learn to live in service to Him.

February 27

His Load Is Easy

TODAY'S READING: Numbers 3:1–4:33

> All their service, whether carrying or doing other work, is to be done under the direction of Aaron. *Numbers 4:27,* NIV

In His instruction to Israel, God demonstrated His character and indicated how He would later instruct His church, including you and me. For example, God gave two Levite families, the Kohathites and Gershonites, detailed instructions regarding their service to the Lord. Both of these priestly families were called to carry (and not to carry) specific objects for use in the tabernacle (Num. 4:15, 24). Carrying a burden God had not called them to carry would bring death (v. 20). And everything they did was to be completed under the watchful eye of Aaron, the high priest.

As followers of Jesus, you and I are called "a chosen generation, a royal priesthood" (1 Pet. 2:9). Like those Levites, we are set apart for God's service. And just like them, all that we do is to be completed under the direction and watchful guidance of our great high priest, Jesus (Heb. 4:14–16).

As He did for the Kohathites and Gershonites, God has instructed us as to the things we are to carry and those we are not to carry. We are to carry our cross (Luke 9:23).

> Whoever does not carry his own cross and come after Me cannot be My disciple. (14:27, NASB)

But we are told to lay down our burdens (Matt. 11:28–30).

> Give all your worries and cares to God, for he cares about you. (1 Pet. 5:7, NLT)

Jesus bore the weight of the world on His shoulders (1 Pet. 2:24; Isa. 53:4). He carried away our sins so our load could be light. He calls us to lay down our own lives as He gathers us in His arms (1 John 3:16; Isa. 40:11; John 10:11–18).

Today, remember that you live under the tender, watchful care of your great high priest who carries you so you can carry on.

Brought Back into the Camp

February 28

TODAY'S READING: Numbers 4:34–6:27

The children of Israel did so, and put them outside the camp; as the LORD spoke. *Numbers 5:4,* NKJV

We've seen repeatedly that the Old Testament previews New Testament principles, so it's no surprise to find another powerful picture in today's reading. Numbers 5 records God's instructions to Israel regarding leprosy. Leprosy often represents sin in the Scriptures, in that it cannot be cured and makes the afflicted person unclean.[35] Both sin and leprosy affect the whole of a person as well as the whole of that person's house. Therefore, God commanded that anyone with leprosy must be put out from Israel's camp.

> Put out of the camp every leper . . . that they defile not their camps, in the midst whereof I dwell. (vv. 2–3)

Why such an extreme measure? Practically, God was protecting Israel from the spread of infectious disease. But beyond the practical is a picture of God's holiness. Where God dwells there can be no impurity, whether of flesh or of spirit (1 John 1:5). And herein lies our desperate need for Jesus.

Like the leper in the Old Testament, the unsaved person is hopelessly defiled and unclean, living outside of a relationship with God (Rom. 3:23). But Jesus showed His love and power as He touched and healed the leper (Luke 17:11–19; Matt. 8:1–4).

The Old Testament high priest would pronounce a person clean or unclean, while our great high priest, Jesus, has taken away our sin and proclaimed us righteous (John 3:36; Rom. 3:22; 1 John 1:9). By the blood of the Lamb, you no longer live outside of God's "camp" but are given favor and fellowship (Eph. 2:13).

No Ordinary Offering

TODAY'S READING: Numbers 7

> They shall offer their offering, one leader each day, for the dedication of the altar. *Numbers 7:11,* NKJV

Today's reading may seem overly repetitive, but we find profound encouragement tucked away in these verses. Numbers 7 describes twelve leaders, one from each of the twelve tribes of Israel, coming to the tabernacle with offerings of dedication. Here is what's so interesting: every single offering is identical. Twelve times we read of an offering that mirrors precisely the one given before. There isn't anything different or unique about any of them. All are exactly the same. Yet God records each one individually. He documents every single offering and who brought it. Then He accepts it and uses it for His glory. Why? Because every gift and giver matters to Him. This is a great encouragement to an ordinary person like me.

If you've ever been saddened by your lack of something extraordinary to offer the Lord, take heart. Nothing was extraordinary about the twelve offerings in Numbers 7 except that each was brought by an individual acting in obedience to God. Every single act of obedience is seen and counted by the Lord!

This reminds me of an offering we find in the New Testament as well. Do you recall the boy who gave Jesus his five loaves and two fish? There wasn't anything extraordinary about his lunch, but when it was placed in Jesus's hands, a miracle took place (John 6:9).

What do you have today that you can offer to the Lord? Whatever you offer is profoundly significant once it is placed in His hands.

Keep Cool

TODAY'S READING: Numbers 8–10

> At the commandment of the LORD they rested . . . and at the commandment of the LORD they journeyed. *Numbers 9:23*

God led the Israelites through the wilderness, parted the seas, fought their battles, and provided for them every step of the way. All the people had to do was follow His lead. The Israelites were covered by God's Spirit via a cloud (Exod. 13:21–22), and this covering kept them safe from the desert's scorching sun (Ps. 105:39). What an obvious and practical indication of God's direction and guidance! All Israel had to do to "cool down" and to "chill out," so to speak, was stay under the cloud.

> Whether it were two days, or a month, or a year, that the cloud tarried . . . , the children of Israel abode . . . and journeyed not: but when it was taken up, they journeyed. . . . At the commandment of the LORD they rested . . . and at the commandment of the LORD they journeyed. (Num. 9:22–23)

As New Testament believers, we are led by the same protective Spirit of the Lord. Jesus promised to send the Holy Spirit, who would comfort, teach, and lead (John 14:26). Just as Israel remained under the cloud, we abide in Christ and are under the shadow of His wing (Ps. 36:7). Jesus sent His Spirit, who testifies and continually points us to the Son (John 15:26; 1 John 4:13).

> The Comforter . . . shall teach you all things, and bring all things to your remembrance, whatsoever I have said unto you. (John 14:26)

May you allow Jesus, through His Spirit, to guide you through your wilderness and protect you from the heat of the day. May you submit to God's practical leading and guiding and in so doing abide under the "cool" cloud of His counsel.

March 3

Adversity Is Opportunity

TODAY'S READING: **Numbers 11–13**

Let us go up at once and take possession, for we are well able to overcome it. *Numbers 13:30,* NKJV

In the midst of great adversity and seeming impossibility, God moved on behalf of His people. Remember, God promised the people of Israel land and victory over their enemies (Gen. 13:15; Exod. 23:20–23). Yet Israel's bravest men were afraid to face the giants living in that Promised Land. Out of twelve spies sent to survey the land of Canaan, only Joshua and Caleb came back ready to fight for and take possession of it. The people sided with the rest of the spies, with the doubters. We'll see tomorrow, in Numbers 14, how that doubt and unwillingness to obey God's leading caused the whole camp to trade sweet victory in the Promised Land for the bitterness of forty years in the wilderness.

You see, God had already promised to fight for the Israelites (Deut. 3:22). He had already promised to give them the land and lead them along the way. All they had to do was trust Him and stand firm. This is the same promise He gives to you and me today. Here in Numbers 13 we find a reminder that Jesus Christ has fought the battle—and won! The giants in our lives have been conquered by the blood of Christ. Our Enemy no longer rules over us; he was defeated on the cross of Calvary. Like the people of Israel, all we have to do is trust Him and stand firm in the armor He has provided (Eph. 6:13–17).

I encourage you to adopt Joshua and Caleb's response to the giants in your life. Be strong and courageous. Your adversity is simply an opportunity for God to fight for you.

Missed Opportunity

TODAY'S READING: Numbers 14–15

In their presumption they went up toward the high hill country. *Numbers 14:44,* NIV

God's instructions are not subject to our timeline and are often anything but convenient. Yet the results of disobedience can be dire. Opportunities to obey the Lord are time sensitive. God had brought the people of Israel to the very doorstep of victory, but they refused to enter because they feared the giants in the land. Israel chose fear over faith, grumbling over praise, and defeat over victory (Num. 14:2–3). As a result, God declared He would not allow this generation to enter the Promised Land. Instead of walking into the land flowing with milk and honey, they would wander in the wilderness.

Upon hearing their punishment, the people decided to obey, but it was too late. Their opportunity had expired. Now they had a new opportunity: trusting God as He walked with them through the wilderness (vv. 20–23).

You see, God grows His people through obedience. Even Jesus learned obedience through the things He suffered (Heb. 5:8). And Jesus emphasized the timing of obedience, saying, "Now the time has come" (John 12:23, NLT).

Like the Israelites, we may miss opportunities to obey, but we take comfort in knowing that God's grace abounds and Jesus Christ paid the price for all our missed opportunities.

I'm so thankful that Christ obeyed the Father, even unto death (Phil. 2:8). His obedience has brought us life (Rom. 6:4).

When surrender is difficult and the cost of obedience seems too great, turn your eyes upon Jesus! Remember what He chose to do for you and listen to His words: "Now the time has come."

Between the Living and the Dead

TODAY'S READING: Numbers 16–18

> He stood between the dead and the living; and the plague was stayed. *Numbers 16:48*

These three chapters are full of lessons, exhortations, examples, and a powerful picture of Jesus. A group of men rose up among the Israelites, questioned God's instruction, caused division, and led an insurrection. In keeping with His character of love and grace, through Moses, God gave His people a choice and an opportunity to move away, quite literally, from sin.

> He warned the assembly, "Move back from the tents of these wicked men! Do not touch anything belonging to them, or you will be swept away because of all their sins." (Num. 16:26, NIV)

Through Jesus, God offers the same choice to us today. God loves us and knows that sin leads to death, so He warns us to move away from it. It will swallow you up, as the Israelites soon learned (v. 31).

As a result of Israel's sin, a plague swept through the camp. But even in the middle of discipline, our merciful God provided a way out. Aaron grabbed his staff and ran to pray for the people, and the plague was stopped (v. 48).

What a powerful picture of Jesus! Just as Aaron, Israel's high priest, stood between the living and the dead, Jesus, our great high priest, stands making "intercession for us" (Rom. 8:34). The plague of sin that threatened our lives has been stopped through the power of His atoning blood. Jesus stands, arms outstretched, beckoning us to come to Him and find life (John 3:16–18; Col. 2:13).

> He who hears My word and believes in Him who sent Me has everlasting life, and shall not come into judgment, but has passed from death into life. (John 5:24, NKJV)

Today, if you are standing near sin, move away. Jesus is your remedy! Cling to Him and find life.

Speak to the Rock

March 6

TODAY'S READING: Numbers 19–21

> Speak to the rock before their eyes, and it will yield its water; thus you shall bring water for them out of the rock. *Numbers 20:8,* NKJV

There is no rock like our God. Jesus is our solid rock and the rock of our salvation. He is a sure foundation and our cornerstone (Matt. 21:42; Acts 4:11; 1 Cor. 3:11; Eph. 2:20). As we saw previously, He Himself is the rock that followed Israel in the wilderness.

> They drank from the supernatural Rock which followed them, and the Rock was Christ. (1 Cor. 10:4, RSV)

The first time God provided water from the rock, He instructed Moses to strike the rock (Exod. 17:6). This foreshadowed Jesus, smitten at Calvary and from whose sacrifice flows the gift of salvation. But here, God told Moses to speak to the rock. Why? Because Christ was smitten once for all (Heb. 10:10). His sacrifice was sufficient for all eternity. He is not to be struck again. This time the rock was to be spoken to (Num. 20:8).

As we follow Christ, the rock of ages, we find living water (John 4:14) when we approach Him in prayer and praise. There, in sweet fellowship, we receive the abundance of living water and the Holy Spirit pouring out upon us.[36]

Like the Israelites, we are sojourners in the desert of this world. The literal water we drink sustains us for only a short time. Jesus, however, the supernatural rock of our salvation, offers us living water so we can drink and never thirst again—and all we need to do is speak to Him.

March 7

Whom He Blesses

TODAY'S READING: Numbers 22–24

> The LORD opened the mouth of the donkey. *Numbers 22:28,* NKJV

We see clearly God's power, mercy, and creativity throughout the account of Balaam and his talking donkey. One lesson that stands out is God's faithfulness both to Balaam as he heads down the wrong path and to His people Israel, whom Balaam is attempting to curse. Certainly, the Israelites at times needed correction, but God blessed His people not on account of their worthiness but on account of His faithfulness (Num. 23:21). God would not stand by and allow Balaam to curse His people, so He sent an angel and a talking donkey to thwart Balaam's plan.

> The angel of the LORD stood in the road to oppose him. (22:22, NIV)

Perhaps you feel as if nothing ever works out right for you or as if someone or something is trying to curse you. Take heart! Just as God saved Israel from Balaam's curse, He has come to save you.

> Christ hath redeemed us from the curse of the law, being made a curse for us. (Gal. 3:13)

Just as Israel belonged to the Lord, so do we! You and I belong to Christ. We are sealed by the New Covenant, not only beneficiaries of His blessings but also heirs to His kingdom.

Just as God protected Israel (Num. 23:23), He shelters and protects us—His people, His heirs, His children (Rom. 8:17). You are blessed and not cursed! So today, live in confidence and comfort of His blessing and His favor—in Jesus's name.

A Sword and Zeal

TODAY'S READING: Numbers 25–26

He was zealous for my sake. *Numbers 25:11*

Today's reading prompts me to ask myself, *How zealous am I to cut sin out of my life?* A genuine zeal for the Lord and a determination to follow and obey Him will bring great blessings.

God had clearly instructed His people, the Israelites, to abhor the wicked practices of the nations and culture around them. He told His people not to adopt their lifestyles, not to worship their false gods, and not to engage with their women. Prone to wander, however, Israel did the complete opposite.

> While Israel remained at Shittim, the people began to play the harlot with the daughters of Moab. For they invited the people to the sacrifices of their gods, and the people ate and bowed down to their gods. (Num. 25:1–2, NASB)

What a mess! In disobedience Israel had brought the Moabite women (a picture of the world) right into God's temple and as a result suffered severe consequences.

But God showed mercy because of a man named Phinehas, who responded to Israel's sin with great zeal by getting right to the point of the problem at hand (vv. 7–11).

What a wonderful picture of the work Jesus does in our lives! You see, our lives are, in essence, the camp of Christ (1 Cor. 6:19–20). Like Phinehas, we have a sword—the Word of God, which is "the sword of the Spirit" (Eph. 6:17)—that cuts the sin out of the camp. Jesus is the Word made flesh (John 1:14), and He told us in John 15:3 that we are cleansed through His Word (Eph. 5:26).

Dear Christian, won't you follow the lead of Phinehas (Ps. 106:30–31) and zealously take hold of the sword of the Spirit today? Allow Jesus, through His Word, to cut away the sin in the camp of your life. For God's Word is quick and powerful, "sharper than any two-edged sword" (Heb. 4:12, NKJV).

Listen for That Trumpet Sound

TODAY'S READING: Numbers 27–29

It is a day of blowing the trumpets. *Numbers 29:1*

Just as there was purpose in every law and the promise of a redeemer in the sacrifice, God also demonstrated His kingship over the times and seasons through the feasts He established. These feasts reveal not only His rule over nature's physical seasons but also His creation and dominion over spiritual seasons. Let's look at one of the most anticipated celebrations—the Feast of Trumpets.

Throughout the Scriptures God uses a trumpet to proclaim victory and liberty. Take, for example, Joshua's miraculous victory at Jericho (Josh. 6), the Day of Atonement as the people were freed from the guilt of sin (Lev. 25:9), and the indication of liberty from bondage during the year of jubilee (vv. 8–11).

But here, for the Feast of Trumpets, the trumpet itself takes center stage. The trumpet's sound indicated that the time of harvest had ended, rest was to be celebrated, and the people were presented to God.

As believers in Jesus Christ, we listen for the sound of a greater trumpet call, marking the fulfillment of the Feast of Trumpets, when we will be caught up into heaven to be with the Lord forever.

> The Lord Himself will descend from heaven with a shout . . . and with the trumpet of God. And the dead in Christ will rise first. Then we who are alive and remain shall be caught up together with them in the clouds to meet the Lord. (1 Thess. 4:16–17, NKJV)

Like the ancient Israelites, we await the trumpet sound! We are busy reaping the harvest (John 4:35; Luke 10:2), but when God blows His trumpet, we'll be caught up and it will be time to leave the field and enter the Temple to worship Him forevermore.

Mercy in the Fire

TODAY'S READING: Numbers 30–31

All that cannot endure fire you shall put through water.
Numbers 31:23, NKJV

In today's reading we see that God commanded the Israelites to purify by fire whatever was brought into their camp. We now know that heat kills impurities. But what about those items that were too fragile to withstand the heat? Those were to be purified with water.

Remember, everything in the Old Testament is a picture of a New Testament principle. Today's reading pictures our sanctification. Like the treasure brought into Israel's camp, we were once outsiders but have been brought into God's family by the blood of Jesus (Eph. 2:13). Just as Israel's possessions were cleansed, we, as Christ's precious possessions, are purified and washed in the water of His Word (Eph. 5:26; John 15:3).

Like the gold and silver in today's reading, we are taken through the purifying process of sanctification, which sometimes includes a fiery trial. In the midst of difficult times, we can be sure that God is getting rid of impurities that would otherwise stunt our spiritual growth.

> That the trial of your faith, being much more precious than of gold . . . though it be tried with fire, might be found unto praise and honour and glory at the appearing of Jesus Christ. (1 Pet. 1:7)

Even in the midst of the fire, God's overwhelming mercy and lovingkindness are revealed. God knows we are frail, and He shelters us from heat and trials that would otherwise consume us. If you are in the middle of a fiery trial, remember that God uses all things for our benefit (Rom. 8:28). His intent is never to burn His children but to prepare them to be healthy, holy, sanctified, set apart.

If, instead, you're in a season of calm, enjoy the refreshing water of His Word and let it sanctify your heart and cleanse your mind (Eph. 5:26; Rom. 12:2).

Keep Moving Forward

TODAY'S READING: Numbers 32–33

Why do you discourage the Israelites from going over into the land the LORD has given them? *Numbers 32:7,* NIV

God has given us exceedingly "great and precious promises" (2 Pet. 1:4)! He has promised to take us to a land of blessing and to provide for us. But, like Israel, we have battles to fight and enemies to defeat along the way. In today's reading we find two tribes in Israel—the Gadites and the Reubenites—considering a seemingly easier option. They had found a comfortable stopping point and were prepared to settle down rather than join the rest of the Israelites in crossing over Jordan to take possession of the Promised Land. Moses warned them that their stopping short of the final goal would discourage the rest of God's people from fully engaging in the fight for the Promised Land.

Right here is a truly poignant Old Testament picture of our New Testament life in Christ! As Christians, we encounter many tempting stopping points. And just like the Gadites and Reubenites, we can choose to stop short of the goal. However, if we settle there, we'll miss out on so much! This is why the apostle Paul repeatedly encourages us to run the race and to finish strong (1 Cor. 9:24; 2 Tim. 4:7). God has new territory, triumphant victories, and abundant blessings as we continue on with Him.

I'm so thankful Jesus completed the work He was sent to do (John 17:4). Because Christ didn't stop short, we have been redeemed. He is now "the author and finisher of our faith" (Heb. 12:2). His strength is made perfect in our weakness (2 Cor. 12:8–10).

Don't stop short, friend! Not only will you miss out on blessings intended for you, but you might also discourage others from being brave in their battles. So pick up that sword of the Spirit, which is the Word of God, and let it strengthen you for today's work.

Our City of Refuge

March 12

TODAY'S READING: **Numbers 34–36**

They shall be cities of refuge for you from the avenger.
Numbers 35:12, NKJV

We can't outrun our past mistakes or hide from a life of regret. What we need is a refuge. Our heavenly Father knows this and provides what we need "according to his riches in glory" (Phil. 4:19).

In the Old Testament God instructed Israel to set aside six Levitical towns to serve as places of refuge, where someone who had killed someone else could flee to safety before standing trial. Please don't misunderstand; this was not Israel's version of a get-out-of-jail-free card. It was the means by which God provided an escape from the avenger's wrath and through which justice could prevail.

What a powerful picture of the gospel! We have broken the law (James 2:10) and are in desperate need of refuge. Not only did God provide that refuge for His people, but upon trial, His Son took our rightly deserved judgment. That is good news indeed! We who broke the law are now hidden in Christ (Col. 3:3). Justice was accomplished when He bore the penalty we deserved and paid the debt we owed (Rom. 8:1–2).

> That I may . . . be found in him, not having mine own righteousness, which is of the law, but that which is through the faith of Christ, the righteousness which is of God by faith. (Phil. 3:8–9)

Jesus is not just the fulfillment of the city of refuge; He *is* our refuge (Ps. 91:2).

We have escaped our enemies, sin and death. In Christ, we are secure. Only He can redeem our lives, forgive our pasts, cover our sins, justify our failures, and set our feet in a secure place.

March 13

All the Way

TODAY'S READING: Deuteronomy 1:1–3:11

> . . . in the wilderness where you saw how the LORD your God carried you, as a man carries his son, in all the way that you went until you came to this place. *Deuteronomy 1:31,* NKJV

In Deuteronomy 1 God instructed the people of Israel to look back and remember how carefully and tenderly He provided and cared for them during their years of wandering. Now Israel stood on the brink of a new chapter. Their forty years of wandering had come to a close. The doubting generation had died in the wilderness. A new generation was poised to take possession of the land God had promised. But before they did, He directed them to be mindful of the things He had already done for them.

This brings us to the whole point of the book of Deuteronomy: it's a book of remembrance, a catalog of the laws, miracles, provisions, warnings, and blessings God had previously given to His people.

In the midst of life's events, you and I have the tendency to forget how God has met us in the past. Just as Moses reminded the Israelites that God had carried them all the way to the Promised Land (1:31), we need to pause, look back, and remember how Jesus has carried us in the wilderness of our lives. As the good shepherd, Jesus has promised that He holds each of us and will not lose a single one of His sheep (John 6:39; 10:28). We are never outside His care, and He doesn't drop us along the way.

> Being confident of this very thing, that he who began a good work in you will complete it until the day of Jesus Christ. (Phil. 1:6, WEB)

As seasons come and go, notice what Jesus is doing for you. Remember His good deeds, His loving-kindness, His provision. Don't forget His faithfulness, dear friend!

The Good No

TODAY'S READING: **Deuteronomy 3:12–5:33**

The LORD said to me: "Enough of that! Speak no more to Me of this matter." *Deuteronomy 3:26,* NKJV

Moses desperately wanted to see the Promised Land, to join the Israelites as they crossed over the Jordan and into Canaan. But God had told Moses that he would not be allowed to enter the Promised Land because he disobeyed God's instruction and struck the rock at Meribah (Num. 20:12). Despite Moses's pleading, God still said no.

When it comes to hearing no from the Lord, we can find solace in knowing that God is a good Father. Unlike a tired parent, God never says no out of weariness. He always has a purpose, sound reasoning, and a plan. He is never dismissive or inattentive to our requests (Luke 11:13).

Regarding Moses, God's no had eternal significance. You see, Moses represents the law and highlights our inability to keep it perfectly. As good as the law was (Rom. 7:12), it could not lead Israel into the Promised Land. Ultimate victory needed to come by Joshua, whose very name means "Jehovah is salvation"[37] and who is a picture of the One who is greater than the law. Joshua, foreshadowing our Savior, would lead Israel over the Jordan and into the Promised Land.

So, too, the Old Testament law cannot lead us to victory. Jesus Christ alone is our salvation and the very fulfillment of the law (Matt. 5:17).

God, in His infinite wisdom, told Moses no so that His masterpiece, His story, would point all humanity to His Son.

March 15

Remember and Speak

TODAY'S READING: Deuteronomy 6–8

> Be careful that you do not forget the LORD, who brought you out of Egypt, out of the land of slavery. *Deuteronomy 6:12,* NIV

God consistently reminded Israel not to forget Him. Time and time again, He stirred them to remember His faithfulness. Through His servant Moses God gave the people of Israel a written account of His mighty deeds and great love for them. As we have seen, that is the purpose of the book of Deuteronomy—to encourage His people to remember God's works, remember His deliverance, remember His promises, remember His commands, and then share them with our kids, with our community, with ourselves!

> You shall teach them diligently to your children, and shall talk of them when you sit in your house, and when you walk by the way, and when you lie down, and when you rise. (6:7, ESV)

Like Israel, we tend to forget. It's easy to lose sight of who we were before we were born again. But God, who knows our frailty, is faithful to give us reminders that stir our hearts and renew our perspective. What reminder has He given to you? Consider the communion table, the Lord's Supper, as one of His greatest reminders.

> He took bread, and gave thanks, and brake it, and gave unto them, saying, This is my body which is given for you: this do in remembrance of me. (Luke 22:19)

Today, remember who you were before Jesus Christ. Recall His saving grace. Reminisce about His mighty deeds and answered prayers. How? Remember His body broken for you. Reflect on His blood shed for you. Then share those truths with someone who needs to hear about them.

Giants, Walled Cities, and a Fierce River

March 16

TODAY'S READING: Deuteronomy 9–11

The LORD thy God is he which goeth over before thee.
Deuteronomy 9:3

Israel was facing the impossible: giants, walled cities, and a fierce river. But these things did not concern God. He created all of them and intended to use each of them to show Israel His mighty power.

> Hear, O Israel. You are now about to cross the Jordan to go in and dispossess nations greater and stronger than you, with large cities that have walls up to the sky. The people are strong and tall—Anakites! You know about them and have heard it said: "Who can stand up against the Anakites?" But be assured today that the LORD your God is the one who goes across ahead of you like a devouring fire. (Deut. 9:1–3, NIV)

God warned the Israelites not to look back at their victories and take any credit. God and God alone went before the people of Israel and won them the victory.

Likewise, Jesus has gone before us. He has defeated the Enemy, brought down the walls of our hearts, and leads us into the Promised Land of salvation. It's important to always remember that it's not on account of our righteousness but because of His great love for us that He fought the fight on Calvary and won the victory over sin and death (Phil. 3:9).

What an awesome God! He holds all power and righteousness yet faithfully demonstrates His kindness in defending and upholding the cause of His people. Like Israel, we face giants, but God promises that neither height nor depth nor any creature can separate us from His love in Christ Jesus (Rom. 8:39). Giants, walled cities, and raging rivers—whatever challenges you may find daunting, intimidating, or even life threatening—are nothing compared to the power of our God! In Christ we are more than conquerors (v. 37).

March 17

Cast Down Those Idols

TODAY'S READING: Deuteronomy 12–14

> You shall walk after the LORD your God and fear him and keep his commandments and obey his voice. *Deuteronomy 13:4,* ESV

The time was drawing close for the Israelites to take possession of the Promised Land, and God was preparing their hearts and minds. As they stood on the cusp of entering, God gave them the same direct, simple instructions He gives you and me today: remain faithful to the Lord your God and worship Him only.

> Destroy completely all the places . . . where the nations . . . worship their gods. Break down their altars, smash their sacred stones . . . ; cut down the idols . . . and wipe out their names. (Deut. 12:2–3, NIV)

You probably don't have little idols lying around that you believe are gods. But the Bible tells us that we are just as prone to setting up idols in our hearts and minds and souls. An idol can be anything that we esteem more than following Christ.

Jesus demonstrated this very lesson when He admonished the rich young ruler to sell his possessions and follow Him (Matt. 19:16–26; Mark 10:17–27). That young man was unwilling to let go of what he had. Jesus wants not only our lip service but also the desires of our hearts, the affections of our souls, and the thoughts of our minds (Matt. 22:37).

Today, as Jesus followers, may we heed the apostle Paul's instructions and cast down anything that exalts itself above Christ.

> Casting down imaginations, and every high thing that exalteth itself against the knowledge of God, and bringing into captivity every thought to the obedience of Christ. (2 Cor. 10:5)

As it was for Israel, our Promised Land is just ahead. May the true and living God be the only one exalted in your heart and mind.

Canceled Debts

TODAY'S READING: Deuteronomy 15–18

The LORD's time for canceling debts has been proclaimed.
Deuteronomy 15:2, NIV

From Genesis to Revelation, from the giving of the law to the coming of the Redeemer, we find the culmination of Scripture to be the unveiling of Jesus Christ and Him crucified. It really is one big picture book, given that we see Jesus in it from cover to cover. Consider the beautiful picture painted by today's reading:

> Every creditor who has lent anything . . . shall release it; he shall not require it of his neighbor . . . because it is called the LORD's release. (Deut. 15:2, NKJV)

Every seven years Israel was to forgive debts and in that way "rest." Can you imagine? All debts paid, canceled, forgiven! This financial reality for the Israelites foreshadows a spiritual reality for us. You and I owed a debt of sin we simply couldn't pay, but now the Lord's time for canceling our debt has been proclaimed.

He has provided forgiveness and rest. Our debt has been canceled, and we rest from carrying the burden of unforgiven sin, the weight of our failure to live up to the law.

> Having cancelled and blotted out and wiped away the handwriting of the note (bond) with its legal decrees and demands which was in force and stood against us (hostile to us). This [note with its regulations, decrees, and demands] He set aside and cleared completely out of our way by nailing it to [His] cross. (Col. 2:14, AMPC)

You can celebrate today! Your debt of sin is canceled. You've been set free from those charges, and you can rest knowing that Jesus took your debt on Himself and paid it all on the cross.

Our Curse, Nailed on His Tree

TODAY'S READING: Deuteronomy 19–22

He that is hanged is accursed of God. *Deuteronomy 21:23*

Every law given by God has significance. No instruction is misplaced or without purpose (Ps. 19:7–11). Each detail of God's instruction highlights some aspect of His goodness, His provision, or His plan of redemption. Just consider this passage from today's reading.

> His body shall not remain all night upon the tree, but thou shalt in any wise bury him that day; (for he that is hanged is accursed of God). (Deut. 21:23)

As Moses laid down the law, directed by the Spirit, we see him hammer home the humiliation of being hanged. So detestable was this penalty that Moses equated it with being cursed by God. *Hanged on a tree. Cursed by God.* Sound familiar? God foretold the shame His beloved Son would bear centuries before the crucifixion. In his classic commentary on the Scriptures, Matthew Henry said of this passage "that it might afterwards be applied to the death of Christ, and might show that in it he underwent the curse of the law for us."[38]

Even beyond being cursed, the Bible tells us that Christ *became* a curse for us.

> Christ hath redeemed us from the curse of the law, being made a curse for us: for it is written, Cursed is every one that hangeth on a tree. (Gal. 3:13)

You and I deserved to be cursed by God for our sin and rebellion. But Jesus willingly hung on the cross instead, not only removing our guilt and taking our shame but also completely fulfilling the law, just as Jesus said He would do (Matt. 5:18). He bore your shame. He took your curse. Truly, because of Christ, it is finished.

His Special People

TODAY'S READING: Deuteronomy 23–26

Today the Lord has proclaimed you to be His special people, just as He promised you, that you should keep all His commandments. *Deuteronomy 26:18,* NKJV

Today's reading has a lot to do with the consequences of sin. God knows what heartbreak sin brings. He knows it is a destroyer and has global consequences (Gen. 3:16–19), national consequences (Prov. 14:34), physical consequences (v. 30; James 1:15), spiritual consequences (Isa. 59:1–2), and eternal consequences (2 Thess. 1:7–9). God's warnings are rooted in His love.

He chose Israel to be His special people and, as such, defended them, provided for them, and warned them of danger. I love the fact that here in Deuteronomy, God first reminds Israel of His love and affection—then reminds them to keep His commandments.

Just as God declared Israel to be His special people, Jesus proclaims us to be His treasured possession. You are His "pearl of great price" (Matt. 13:45–46). God cared about the well-being of His people in the Old Testament, and He certainly cares about our well-being as His redeemed children. So just as He instructed Israel to keep His commandments, He tells us to walk in His ways.

For ye are bought with a price: therefore glorify God in your body, and in your spirit, which are God's. (1 Cor. 6:20)

God's love for us is wrapped up in the commandments He gives to us (1 John 5:3). As loving parents provide instruction to their kids, so, too, our loving heavenly Father reminds us how to avoid danger by obeying Him. If the Holy Spirit convicts your heart today of sin, listen and obey. He is warning you because He loves you. You are special to Him.

March 21

A Guide to Blessing

TODAY'S READING: Deuteronomy 27–28

> All these blessings shall come on thee, and overtake thee, if thou shalt hearken unto the voice of the LORD thy God.
> *Deuteronomy 28:2*

The voice of the LORD thy God." I like that. What do we know about the voice of the Lord our God? We know that it was through His voice that Moses heard the law. Today's reading speaks of the blessings that abound from being obedient to the voice of the Lord. You see, the laws God instituted were not just for Israel's benefit but for ours as well. As we look into them, we see both our Savior and our need to be saved. Remember, Jesus is the perfect fulfillment of the law (Matt. 5:18). The law is holy, just, and good (Rom. 7:12), and the law is "our schoolmaster to bring us unto Christ" (Gal. 3:24).

God desired to bless His people immensely. So He gave them a road map to success—His commandments—that guided them in daily life and pointed them to the Messiah for eternal life. Simply walking in obedience brought Israel blessing.

God also desires to bless us New Testament believers immensely. So He has given us a road map—His Word.

> One who looks intently at the perfect law, the law of liberty, and abides by it, not having become a forgetful hearer but an effectual doer, *this man will be blessed* in what he does. (James 1:25, NASB, emphasis added)

Let's remember that we look to Jesus as the fulfillment of the law. Outside of Him we cannot follow the perfect law of liberty. So fix your eyes on Jesus, listen for "the voice of the LORD thy God," and be abundantly blessed by simply obeying Him.

Second Chances

TODAY'S READING: **Deuteronomy 29:1–31:29**

The LORD, he it is that doth go before thee; he will be with thee, he will not fail thee, neither forsake thee: fear not, neither be dismayed. *Deuteronomy 31:8*

In today's reading we find Israel coming full circle. They are right back where they were forty years previously, camped across the Jordan facing Jericho. Now, we know how the story ends, how the walls of Jericho came tumbling down. But put yourself in Israel's sandals. This is the place that caused them great distress and doubt, which led to forty years in the wilderness. But God is a God of forgiveness and second chances. He was faithful to bring them back to where they started as a means to teach them to trust Him and to walk in faith.

Herein is a great lesson for you and me: God is faithful to bring us back to our personal "Jordans" and give us a second chance. Consider Peter. Filled with discouragement after having denied Jesus, Peter returned to what he knew before he followed Christ: fishing (John 21:3). Sitting on the shore, the resurrected Jesus met Peter, cooked him a meal, and gently gave him another opportunity to profess his love for Him. Peter had denied Jesus three times (Luke 22:54–62), and three times Jesus asked him, "Do you love Me?" (John 21:15–17, NKJV).

Where is the Lord leading you today? Are you, like Israel, facing a daunting challenge? Or perhaps, like Peter, you just need to sit and tell Jesus you love Him. Whatever your situation, don't shrink back, friend! God promises to go before you (Deut. 31:8) and to never leave you or forsake you (Heb. 13:5).

March 23

Moses and Jesus

TODAY'S READING: Psalm 90; Deuteronomy 31:30–32:52

Moses spake in the ears of all the congregation of Israel the words of this song, until they were ended. *Deuteronomy 31:30*

The account of Moses's life ends with his song, in which he recounts God's faithfulness, ponders His power, and encourages God's people to remember the Lord's favor and walk righteously.

We've seen how Moses was a type of the law and how, like the law, he was unable to lead the people into the Promised Land. But there are similarities between Moses and Jesus that should be considered, especially here as Moses sings his final song.

- As infants, Moses and Jesus were threatened by reigning rulers (Exod. 1:15–16; Matt. 2:16).
- Moses gave up his royal Egyptian inheritance, while Jesus left His place in heaven (Exod. 33:1; John 6:38).
- Moses shepherded sheep, while Jesus shepherds men (Exod. 3:1; John 10:14, 16).
- Both were noted for meekness (Num. 12:3; Matt. 11:28–30) and were burdened by Israel's sin (Exod. 32:31–32; Luke 19:41–44).
- God told Moses that bread would come down from heaven (Exod. 16:11–15). Jesus fulfilled this picture as He fed the multitude (Matt. 14:13–21); He is "the bread of life" (John 6:35).
- Moses saw the glory of God on a mountain, while Jesus displayed His glory on the mount of transfiguration (Exod. 34:29, 35; Matt. 17:2; John 1:14).
- Moses spent forty years in the wilderness, and Jesus spent forty days in the wilderness (Num. 32:13; Matt. 4:1–2).
- Moses was a mediator between God and Israel, and Jesus is the "one mediator between God and men" who intercedes on our behalf (Exod. 20:18–21; 1 Tim. 2:5; Rom. 8:34).

Indeed, Moses had reason to end his life with a song! For his life was a reflection of Jesus. May we, too, be filled with His praise and His song of faithfulness all our days.

Rahab's Scarlet Cord

March 24

TODAY'S READING: Deuteronomy 33–34; Joshua 1–2

Bind this line of scarlet thread in the window which thou didst let us down by. *Joshua 2:18*

Today we venture into the book of Joshua, the victorious consummation of Israel's redemption out of Egypt and into the Promised Land.[39] How appropriate that we find a picture of redemption in the opening chapters!

Having spied out the land himself forty years earlier (Num. 13:16), Joshua again sent spies into Jericho. When the spies entered Jericho, their hazardous mission was aided by Rahab, a harlot whose house was built into the wall (Josh. 2:15). Rahab was God's unlikely instrument of protection and a picture of Jesus's coming redemption.

In chapter 2 we find Rahab hiding the spies, professing her belief in God's power, and petitioning for protection (vv. 4–13). What a wonderful pattern of salvation! As followers of Jesus, we believe in our hearts, we confess with our mouths, and in humble petition we receive Jesus's free gift of salvation—protection for our souls (Rom. 10:9–10).

The spies instructed Rahab to hang a scarlet cord out her window on the day they were to conquer Jericho. That lifesaving scarlet cord is a clear picture of Jesus's precious lifesaving blood, which flowed to save us as He hung on the cross (Matt. 26:28; 1 John 2:2).

Rahab, a Gentile and prostitute, was saved by faith (Heb. 11:31). She is included in the genealogy of Jesus—a member of the Savior's family tree (Matt. 1:5)! So, too, we were outsiders, brought into God's family, made heirs with Jesus, and our names are written in the Lamb's Book of Life.

March 25

Step Out

TODAY'S READING: Joshua 3–6

> The priests that bare the ark of the covenant of the LORD stood firm on dry ground in the midst of Jordan, and all the Israelites passed over on dry ground. *Joshua 3:17*

Have you ever felt like God was calling you to step out into what seemed to be a deadly deluge? That's exactly what He called the people of Israel to do as they moved at last into the Promised Land. Israel was camped across the Jordan River from Jericho. Joshua 3:15 tells us that the river was at flood stage. This happens annually during the harvest season, when the fast-flowing waters swell many times their normal size. Plus, the Jordan is an extremely steep river, descending rapidly into the Dead Sea, which, especially at flood stage, creates treacherous conditions.

Nevertheless, God told Joshua to have the priests step into the torrent and watch as He, "the LORD of all the earth," cut off the waters and stood them up in a heap (v. 13).

When the priests stepped into the waters in faith, God completely stopped the river and Israel "stood firm on dry ground" (v. 17). Amazing! God can do that because He is the Lord of all. He is the creator of everything and is mightier than the rushing of many mighty waters (Ps. 93:4).

Doesn't this remind you of a time in the New Testament when Jesus called His disciple Peter to step out onto the water (Matt. 14:22–33)? In faith Peter began to walk on the Sea of Galilee, but intimidated by the boisterous conditions, he became afraid and began to sink. Jesus immediately reached out and caught him.

Jesus still calls His disciples to step out in faith. Just as God stopped the waters of the Jordan River upstream and out of sight (Josh. 3:16), He often works on our behalf "upriver" where we can't quite see. So step out and follow our Lord! Just as it did for Israel, a great victory awaits you.

Victory in Jesus

TODAY'S READING: Joshua 7–9

Fear not, neither be thou dismayed: take all the people of war . . . and arise, go up. *Joshua 8:1*

Joshua was anointed and appointed to lead Israel after Moses had died. As Israel's courageous captain, Joshua offers a picture of the great captain of our salvation, Jesus (Heb. 2:10).

As we've noted, Moses symbolized the law. Neither he nor the law could lead God's children to victory or bring them into the peace of the Promised Land. For that they needed Joshua, the one whose name meant "Jehovah is salvation."[40] In the same way, we need Jesus, our Jehovah-Savior, to lead us to victory, to take us into our Promised Land.

Thanks be to God, which giveth us the victory through our Lord Jesus Christ. (1 Cor. 15:57)

Jesus is the ultimate conqueror who defeated both sin and death on the cross (Col. 2:15; 2 Tim. 1:10; 1 Cor. 15:4, 55). It is Christ who ushers us into new life (Eph. 4:8; Rom. 6:4).

Joshua and the Israelites marched all night, maneuvered troops, used their swords, and set siege to cities. Ultimately, however, it was God who won every battle for them. Whether by hail (Josh. 10:11), the sun standing still (v. 13), or divine instructions (11:6), it was God who intervened and, with a mighty hand and outstretched arm, defeated every one of Israel's enemies.

The same is true for you. You are called to put on the whole armor of God, to pick up the sword of the Spirit, which is the Word of God, and to do battle in prayer (Eph. 6:13–18). But it is God who does the fighting for you. You stand victorious in Christ, dear Christian. It is Jesus who won the battle on Calvary, and you and I have the victory we need for today in and through Him!

March 27

Nothing Left Undone

TODAY'S READING: Joshua 10–12

> Joshua . . . left nothing undone of all that the LORD commanded. *Joshua 11:15*

Joshua is the perfect picture of our conquering king, our mighty Jesus. We can rejoice because the Bible tells us that Jesus did it all! As foreshadowed by Joshua, He left nothing undone. He conquered sin and death and redeemed our lives.

> Jesus, knowing that all things were now accomplished, that the Scripture might be fulfilled . . . said, "It is finished!" (John 19:28, 30, NKJV)

Joshua fought the battles, and as a result, the land had rest. So, too, Jesus has finished the work and has brought us rest for our souls.

> Take my yoke upon you, and learn of me; for I am meek and lowly in heart: and ye shall find rest unto your souls. (Matt. 11:29)

God accomplished His mighty work through Joshua, and He has accomplished His perfect work through His Son, Jesus—and He will complete His work in you.

> Being confident of this very thing, that he which hath begun a good work in you will perform it until the day of Jesus Christ. (Phil. 1:6)

Jesus did it! He left nothing undone. You can rest in His finished work.

Expanded Territories

March 28

TODAY'S READING: **Joshua 13–15**

I am still as strong today as the day Moses sent me out;
I'm just as vigorous to go out to battle now as I was then.
Joshua 14:11, NIV

In today's reading Joshua recounts the territories God had given to Israel. Can you imagine the testimonies and memories this time of reflection would have conjured in the minds of those who fought these battles? These soldiers had had the privilege of standing on the front lines, watching God work on their behalf to deliver their enemies into their hands.

Consider Caleb. What a wonderful picture of Jesus and our potential in Christ. His determination, strength, and hope in the Lord endured. Even in his old age, Caleb stood ready and eager to fight the good fight.

Jesus desires to fill us with this same strength. Jesus fought the good fight and finished the work He was sent to do (John 17:4; 19:30). Now His strength is made perfect in our weakness (2 Cor. 12:9).

Take time to think of the victories God has given you. Answered prayers, old habits kicked, new behaviors created, guilt gone, and new life experienced—that is your story and your expanded territories!

This is the victory that overcometh the world, even our faith.
Who is he that overcometh the world, but he that believeth
that Jesus is the Son of God? (1 John 5:4–5)

God continues to expand our boundaries this side of heaven. Like Caleb, let's refuse to grow "weary of doing good" (Gal. 6:9, ESV). Our Promised Land awaits, and we are on our way to meet our great high captain, Jesus Christ.

March 29

Keep Going

TODAY'S READING: Joshua 16:1–19:9

> How long are ye slack to go to possess the land, which the LORD God of your fathers hath given you? *Joshua 18:3*

God ordained a vast territory for Israel's inheritance. In a wave of initial enthusiasm, the people of Israel began to take possession of the Promised Land. Once they gained some ground, however, they grew comfortable and a bit complacent and began to slow down their conquest.

In today's reading Joshua admonishes Israel to keep going and to take possession of the entire land—all God's promises. We find the same admonishment in the New Testament when Paul encourages us to run this life race well, not giving up or slowing down but rather throwing off anything that would hold us back—in other words, not getting comfortable in our conquest over the flesh.

> Let us lay aside every weight, and the sin which doth so easily beset us, and let us run with patience the race that is set before us, looking unto Jesus the author and finisher of our faith. (Heb. 12:1–2)

The Promised Land required battles and sanctification. Our hearts require the same. God fought Israel's battles, and Jesus has fought ours. He died on the cross so we could live. He conquered sin and death to bring us victory. We are free from our old selves and have victory over sin. Yet, like Israel, we have the propensity to grow comfortable and leave much heart territory unconquered.

Today, if you hear His Spirit nudging you to take possession of some "Promised Land" in your life, keep going in enthusiasm! These are promised territories and sure victories in Jesus.

Not a Word Failed

TODAY'S READING: Joshua 19:32–21:45

Not a word failed of any good thing which the LORD had spoken. . . . All came to pass. *Joshua 21:45,* NKJV

God is faithful. He always keeps His promises. Not a word He has spoken fails. We've seen throughout the Old Testament how God established covenants, gave assurances, and told Israel to watch as all His promises came to pass.

God continually encouraged His people and reminded them of His faithfulness. He told them to create monuments so they could look back and remember His mighty deeds (Josh. 4:5–6). He gave them feasts to prompt them to reflect on all He had done and be reminded of all He promised to do. God worked through Israel, picturing the rest and victory He would give us through His Son, Jesus.

The people of Israel watched as God performed miracles and orchestrated His plan throughout their journey. Similarly, Jesus has given us "great and precious promises" (2 Pet. 1:4). We have the privilege of watching His plan unfold as we eagerly anticipate Jesus's return.

> The Lord Himself will descend from heaven with a shout, with the voice of an archangel, and with the trumpet of God. And the dead in Christ will rise first. Then we who are alive and remain shall be caught up together with them in the clouds to meet the Lord in the air. And thus we shall always be with the Lord. Therefore comfort one another with these words. (1 Thess. 4:16–18, NKJV)

Today, let's remember His promises—and His faithfulness to keep them. Jesus promised to rise from the dead, and He did. He promised to send His Spirit, the comforter, and He did. He promised to come again, and He will! Not a word will fail of any good thing that the Lord has spoken.

A Stone and a Tree

TODAY'S READING: Joshua 22–24

Behold, this stone shall be a witness unto us. *Joshua 24:27*

As the end of his life drew near, Joshua gathered Israel and recounted all the Lord had done—His victories, His faithfulness, and His commands. In response Israel promised to follow God, to remain faithful to Him, and to reject other gods. Joshua then took a large stone and set it up under an oak tree near the holy place of the Lord as a visual reminder of God's unbreakable promises (Josh. 24:26).

Little did Joshua know the powerful portrait of Israel's future redeemer he was providing that day! For you see, Joshua set up a reminder, a stone, under a tree. Jesus Christ, our chief cornerstone (1 Pet. 2:6), hung on a tree. Joshua recounted the victories God gave them—but those victories were mere shadows of the ultimate victory God would bring through His Son, Jesus Christ. Joshua set up his stone near the holy place of the Lord (Josh. 24:26). Jesus Christ, having torn the veil (Matt. 27:51), ushers us into the holy of holies.

> Let us therefore come boldly unto the throne of grace, that we may obtain mercy, and find grace to help in time of need. (Heb. 4:16)

Joshua set up his rock as a witness against the people, so if ever they broke the covenant, they would remember what God had promised and what they had promised in return. Jesus, our rock, took our guilt upon Himself and stands as a witness for us, not against us (Rom. 8:34; Heb. 7:25).

The Israelites looked to Joshua's stone under that oak tree and remembered all God had done for them. So, too, you and I can look to Jesus—our solid rock, our firm foundation, the stone the builders rejected, and see all that God, who spared not His Son in order to secure our salvation, has done for us. Truly, it all points to Jesus.

The Great Judge Who Saves

April 1

TODAY'S READING: Judges 1:1–3:6; Judges 17

The LORD was with the judge, and delivered them out of the hand of their enemies. *Judges 2:18*

The book of Judges describes Israel's behavior between the death of Joshua and the establishment of a king. We find in these pages one fantastic story after another recording the Israelites' propensity for back-sliding in contrast to the persistent grace of God, who provided leaders—judges—to guide Israel in times of crisis.

Although parts of the book are not in chronological order,[41] we will follow the judges as they occurred in the historical time line.

The judges God gave Israel foreshadow our great judge, Jesus. God used these fascinating men—and one wonder woman—to deliver the Israelites from their oppressive enemies and to speak truth to His way-ward people. In the New Testament we see Jesus appointed by God as the judge of the whole earth (Matt. 25:31–46; Acts 10:38–42). Like these Old Testament judges, Jesus speaks truth to His people and sets us free from sin (John 8:32).

Israel's judges brought respite for a season, but Jesus's salvation is eternal and His justice is everlasting.

The Bold Lion

TODAY'S READING: **Judges 18; Judges 3:7–4:24**

Don't hesitate to go there and take it over. *Judges 18:9,* NIV

Israel's backsliding, as recorded in Judges, stands as a sign of caution for us as Christians. Their state of degeneration did not follow a season of hardship or oppression but instead came on the heels of their victory in the Promised Land.[42] The book of Hebrews warns against losing our focus, admonishing us as believers to hold firmly to the end what we had at the beginning (3:14). Our Christian life is not to be spent in idle rest but to be marked by the active pursuit of growth in godliness (2 Pet. 3:18).

While Israel stands as a cautionary example of compromise, God also gives us a picture of our perfect remedy: Jesus.

Look at Othniel, Israel's first judge, whose very name means "lion of God."[43] Othniel, the man with a lion's heart, delivered Israel with valor (Judg. 1:12–13; Josh. 15:16–17). Later God would raise up His Son, Jesus, "the Lion of the tribe of Judah," to deliver all those who call upon His name (Rev. 5:5).

Othniel was full of courage and did not hesitate to go and conquer what God had given. In the same way, we can trust that Jesus has made us "more than conquerors" (Rom. 8:37). May we set our sights on our great judge, Jesus, and follow "the Lion of the tribe of Judah" into victory today.

Mighty Warrior

TODAY'S READING: **Judges 5–7**

The Lord is with you, mighty warrior. *Judges 6:12,* NIV

Gideon's story demonstrates that God chooses the weak things of this world to shame the strong (1 Cor. 1:27–29). Fearing the Midianites, Gideon had snuck out and was hiding behind a winepress, attempting to thresh wheat. He must have been startled when the angel of the Lord appeared to him with a bold greeting: "The Lord is with you, mighty warrior" (Judg. 6:12, NIV).

Surely Gideon felt anything but mighty. And his behavior was not that of a warrior. But this was no ordinary angel who declared Gideon a "man of valor" (ESV). It was the preincarnate Son of God, Jesus Christ, the eternal Word talking to Gideon face to face!

When Gideon realized whom he spoke with, he was again filled with fear. But the Lord comforted Gideon, "Peace be unto thee; fear not: thou shalt not die" (v. 23)

Here we see the preincarnate Son of God speaking peace over Gideon. Later in the Gospels we find Jesus—the eternal Word made flesh—appearing to doubting Thomas with similar words of assurance and challenge.

> Peace be with you! . . . Put your finger here; see my hands. Reach out your hand and put it into my side. Stop doubting and believe. (John 20:26–27, NIV)

The Lord has called each of us, like Gideon, by names we cannot fathom—righteous (2 Cor. 5:21), beloved (1 Thess. 1:4), glorious (Eph. 5:27), faultless (Jude 24). Praise the Lord for choosing the weak and foolish things of this world to accomplish His mighty plans!

Endurance

TODAY'S READING: **Judges 8–9**

> Gideon and his three hundred men, exhausted yet keeping up the pursuit, came to the Jordan and crossed it. *Judges 8:4,* NIV

God had placed a challenging call on Gideon's life. A call that required fortitude and perseverance. Yesterday we saw how God Himself fortified Gideon in the midst of his fear. Today we see God create in Gideon a commitment to continue until the end.

Gideon and his men had experienced a miraculous victory over the Midianites, but two kings (Zebah and Zalmunna) escaped and were on the run (Judg. 8:5). Gideon determined to see the battle through. He would not be content until those two kings were captured, so he and his men continued their pursuit, despite their exhaustion.

When considering Gideon, I cannot help but think of Jesus, who ran the race, accomplished His task, and proclaimed, "It is finished" (John 19:30). Gideon's story also mirrors our spiritual lives. Through Jesus we've been given a great and mighty victory, but we are still required to run the race set before us.

> We also, since we are surrounded by so great a cloud of witnesses, let us lay aside every weight, and the sin which so easily ensnares us, and let us run with endurance the race that is set before us. (Heb. 12:1, NKJV)

God gave us the accounts of these Old Testament men and women so that we would find encouragement for our personal races (Rom. 15:4). May you lay aside your weariness today and trust the Lord to give you the endurance through His Word, by His Spirit, to run your race well.

The Way That Leads to Peace

April 5

TODAY'S READING: Judges 10–12

They put away the strange gods from among them, and served the LORD: and his soul was grieved for the misery of Israel.
Judges 10:16

We have seen throughout the Old Testament how God blessed the Israelites abundantly when they walked in obedience. God, who had promised victory, blessings, peace, and His presence if they would stay close to Him, was faithful to keep His promise.

However, at times Israel walked away from the true and living God and began to worship false gods (Judg. 10:13–14). As a result, the nation experienced war and oppression (vv. 7–8), family feuds (11:1–3), unwise promises made (vv. 30–31), lack of discernment (13:16), and confusion regarding what God had said (v. 22).

God's Word is true, friend! His promises will come to pass, including the consequences of sin He so strenuously warns us about. It's important to understand that sin is not bad because it's sin. Sin is sin because it's bad—it hurts us.

Consider how Jesus warned His disciples to avoid the Pharisees and have nothing to do with their sin, with the "leaven," or yeast, of hypocrisy (Matt. 16:6–12; Luke 12:1). Why? Because the Pharisees pretended to be devoted to God and His truth, but in reality they were unwilling to obey the truths God had given. They preferred their way over God's, their ideas over God's Word. As the apostle Paul noted, "A little leaven leavens the whole lump" (Gal. 5:9, NKJV). Allowing in even a little sin leads to ruin.

That is the lesson in today's reading. Jesus told us that His truth sets us free (John 8:32). Let's trust that He knows best and that obedience to His ways will lead to peace (Gal. 5:22).

Keep reading: Judges 19–20

April 6

The Power of a Consecrated Life

TODAY'S READING: Judges 13–16

The child shall be a Nazarite unto God from the womb.
Judges 13:5

The story of Samson[44] is one of sad syncretism, the result of intermingling holiness with human desire, and spiritual power with sin. Samson's life began beautifully. An angel announced his conception. He had a divine purpose and was set apart to God from the womb (Judg. 13:3–5). He was anointed by the Spirit with unsurpassed strength. His life was full of potential. Yet Samson chose to mingle the godly with the ungodly, the consecrated with the defiled. As a result, Samson ended his life in captivity, blind and tied to a grindstone (16:21–22).

Despite Samson's shortcomings God gave him a final victory over the Philistines (vv. 23–31) and counted Samson faithful (Heb. 11:32–33).

Samson's life certainly foreshadows Jesus to a degree. Both births were unexpected by their mothers and announced by an angel (Judg. 13:2–5; Luke 1:26–38). Both were set apart and divinely appointed (Judg. 13:7; Heb. 10:10–12). Both were sent to deliver Israel (Judg. 13:5; Matt. 1:21). But where Samson fell short and failed in his assigned role, Jesus triumphed and finished the work.

It is a solemn reality for us to consider the effect of compromise in our lives. It hinders our full potential, blinds us spiritually, and leaves us tied to the grindstone of sin.

Dear Christian, don't underestimate the power of a consecrated life. While Samson taught us the danger of compromise, Jesus gave us power over it.

Brought into His Family

TODAY'S READING: Ruth 1–2

Naomi had a kinsman of her husband's, a mighty man of wealth, . . . and his name was Boaz. *Ruth 2:1*

The book of Ruth portrays Christ's love for you and me, His bride, on every single page. This is an amazing story of a Gentile bride loved by a Jewish man, wooed by kindness and provision, and redeemed through the fulfilling of the law. Sounds familiar, doesn't it? That's our story.

Boaz loved Ruth, and as we'll see, he pursued her with kindness and provision. Ephesians chapter 2 and Colossians 2:13 tell us that we were once outsiders, Gentiles who were so deeply loved by Christ that He pursued us by bearing our iniquities on the cross (1 Pet. 2:24) and providing all we need for a life of godliness and salvation (Phil. 4:19).

Boaz was required to follow the law in order to have the legal right to marry Ruth and bring her into his family. Jesus completely fulfilled the law (Matt. 5:17) and is therefore, according to the law, the only man able to redeem you and me (1 Pet. 1:18–19).

Boaz brought Ruth into his family, and their marriage produced a great-grandson who became King David, which means Ruth is in the lineage of Jesus. This remarkable woman is forever written into the Lord's earthly genealogy. What a wonderful story!

Ruth's story is our story too. We were brought into God's family (Rom. 8:17), and just as Ruth's name is recorded in Christ's genealogy, our names are recorded in the Lamb's Book of Life (Luke 10:20; Rev. 21:27). As you read the book of Ruth, remember: you have been made Jesus's bride and will spend forever by His side.

Keep reading: Judges 21; 1 Chronicles 6:4–15

April 8

Kinsman-Redeemer

TODAY'S READING: **Ruth 3–4**

> Blessed is the LORD who has not left you without a redeemer today. . . . May he also be to you a restorer of life and a sustainer of your old age. *Ruth 4:14–15,* NASB

Today's reading is full of good news! Ruth is "redeemed" as her hero, Boaz, fills the role of her kinsman-redeemer. What a sweet picture of Jesus, our bridegroom, stepping up to redeem His bride, the church.

The first mention of the legal role of a kinsman-redeemer is found in Deuteronomy 25. There God graciously provides for a widow left without a son. In such an event the closest available and willing relative had the option of marrying the widow and producing a son who would be named after the deceased father (Deut. 25:5; Lev. 25:25; Ruth 3–4).

Ruth was a Moabitess, from a wicked line and a cursed people (Jer. 48:11–13). She had nothing to offer Boaz—no riches, no land, not even a decent family heritage. Yet Boaz pursued her and claimed her as his own.

How could Boaz have known that his acts of love and provision for this Gentile woman were painting a picture of the greatest love story ever written—the story of Jesus, our great kinsman-redeemer, who took for Himself a Gentile bride who had nothing to offer Him yet loved her to death anyway?

May you know today that you are loved, you've been redeemed, your kinsman-redeemer fulfilled all the requirements, and you are His beloved bride.

Keep reading: 1 Chronicles 2:3–16

Reason to Rejoice

TODAY'S READING: 1 Samuel 1–2; Psalm 113

My heart rejoiceth in the LORD . . . because I rejoice in thy salvation. *1 Samuel 2:1*

Answered prayer is a call to rejoice! God had answered Hannah's deepest desire by giving her a son, Samuel. After years of pain from being barren, her heart overflowed with praise into a sweet song of thanksgiving.

> Her countenance was no more sad. . . . Hannah had conceived, . . . she bare a son, and called his name Samuel, saying, Because I have asked him of the LORD. (1 Sam. 1:18, 20)

"Well, I'm glad for Hannah," you might say. "But what about my prayers that never get answered?" Understand, dear friend, that no prayer is ever unanswered, even if it seems that way!

Remember, you and I are children of the King. What a privilege! But we're still children. And as a good Father, sometimes God tells us no or simply to wait.

Even so, God's Word tells us that He doesn't withhold any good thing from us (Ps. 84:11). When a prayer is not answered the way we had hoped, that does not change the truth: God is holy, He is good, He is loving, and He knows what's best for us.

God the Father knew we needed a savior, so He answered with a resounding yes by sending His Son, through whom He "has given to us all things that pertain to life and godliness, through the knowledge of Him who called us by glory and virtue" (2 Pet. 1:3, NKJV).

As it did for Hannah, the answer to our most desperate prayer came through the birth of a baby boy—God's Son, Jesus Christ.

> He that spared not his own Son, but delivered him up for us all, how shall he not with him also freely give us all things? (Rom. 8:32)

Positioned to Hear

TODAY'S READING: 1 Samuel 3–5

> The LORD came, and stood, and called as at other times, Samuel, Samuel. Then Samuel answered, Speak; for thy servant heareth.
> *1 Samuel 3:10*

The nation of Israel was going through a spiritually dry time, and the Word of the Lord was scarce.

> The word of the LORD was precious in those days; there was no open vision. (1 Sam. 3:1)

These same words could well describe these last days. Many people talk about God, but it's rare to find a person searching and relying on the Word of God. Yet our hearts yearn to know that God hears us, and we need to hear Him.

> Bow down thine ear, O LORD, hear me: for I am poor and needy. (Ps. 86:1)

Have you ever asked where God is or wondered why you aren't experiencing Him in a fresh way? These seasons of spiritual dryness, when our souls cry out in need of God's presence, should prompt us to consider whether we've positioned ourselves to hear His voice.

Samuel was in a position to hear from God—He was in the tabernacle, serving the Lord. He was where God was.

Jesus followed this pattern of position as well. He rose up early to pray (Mark 1:35), sought out quiet places (Luke 5:16), was continually in the temple, His Father's house (2:49; John 2:17), and knew and applied the written Word of God (Luke 4:32; 10:27; Matt. 4:1–11).

So today, position yourself to hear from the Lord. Keep opening His Word to look for Jesus, spend time in prayer, go to His house, and fellowship with His people.

In Time of Need

TODAY'S READING: 1 Samuel 6–9

The LORD heard him. *1 Samuel 7:9*

Samuel and the Israelites were facing some daunting attacks and even more daunting discouragement. With their enemy, the Philistines, breathing down their necks, they were afraid, concerned, feeling the threats. But Samuel shows us how to face our foes and defeat discouragement.

> Samuel took a sucking lamb, and offered it for a burnt offering wholly unto the LORD: and Samuel cried unto the LORD for Israel; and the LORD heard him. (1 Sam. 7:9)

Does this offering sound familiar? Jesus is the lamb of God (Rev. 5:12), offered for us so we can approach God's throne, confident of His response.

> Let us therefore come boldly unto the throne of grace, that we may obtain mercy, and find grace to help in time of need. (Heb. 4:16)

When Samuel looked to God and the sacrifice He provided, Israel experienced victory. Similarly, Jesus is the provision for whatever need we face. When discouragement threatens to dim the truth of God's goodness and faithfulness, remember to set your eyes on Jesus!

> I will remember the works of the LORD: surely I will remember thy wonders of old. I will meditate also of all thy work, and talk of thy doings. Thy way, O God, is in the sanctuary: who is so great a God as our God? (Ps. 77:11–13)

April 12

Governed by God

TODAY'S READING: 1 Samuel 10–13

The people shouted, "Long live the king!" *1 Samuel 10:24,* NIV

As Samuel grew older, the task of leading Israel became more difficult. In an attempt to lessen the burden, he appointed his sons as administers of justice. This did not work out because Samuel's sons were not walking with the Lord (1 Sam. 8:3). The elders of Israel grew tired of the injustices done by Samuel's sons, so they came up with their own idea: a king, just like all the nations around them had.

The problem was, Israel had the opportunity to be governed by the King of kings. God Himself desired to rule Israel in what we call today a theocracy. He wanted the people to seek Him directly and be led by His Spirit. But they chose to be governed by mere men, imitating the nations around them.

What a great lesson for us! We know that God's Word is a lamp to our feet and a light to our path (Ps. 119:105) and that God writes His Word on our hearts (Rom. 2:15). We also know that the Holy Spirit lives and abides in us, quickening our conscience (2 Cor. 1:12). This is God's plan for our lives—that every single day we listen, seek, and obey the leading of His Spirit as we take in His Word and rely on His guiding.

Like Israel, however, we have a tendency to want to be governed by what we can see and touch. We want a list we can check off rather than seeking out His will daily. As you look into God's Word today, listen to what the Spirit lays on your heart and obey. You and I are His people and have the privilege of being led by the Spirit of the living God.

What a thrill to walk with Jesus—to have Him sit on the throne of our hearts as king, to listen to His voice, and to be governed by the Spirit of the living God!

By Many or Few

TODAY'S READING: 1 Samuel 14

> It may be that the LORD will work for us: for there is no restraint to the LORD to save by many or by few. *1 Samuel 14:6*

Is your heart, like Jonathan's, filled with anticipation of what God can accomplish in your life? Jonathan positioned himself for victory out of a fervent faith in his heavenly Father.

Jonathan determined to surprise a garrison of wicked Philistines, but to approach them he had to cross over a dangerous pass flanked by sharp rocks, putting him directly in the enemy's line of sight (1 Sam. 14:4–5). Despite the seemingly impossible situation, Jonathan believed that if God was with him nothing could stand against him.

> If they say to us, "Wait until we come to you," then we will stand still in our place, and we will not go up to them. But if they say, "Come up to us," then we will go up, for the LORD has given them into our hand. And this shall be the sign to us. (vv. 9–10, ESV)

Jonathan and his armor-bearer scaled the cliffs, fearlessly faced their foes, and defeated Israel's enemy with an army of two—under the protection of the Almighty. God doesn't need a garrison to accomplish His purposes, just a willing heart and eyes of faith.

We serve the same God that Jonathan did. Through Christ you are more than a conqueror. The battle has been won; your foe was defeated on the cross (Col. 2:15).

> Thanks be to God, who in Christ always leads us in triumphal procession, and through us spreads the fragrance of the knowledge of him everywhere. (2 Cor. 2:14, ESV)

The Enemy may be looking down on you, assuming you're already defeated. Stand firm like Jonathan, my friend. Jesus is leading you in a glorious procession of victory.

Keep reading: 1 Chronicles 8:1–9:1

April 14

He Cares About Your Heart

TODAY'S READING: 1 Samuel 15–16

Behold, to obey is better than sacrifice. *1 Samuel 15:22*

For the Lord, the heart of the matter is always a matter of the heart. Only God can see a person's hidden motives, and that's what He cares about. Today's reading highlights the dangers of compromise cloaked as obedience.

We are people with misguided hearts (Jer. 17:9), and we have a tendency to substitute or mistake our own religious ritual for what God truly called us to do. Like King Saul, we find ways to "sanctify" compromise by cloaking it in self-obligatory sacrifice, which masquerades as true worship.

God told King Saul not to take any plunder from their defeated enemy, the Amalekites. But Saul saw the sheep and cattle and decided to let his men take those. After all, they could be used to make sacrifices to the Lord, right?

> Samuel said, "Has the Lord as much delight in burnt offerings and sacrifices as in obeying the voice of the Lord? Behold, to obey is better than sacrifice. . . . Because you have rejected the word of the Lord, He has also rejected you from being king." (1 Sam. 15:22–23, NASB)

Time and again Jesus focused on the motives of the heart. He rebuked the Pharisees not for their outward rituals but for their inward sin, calling them whitewashed tombs (Matt. 23:27–28). When the poor widow gave only two small coins, Jesus saw her heart and knew she gave all she had (Luke 21:1–4).

Jesus's focus on the heart means we can apply Saul's story to our lives: may we not embrace things contrary to God's Word with the excuse that they will be used to benefit the Lord. God sees right through this sort of compromise. May our hearts be filled with a genuine willingness to obey our Lord today.

Keep reading: 1 Chronicles 5:7–10, 18–22; 9:35–44

The Victorious Shepherd

TODAY'S READING: 1 Samuel 17; Psalm 144

David prevailed over the Philistine with a sling and with a stone. *1 Samuel 17:50*

David's bravery and victory as he toppled the mighty giant Goliath is a classic Sunday school story. In a surge of knee-high enthusiasm, many a little tyke has come out whirling his or her sling. As a moralistic or inspirational narrative, this miraculous account of David and Goliath often concludes with "Be brave and courageous." But if we look more closely, we will discover a treasure trove of rich redemptive pictures of our shepherd and king, Jesus, the Son of David.

- David faced Goliath, who had taunted Israel for forty days, and Jesus resisted Satan after fasting in the wilderness for forty days (1 Sam. 17:16; Matt. 4:1–11).
- David was criticized by his brothers, just as Jesus came to His own and was not received by them (1 Sam. 17:28; John 1:11).
- Goliath demanded a sole victor, one representative from Israel who determined the entire outcome of the battle. By one man, Adam, sin entered into the world, but through one man, Jesus, our victory was won (1 Sam. 17:8–10; Rom. 5:18–19).
- David cut off Goliath's head, winning the day. Jesus has crushed the serpent's head for all eternity (1 Sam. 17:51; John 12:31; Rev. 20:7–10).
- David's victory came through God, just as our victory comes through Christ. We are like the cowering Israelites—only after David defeated Goliath did they pursue the enemy (1 Sam. 17:52; 1 Cor. 15:57).

The moral of the story, "Be brave and courageous," remains, but keep Jesus at the forefront. Only because He has gone before us can we follow Him into battle—and victory!

Heart of Wisdom

TODAY'S READING: 1 Samuel 18–20

David behaved himself wisely. *1 Samuel 18:14*

God's Word is constant, consistent, and enduring. The Word of God is alive and powerful in our lives (Heb. 4:12). That is why you can read a passage of Scripture over and over and each time gain something new.

Through his understanding of and reliance on God's Word, David was able to behave wisely (1 Sam. 18:14). God's Word contained the wisdom and counsel David needed.

> Thou shalt guide me with thy counsel. (Ps. 73:24)
>
> Thy word have I hid in mine heart, that I might not sin against thee. (119:11)

Because David esteemed God's Word, he knew how to respond to King Saul's jealousy. This is wisdom in action.

> David behaved himself wisely in all his ways; and the LORD was with him. Wherefore when Saul saw that he behaved himself very wisely, he was afraid of him. (1 Sam. 18:14–15)

Now consider our greatest example of all, Jesus. He knew the Scriptures and answered those who tested Him with wisdom that astounded those who opposed Him (Luke 4:32).

Both David and Jesus were the targets of a jealous king (1 Sam. 19:1–4; Matt. 2:16), but both had an understanding of God's Word that provided wisdom in the face of adversity (Ps. 119:130; Luke 20:20–26).

Knowing, studying, meditating on, and loving God's Word matters! Today, may we be filled with God's Word and act wisely because we know His counsel.

Not a Bone Broken

April 17

TODAY'S READING: **Psalms 5; 34; 59; 133; 1 Samuel 21**

> He keepeth all his bones: not one of them is broken.
> *Psalm 34:20*

David, forced to flee from his country as a result of Saul's jealous rage, found himself hiding in Philistine territory. David's true identity was soon discovered, and, well aware of the danger he was in, David feigned madness. The result was what he had hoped for: the Philistines dismissed him as an unlikely spy and an unrealistic threat. Through his craftiness David navigated a situation that would otherwise have certainly resulted in physical harm at the hands of his enemies.

Out of this experience David penned this praise and thanksgiving: "He keepeth all his bones: not one of them is broken" (Ps. 34:20).

Psalm 34 speaks of God's protection over David and the "righteous" (v. 19), but it should also stir our hearts and cause us to think of the one whom David's life foreshadowed: Jesus.

> Then came the soldiers, and brake the legs of the first, and of the other which was crucified with him. But when they came to Jesus, and saw that he was dead already, they brake not his legs. . . . For these things were done, that the scripture should be fulfilled, A bone of him shall not be broken. (John 19:32–33, 36)

Jesus Himself told us that the Psalms declared His death and resurrection (Luke 24:44), and that is exactly what we find in today's reading—a future picture of our Passover Lamb, pierced but not broken, just as the law required (Exod. 12:46).

April 18

Good, All the Time

TODAY'S READING: 1 Samuel 22–23; Psalms 52; 109

> I trust in the steadfast love of God forever and ever. *Psalm 52:8,* ESV

God is good, all the time! And all the time, God is good! David continued to hide from King Saul. Through this dark season he constantly reminded himself of God's goodness, love, provision, and promise to set all things right in the end. David trusted that God's justice would someday be seen by all men, and this faith gave David hope in the midst of a seemingly hopeless situation.

Whatever difficulties we face, like David, we can (and should) repeatedly remind ourselves to consider these same promises. God is only good. His very nature is good. This great goodness, as demonstrated on the cross, compels His unwavering love for humanity.

> God so loved the world, that he gave his only begotten Son, that whosoever believeth in him should not perish, but have everlasting life. (John 3:16)

Through the Cross God provided a way for us to have peace and forgiveness (Eph. 1:7; 2:14–15), a clean conscience (Rom. 8:1), and new life (2 Cor. 5:17). He has promised to satisfy our spiritual thirst (John 4:14; Rev. 21:6) and meet our every need (Phil. 4:19).

Truly God has kept and will keep every single promise as spoken by David in the Psalms. He showed us His goodness, He satisfies our souls, and even His righteous wrath against sin was satisfied as Jesus took the punishment of the world on Himself.

Whatever injustice you face today, keep your eyes on Jesus. Just as God kept His promises to David, He will keep His promises to you.

The Crucifixion Foretold

April 19

TODAY'S READING: Psalms 13; 17; 22; 54; 1 Samuel 24

They part my garments among them, and cast lots upon my vesture. *Psalm 22:18*

The presence of our Savior is unmistakable in today's reading! David lived approximately one thousand years before Christ and had never heard of death by crucifixion. It would take the Romans another four or five hundred years to invent such a brutal form of execution. Nevertheless, David knew of God's promise to send a messiah (Gen. 3:15), and inspired by the Holy Spirit, David wrote powerfully of the Prince of Peace to come. *The Scofield Reference Bible* highlights how the detailed picture of crucifixion described in Psalm 22 is perfectly fulfilled in the gospel account:

> The bones (of the hands, arms, shoulders, and pelvis) out of joint (v. 14); the profuse perspiration caused by intense suffering (v. 14); the action of the heart affected (v. 14); strength exhausted, and extreme thirst (v. 15); the hands and feet pierced (v. 16); partial nudity with the hurt to modesty (v. 17); are all incidental to that mode of death. The accompanying circumstances are precisely those fulfilled in the crucifixion of Christ. The desolate cry of verse 1 (Matt. 27:46); the periods of light and darkness of verse 2 (Matt. 27:45); the contumely of verse 6–8, 12, 13 (Matt. 27:39–43); the casting lots of verse 18 (Matt. 27:35), all were literally fulfilled.[45]

Jesus truly is the very essence of the Scriptures. He is the alpha and omega, the beginning and the end. The Old Testament points to Him, and the New Testament reveals Him. Open His Word today and find Him, for He is there (Ps. 40:7; Heb. 10:7).

April 20
Our Defender

TODAY'S READING: Psalms 7; 35; 57; 142

Awake, and rise to my defense! *Psalm 35:23,* NIV

Throughout Psalms we find David crying out to God and reminding himself of God's faithfulness. David desperately needed a defender from King Saul's ruthless accusations, threats, and endless attacks.

> Plead my cause, O LORD, with them that strive with me: fight against them that fight against me. Take hold of shield and buckler, and stand up for mine help. (35:1–2)

Even in the face of discouragement, difficulties, and danger, David knew God was his help!

The Bible tells us that our enemy, Satan, is the accuser of the brethren, continually bringing our faults to God's attention (Rev. 12:10). But just as God was faithful to defend David, the Son of David—Jesus Christ—literally rose to our defense. If you've received Jesus as your personal lord and savior, then you, too, have God Almighty on your side. He is for you (Rom. 8:31). You are no longer held captive by your sin (Gal. 4:7) or bound by its condemnation (Rom. 8:1); you have "passed from death unto life" (John 5:24), and because of Christ's atoning blood, God Almighty acts as your advocate.

> My little children, these things write I unto you, that ye sin not. And if any man sin, we have an advocate with the Father, Jesus Christ the righteous. (1 John 2:1)

Like David, you have an advocate who has risen to your defense!

Despite Insult

TODAY'S READING: 1 Samuel 25; Psalm 18

Nabal is his name, and folly is with him. *1 Samuel 25:25*

After spending months in the mountains protecting Nabal's herdsmen and flocks, David sent his messengers to ask Nabal for a favor. Nabal responded to David's men by insulting David and accusing him of being a runaway slave (1 Sam. 25:10–11). How rude!

Nabal's response enraged David, who determined to kill Nabal and his household. This seems an overreaction and out of character for the man who had endured so much persecution under Saul, but as the preacher and theologian A. B. Simpson noted,

> There are times when the bite of a mosquito is more trying than the roaring of a lion. There are little imps in life that worry us more than the larger foes that assail us, and we need more grace to keep our sweetness amid the thousand petty and harassing worries than in the roar of the torrent and the crash of the tempest.[46]

The good news was that Nabal's beautiful wife, Abigail, was well versed in diplomacy and immediately intervened in her foolish husband's affairs. Her wise words convinced David to avoid, as he said, "avenging myself with my own hands" (v. 33, NIV), which would have ended in needless bloodshed. Instead of taking revenge, he sent her home in peace.

Abigail helped David, in this situation, remain faithful as a symbol of Jesus, whose trial was crowned not just with thorns but with the jeering taunts and insults of His accusers (Luke 22:63). He could have, in a moment's time, removed Himself (23:37) or avenged Himself. But He took the blows of insults and rudeness and shed His own blood to give us peace.

April 22

The Coming Deliverer

TODAY'S READING: 2 Samuel 22; 1 Samuel 26; Psalms 14; 53

> The LORD is my rock, and my fortress, and my deliverer.
> *2 Samuel 22:2*

David had waited nearly twenty years to become king. Half of that time he had spent running for his life as he was being threatened by King Saul. But he was finally beginning to see God's promises fulfilled. In today's reading David recounts God's faithfulness in these most precious and powerful words:

> He is my stronghold, my refuge and my savior—from violent men you save me. (2 Sam. 22:3, NIV)

Can you relate to David's heartfelt worship here? As David looks back and meditates on the mercies of the Lord, his heart rejoices and he produces a beautiful prophecy of the coming savior, our Lord Jesus Christ.

> He reached down from on high and took hold of me; he drew me out of deep waters. He rescued me from my powerful enemy. (vv. 17–18, NIV)

Our Savior reached down: He humbled Himself, became a man, walked among us, and died for us in order to save us. Our Deliverer drew us out of the waters of sin and left our sins there in the deep (Mic. 7:19). Our Refuge rescued us from our powerful Enemy by defeating death through redemption by His blood.

Just as David reflected on the mercies, favor, and provision God had granted him, may you and I also make a habit of meditating on the truth of what He's done for us, that He might receive all glory and honor and praise.

What a Savior!

April 23

TODAY'S READING: Psalms 31; 40; 56; 1 Samuel 27

Let all those who seek You rejoice and be glad in You;
Let such as love Your salvation say continually,
"The LORD be magnified!" *Psalm 40:16,* NKJV

In Psalms we often find David crying out to the Lord to save him from his enemies. You and I can relate. Who hasn't had an enemy or two who seems to take pleasure in causing us problems and pain on our pilgrimage through life? But here's the truth, dear fellow traveler: the Bible tells us that our battles are "not against flesh and blood, but against principalities, against powers, against the rulers of . . . this world, against spiritual wickedness" (Eph. 6:12). Moreover, Peter tells us we have an enemy, Satan, who is like a lion looking to devour us (1 Pet. 5:8). "But God, who is rich in mercy," has saved us (Eph. 2:4). God has given us shelter at the foot of the cross, where we find grace to help us in times of need (Heb. 4:16). And that is such good news—that's the gospel!

David was well aware of God's promise to send a savior, and he looked forward to his redemption. We have the boundless blessing of knowing that the promise of redemption has been fulfilled in Christ. David wrote in shadows of events still to come, but we can focus squarely on the Cross, in which we find shelter from the shame of Satan.

David declared,

> In you, O LORD, I have taken refuge; let me never be put to shame. (Ps. 31:1, NIV)

Because of the Cross of Christ, we have been "reconciled to God," never to be put to shame (Rom. 5:10; 2 Cor. 5:19). We are forgiven and justified and will one day soon be glorified with Him (Col. 1:14).

Look to the Cross today and find your refuge in Jesus. Truly the Lord is good. What a savior!

Keep reading: 1 Chronicles 12:1–7, 19–22; 1 Samuel 29:1–11

April 24

A Sign of His Goodness

TODAY'S READING: Psalms 69; 86; 131; 1 Samuel 28

Give me a sign of your goodness. *Psalm 86:17,* NIV

Have you ever prayed for a sign from the Lord? I certainly have, and that inclination seems to be a part of human nature. We want to know if God is at work the way we hope. We want our heavenly Father to fix our faulty, fickle faith with His reassurances.

I am encouraged to know that David experienced the same longing. He stirred his heart to remember God's faithfulness, yet he yearned for a sign of God's continuing goodness.

> Give me a sign of your goodness, that my enemies may see it and be put to shame, for you, O LORD, have helped me and comforted me. (Ps. 86:17, NIV)

God did, in fact, give us the greatest possible sign of His goodness: He gave us Himself! Jesus spoke of this when He addressed the Pharisees and Sadducees who asked for an outward sign of His power. He said that no sign would be given except for the sign of Jonah, pointing to the fact that He would be buried and in three days rise again (Matt. 16:4).

God knows our frailty. He understands that our nature needs signs of His goodness. Keep washing in the water of the Word, and you'll find all the signs you need of God's goodness right there in its pages.

Share and Share Alike

April 25

TODAY'S READING: 1 Samuel 30–31; 2 Samuel 1

The share of the man who stayed . . . is to be the same as that of him who went down to the battle. All will share alike.
1 Samuel 30:24, NIV

David and his men had just returned from battle—only to find their homes ransacked and their families taken captive (1 Sam. 30:3). Understandably, their hearts were filled with despair. But rather than simply reacting, David sought the Lord for instruction. God told him to pursue the enemy. David and his men were already exhausted from fighting, "but David found strength in the LORD his God" (v. 6, NIV).

Once again David and his six hundred men headed out to battle. As they pursued their enemy, they came to a ravine. Two hundred of the men were simply too worn out to cross over (v. 9), so they stayed behind to guard the supplies. David and the others continued on and were victorious. They conquered the Amalekites, rescued their families, and returned with piles of plunder.

What happened next reflects God's heart toward His people. You see, the men who had found the strength to fight did not want to divide the spoils of war with those who had stayed behind. But David reminded his men that it was God who gave them the strength to secure the victory. He instructed them to divide the spoils equally (v. 24).

What a wonderful picture of our precious Jesus! When we were unable to win the war with sin because our flesh was too frail, He fought our battle for us, defeated our Enemy, rose victorious, and made us coheirs with Him (Rom. 8:15–17). We did nothing because we were too weak. Yet we still share equally in the spoils of the war Jesus won on the cross.

Amazing grace!

Keep reading: 1 Chronicles 10

April 26

Patience in the Promise

TODAY'S READING: 2 Samuel 2:1–5:5

> David was thirty years old when he became king. *2 Samuel 5:4,* NIV

After years of hiding from King Saul, fighting for his life, and camping out in caves, David finally experienced the fulfillment of God's promise. He had been anointed as Israel's future king when he was just a boy (1 Sam. 16). Now, at age thirty, David finally walked into the role he'd been appointed to so long before.

> The Lord said to you, "You shall shepherd My people Israel, and be ruler over Israel." (2 Sam. 5:2, NKJV)

As David's story demonstrates, God's timing frequently differs from ours. As time passes between promise made and promise fulfilled, we often forget that His Word is true and He is faithful to do all that He promises.

David's life points to another shepherd who began His ministry at age thirty: Jesus, the good shepherd, who came from the line of David (Matt. 1:1–17). David ruled Israel for forty years, but Jesus Christ will reign forever!

> He shall reign over the house of Jacob for ever; and of his kingdom there shall be no end. (Luke 1:33)

If you're in a season where, like David, you're not able to see how God will keep His promises or when they might ever come to pass, rest assured He will fulfill them in His perfect timing. His Word is true, and He is faithful to bring about everything He has promised to you and to me. He promised to come and redeem us from our sin, and He did. He promises to return and take us to heaven, and He will. Soon and very soon we'll be going to see our King. Have patience as you wait upon His promises. He will keep them!

Keep reading: 1 Chronicles 3:1–4; 11:1–3

The Crowned King

April 27

TODAY'S READING: 1 Chronicles 12:23–40; Psalms 2; 78

They came to Hebron fully determined to make David king over all Israel. *1 Chronicles 12:38,* NIV

The account of the men who came to crown David as king might seem mundane, but if we gloss over it, we risk missing a beautiful picture of you and me standing ready to crown the Son of David as our king.

Remember, every one of the people, details, surroundings, and circumstances that God chose to mention in the Bible is there for a reason, so let's look at the details in today's reading.

We're told that the children of Judah bore "shield and spear" (1 Chron. 12:24). The name Judah means "praised."[47] Just as the children of Judah bore shield and spear while crowning David king, you and I are to praise the Lord through the heavenly armor we are given: "the shield of faith" and "the sword of the Spirit" (Eph. 6:16–17).

Then there were the men of Simeon, the "mighty men of valour" (1 Chron. 12:25). The name Simeon means "hearing with acceptance."[48] Obedience brings victory and is the way of valor. As Jesus followers, we are more than conquerors, victorious in Christ. May we stand ready to listen and obey as we crown Him king.

Then there was the tribe of Benjamin, whose name means "son of the right hand."[49] Until this moment the tribe of Benjamin had remained faithful to Saul, who was one of their own. Oh, the grace of God seen here! Despite their last-minute "conversion," they were counted among David's men, just as that thief on the cross beside Christ was counted among those saved (Luke 23:39–43).

Last but not least was the half tribe of Manasseh. The name Manasseh means "causing to forget."[50] But these men were not forgotten! They were "expressed by name" (1 Chron. 12:31). God has not forgotten you. Your name is listed in the Lamb's Book of Life (Isa. 43:1; Luke 10:20).

So today, see Jesus, the crowned king, in David—and see yourself in the tribes as you take up your armor, listen and obey, and marvel in His grace because your name is listed in His Book of Life!

April 28

None Beside Him

TODAY'S READING: Psalms 16; 101; 2 Samuel 5:6–25

You are my Lord; I have no good besides You. *Psalm 16:2,* NASB

We have so much to be thankful for! God is our refuge, our counsel, our strength, our stability, our song. As you read the Scriptures today, consider how many things God says He is to us and provides for us.

Nothing in this world can really satisfy our souls. Our deep desire for some sort of fulfillment is answered only in the One who calls to you and me and says, "You, follow Me." Only Jesus Christ can give us everlasting life, quench our thirsty souls, and bring eternal satisfaction to our spirits.

David recognized that all the good he had was from God and that apart from Him he had nothing.

> I said to the LORD, "You are my Lord; apart from you I have no good thing." (Ps. 16:2, NIV)

The same is true for you and me. In Christ alone we find all we need (2 Pet. 1:3–4). Jesus is the living water, the bread of life, the light of the world, the great "I am"—which means Jesus is our all in all. He provides for and fulfills our every need, and He gives us every good thing.

> Every good gift and every perfect gift is from above, and cometh down from the Father of lights, with whom is no variableness, neither shadow of turning. (James 1:17)

Echoing David, you can declare, "Apart from you, oh Lord, I have no good thing." As you take in His Word today, consider who He is and what He has done for you. And in Christ alone, find satisfaction for today, tomorrow, and forever.

Keep reading: 1 Chronicles 11:4–9, 15–19; 14:1–2, 8–17; 2 Samuel 23:13–17

The Right Thing, the Wrong Way

April 29

TODAY'S READING: 2 Samuel 6; 1 Chronicles 13; 1 Chronicles 15–16

They set the ark of God upon a new cart. *2 Samuel 6:3*

David wanted to bring the ark of the covenant back to Jerusalem. However, he failed to follow God's explicit instructions (Num. 4:1–15), and the effort ended in a fiasco. David's intentions were good, but good intentions do not trump God's directions.

God had given His people a law, the written record of which was to be carried inside the ark. Instead of supporting it with poles, as God had instructed, David wanted to try something different, to put it on a cart as the Philistines had done (1 Sam. 6:7–8). In their parade back to Jerusalem, the oxen stumbled and the cart carrying the law became unstable. The well-meaning Uzzah reached out and attempted to bear the weight of the law in his own strength. It cost his life.

Do you see the connection to Jesus? Like David's men, we are unable to bear the weight of God's law in our own strength. But God sent us His Son, who followed the law perfectly and carries it for us.

Today, don't try to carry God's law in your own strength or in your own way. You will be crushed under its weight. We must do the right thing in the right way—through the Spirit.

> The law of the Spirit of life has set you free in Christ Jesus from the law of sin and death. For God has done what the law, weakened by the flesh, could not do. By sending his own Son in the likeness of sinful flesh and for sin, he condemned sin in the flesh, in order that the righteous requirement of the law might be fulfilled in us, who walk not according to the flesh but according to the Spirit. (Rom. 8:2–4, ESV)

April 30

Give Thanks

TODAY'S READING: Psalms 15; 19; 24; 65; 68; 110

Blessed be the Lord,
Who daily loads us with benefits,
The God of our salvation! *Psalm 68:19,* NKJV

Through the blood of Jesus, our God has saved us! And through Jesus He daily loads us with benefits. There are seasons, however, when we find it difficult to count our blessings. David knew this firsthand. But instead of letting himself slide into the despair of depression, he listed God's benefits. We, too, are told in difficult times to look to Jesus, "the author and finisher of our faith" (Heb. 12:2), the one in whom we have endless blessings (Eph. 1:3).

David did not know Jesus's name or how God would fulfill His promise of a redeemer, but by the inspiration of the Holy Spirit, he wrote of blessings that we now see embodied in Christ. Therefore, like David, we can walk in the divine instructions of Psalm 68 and

- be glad and in good spirits (v. 3)
- rejoice in the Lord's presence (vv. 3–4)
- sing to God (vv. 4, 32)
- proclaim His Word and His power (vv. 11, 34)
- praise God in His congregation (v. 26)

We find a similar list in the New Testament:

> Rejoice evermore. Pray without ceasing. In every thing give thanks: for this is the will of God in Christ Jesus concerning you. (1 Thess. 5:16–18)

Both the psalmist David and the apostle Paul teach us how to triumph in tough times (for indeed these men knew tough times). Despite the challenges of today, take time to be thankful, to count the blessings you have in Jesus, to praise Jesus's name—for He is worthy.

Keep reading: 2 Samuel 8:1; 1 Chronicles 18:1;
2 Samuel 21:15–18; 1 Chronicles 20:4

A Strong Helper

May 1

TODAY'S READING: Psalm 33; 2 Samuel 10

There is no king saved by the multitude . . . : a mighty man is not delivered by much strength. *Psalm 33:16*

Today's reading details battles, stories of personal conflicts, stressful situations, enemy engagements, and all kinds of adverse conditions. But the Lord sent David mighty men, for camaraderie and fellowship, but most of all to fight valiantly and loyally alongside their king.

The companionship of those strong men reminds me of how Jesus sent us the Holy Spirit to be our comrade, to bring us into fellowship with the Father, and to fill us with strength and power. This is why Jesus said, "Greater is He who is in you than he who is in the world" (1 John 4:4, NASB). God Himself dwells in you.

Like David, we are engaged in a battle.

> We wrestle not against flesh and blood, but against principalities, against powers, against the rulers of the darkness of this world, against spiritual wickedness in high places. (Eph. 6:12)

In our own strength we aren't equipped for victory, but we fight alongside the mightiest defender of all: Jesus, the Lord of hosts. He is our conquering king, and through the power of His name, darkness flees, the blind see, the deaf hear, and the lame leap for joy (Matt. 11:5).

Aren't you thankful today to be on the winning side of this battle? Regardless of how you feel, regardless of your immediate circumstances or struggles, you can be sure that God has already won the battle and triumphed victoriously (John 16:33). He equips His saints for war and has given you the mighty Holy Spirit as your companion.

Keep reading: 2 Samuel 23:8–12; 1 Chronicles 11:10–14; 2 Samuel 21:19–22; 1 Chronicles 20:5–8; 19

May 2 The Completeness of God's Forgiveness

TODAY'S READING: 2 Samuel 11–12; Psalms 6; 32

> Blessed is he whose transgression is forgiven, whose sin is covered. *Psalm 32:1*

David was wallowing in the aftermath of sin: guilt, condemnation, and consequences. But God, who is rich in mercy, allowed David to experience repentance and the reassurance of forgiveness.

> I acknowledged my sin to You, and my iniquity I have not hidden. I said, "I will confess my transgressions to the Lord," and You forgave the iniquity of my sin. Selah. (Ps. 32:5, NKJV)

David could not undo his sin. His only remedy was a gracious gift from God: the gift of forgiveness.

We have all sinned and endured the guilt and consequences and misery it brings. Each of us owed a penalty far beyond what we could ever repay. Like David, we cannot undo our sin (Rom. 3:20–23; Gal. 3:11; James 2:10). But Jesus offered Himself as the payment for the penalty we owed so we could be restored, be forgiven, and have the record detailing our faults destroyed (Ps. 103:12; Isa. 43:25). Just as David experienced God's forgiveness, we can too!

The Greek word for *forgiven* is *charizomai,* which means "to grant forgiveness, to pardon, to give graciously, give freely, bestow, . . . graciously to restore one to another."[51] This is the completeness of God's forgiveness—charizomai! Yes, you are forgiven, but also pardoned, shown favor, and restored!

David experienced the wholeness and restoration that the reality of God's forgiveness brings. May you, too, dear Christian, who have been bought, washed, and cleansed in the blood of Jesus Christ, enter into the full realization of God's complete forgiveness.

Hyssop

TODAY'S READING: Psalms 21; 38; 51

Purge me with hyssop, and I shall be clean: wash me, and
I shall be whiter than snow. *Psalm 51:7*

The slightest details in God's Word can open our eyes to the grandest truths of grace. Take for instance David's reference in Psalm 51:7. After sinning terribly with Bathsheba, David was desperately grieved and pleaded with the Lord for forgiveness. He asked God to purge him with hyssop.

Hyssop was a little shrub with a significant purpose. Think back to Leviticus 14:1–7. There, a sprig of hyssop would be dipped in water and blood as purification was applied to a person healed of leprosy. This ceremonial law shadowed the complete forgiveness that would come through Christ and Christ alone.

In the Old Testament leprosy often symbolized sin, as it was deadly, extremely infectious, and affected the whole person. There was no remedy apart from a miracle (2 Kings 5). The symbolism fits! We had no remedy apart from Christ.

The cleansing of the hyssop foreshadowed the complete forgiveness we find in Jesus. He purged our guilty conscience as He covered us in His redemptive blood (Heb. 9:14). But He also washes us in the water of His Word, cleansing us from the defilement of sin (John 15:3; Eph. 5:26) and making us white as snow (Eph. 5:27).

God raised up for David "a righteous Branch" (Jer. 23:5–6), who brought us complete forgiveness. I believe it to be no coincidence that the drink offered to Jesus Christ on the cross was extended to Him on a branch of hyssop (John 19:29). The One who fulfilled the law drank from the very thing that represented purification, as He bore our sins upon Himself.

Like David, you can pray today, "Purge me with hyssop, and I shall be clean," knowing it is Jesus Himself who washes you and makes you whiter than snow.

Keep reading: Psalm 103; 1 Chronicles 20:1–3;
2 Samuel 8:2–8; 1 Chronicles 18:2–8

May 4

Because He Loved Them

TODAY'S READING: Psalms 20; 44; 60; 108; 124

It was not by their sword that they won the land,
nor did their arm bring them victory;
it was your right hand, your arm,
and the light of your face, for you loved them. *Psalm 44:3,* NIV

In Psalm 44 the psalmist praised God for the victories He brings. The words he penned also served as magnificent prophecies pointing to our Savior. Inspired by the Holy Spirit, he painted a picture of our Redeemer and His outstretched arms that brought you and me ultimate victory as a result of His ultimate love.

Just as this psalm says, it was not by our own sword that we won the victory; it was God's right hand and His arms that defeated our foe. Through the outstretched arms of Jesus on Calvary, we are washed clean and made whole. His hands were nailed to the cross so that we, through believing in and receiving His gift of love, would be set free.

He said to Thomas, "Reach your finger here, and look at My hands; and reach your hand here, and put it into My side. Do not be unbelieving, but believing." (John 20:27, NKJV)

Psalm 44 says Israel's victory came by God's arm and the light of His face, because He loved them. In the same way, we find victory through His Son, Jesus Christ—the light of the world. Through Him we no longer walk in darkness, but in the light of His face we find life everlasting.

Then spake Jesus again unto them, saying, I am the light of the world: he that followeth me shall not walk in darkness, but shall have the light of life. (John 8:12)

May you walk in the light of His face and His ultimate love today.

Keep reading: 2 Samuel 8:9–14; 1 Chronicles 18:9–13

Brave Benaiah

TODAY'S READING: 2 Samuel 23:18–39; 8:15–18

Benaiah . . . performed great exploits. *2 Samuel 23:20,* NIV

The ancient account of the brave Benaiah holds an encouraging truth for us today regarding our God who gives His people strength and victory.

> Benaiah . . . performed great exploits. He struck down two of Moab's best men. He also went down into a pit on a snowy day and killed a lion. And he struck down a huge Egyptian. Although the Egyptian had a spear in his hand, Benaiah went against him with a club. He snatched the spear from the Egyptian's hand and killed him with his own spear. (2 Sam. 23:20–21, NIV)

Consider the Bible typology in this scene. Benaiah killed a lion, and our Enemy is likened to a roaring lion seeking to devour us (1 Pet. 5:8). Benaiah also took down the mightiest of the Moabites and Egyptians, both pictures of the heavyweight enemies the world will throw at us. But just as God gave Benaiah victory, He also has given victory to you and me!

Benaiah, one of David's mighty men, was seemingly outmatched and in a vulnerable place—in a pit. Yet God empowered him to defeat his enemies.

When we find ourselves in a pit and under threat, we can remember God's promises. Because of Jesus Christ nothing "will be able to separate us from the love of God" (Rom. 8:39, ESV).

Just as Benaiah faced his foes and ventured into frightful battles in great faith, you can allow the Lord to strengthen your arms and clothe you in His armor (Eph. 6:13–17) with faith that He's already won the battle.

Remember, God uses the weak of this world to make manifest His might (1 Cor. 1:27), and you are more than a conqueror through Christ Jesus who strengthens you (Rom. 8:37).

Keep reading: 1 Chronicles 11:20–47; 18:14–17; 17

May 6

Confess to Move On

TODAY'S READING: Psalms 8; 138–139; 145; 2 Samuel 21:1–14; 9

> The LORD is gracious and compassionate, slow to anger and rich in love. *Psalm 145:8,* NIV

Israel had been suffering through a famine for three years. When David prayerfully sought the reason, God answered: the famine was a result of King Saul's wicked treatment of the Gibeonites, breaking a long-ago promise of Israel to protect them. Even though Saul was dead, the nation as a whole needed to face up to, confess, and repent of its sin (2 Sam. 21:1–3).

The fact that God purges sin from both individuals and nations is a blessing because the Bible teaches that sin leads to death and leaves devastation in its wake. God chastens those He loves (Heb. 12:6), and through His chastisement we see that He loves mankind!

It may be difficult for us to reconcile love and chastisement, but sin always has consequences that need to be addressed. As New Testament believers, we have the joy of knowing that God Himself came and dealt with our sin, paying its ultimate consequence, which is death. Now we look to Jesus, whose blood "cleanse[s] us from all unrighteousness" (1 John 1:9).

Jesus Himself bore our sins and iniquities (1 Pet. 2:24). Sin still brings consequences, of course, and God still chastens those He loves, but forgiveness is readily available.

> If we confess our sins, he is faithful and just to forgive us our sins, and to cleanse us from all unrighteousness. (1 John 1:9)

May you be quick to recognize sin, abandon it, and embrace the forgiveness available through Christ (Rom. 10:9).

Family Conflict

May 7

TODAY'S READING: 2 Samuel 13:1–15:6

David mourned for his son every day. *2 Samuel 13:37*

The Bible says there's "nothing new under the sun" (Eccles. 1:9, NIV). Through His Word God gave us examples, principles, and instructions to shape our perspectives and worldviews and, as a result, help us in every life situation we encounter (1 Cor. 10:6, 11; 2 Pet. 1:3; Col. 2:9).

The quarreling among David's sons is a great example. Here we find a tragic commentary on the devastating way sin fractures relationships. Whether we draw from these examples a warning of what not to do or view them as a lesson in how to rise above a situation, God's Word serves as a compass to help us navigate even the most complicated situations.

The discord within David's family revolved around who would succeed him as king. The love of power and desire for fame is bound tight around the hearts of all people. Even Jesus's disciples were prone to such things, as are we. But the Scriptures provide the proper perspective.

> There was also a dispute among them, as to which of them should be considered the greatest. And He said to them, ". . . on the contrary, he who is greatest among you, let him be as the younger, and he who governs as he who serves." (Luke 22:24–26, NKJV)

Dear Christian, maybe today your family is facing a fracture. The answer, as always, is found in God's Word. God sent His only Son, Jesus, and desires that through Him, His family would walk in unity, responding to one another in humility and serving one another in love. Our goal is not glory of self but rather the glory of God, as we strive to be the servants of all.

Keep reading: 2 Samuel 5:13–16; 1 Chronicles 14:3–7; 3:4–16

May 8

Saved from Wrath

TODAY'S READING: 2 Samuel 24; 1 Chronicles 21

> David built an altar . . . and the plague on Israel was stopped.
> *2 Samuel 24:25,* NIV

Jesus is the alpha and omega, the beginning and the end, the King of kings and Lord of lords, our savior and redeemer. In today's reading we find a beautiful picture of Jesus Christ and His power over the curse of sin.

First Chronicles 21 details a clear pattern of temptation, sin, and consequences, followed by an outpouring of God's mercy and grace. David caved to temptation as he wanted to evaluate his strength in numbers rather than obey God's instructions. David's failure to trust God and his decision to take a census brought devastating consequences. As a result, the people around him were hurt. That is sin's pattern (James 1:15).

Notice, however, that a sacrifice stopped the consequence of David's sin from spreading. What a powerful picture! When we read this story looking for the Son of David, we see the perfect sacrifice, Jesus Christ, who put a stop to the consequence of eternal death that resulted from our sin and through His death brought us eternal life.

> Much more then, being now justified by his blood, we shall be saved from wrath through him. (Rom. 5:9)

David's remedy is your remedy: the sacrifice. God remains faithful to His character and His Word. He was merciful then as He gave a glimpse of the coming redeemer. He is merciful now as you look to His Son the Savior (John 5:24)!

Perspective

TODAY'S READING: 2 Samuel 15:7–16:4; Psalms 3–4; 23; 26

Surely goodness and mercy shall follow me all the days of my life: and I will dwell in the house of the LORD for ever.
Psalm 23:6

Life brings trials and tribulations, but God is greater than all these. He is our strong tower, our shield, and our exceeding great reward! David knew a thing or two about life's trials and tribulations: he was betrayed by Saul; spent years running for his life; suffered the death of his infant son; and saw another son, Absalom, divide the people and launch a rebellion. God was not indifferent to David's struggles. On the contrary God was quite aware and in control. For you see, God would redeem David's trials in the most glorious way—pointing to and foreshadowing the Son of David, Jesus Christ (Matt. 1:1).

Both David and Jesus were betrayed by close friends (2 Sam. 15:31; Matt. 26:14–16). Both left Jerusalem after being rejected by its citizens (2 Sam. 15:13–14; John 1:11). Both climbed the Mount of Olives and prayed (2 Sam. 15:30–32; Luke 22:39–44). But in the end, both did and will return to Jerusalem in triumph (2 Sam. 19:8–15; Rev. 21:1–4).[52]

Through his trials David constantly prayed (Ps. 4:1). He reminded himself of God's faithfulness (3:8), and he continued to find comfort in God's house (26:8, 12). David held on to God's promises to come (2 Sam. 7:8–17), but now we look to Jesus, the fulfillment of all God has promised us (2 Pet. 1:3). What a perspective! God can use all things, even—or perhaps especially—hardship, to bring glory to our King!

May 10 Delight in Him

TODAY'S READING: Psalms 9–12; 27; 36–37

> Delight yourself in the LORD, and he will give you the desires of your heart. *Psalm 37:4,* ESV

The joy of growing closer and closer to our Savior is the greatest happiness we can know this side of heaven. That's not just a sappy sentiment. Haven't you found it to be true? As God becomes your daily delight, you find your soul is truly satisfied and your heart's desires are fulfilled.

> Commit thy way unto the LORD; trust also in him; and he shall bring it to pass. And he shall bring forth thy righteousness as the light, and thy judgment as the noonday. (Ps. 37:5–6)

Committing one's way to the Lord is part of sanctification. Peace comes by way of justification ("just-if-I'd" never sinned), but happiness (our desires fulfilled) comes by way of sanctification. Sanctification is simply the process of being set apart and becoming more like Jesus Christ.

God's ways are pure, peaceable, and full of life. David knew this when he penned the psalms, and Jesus reminded us of this in His Sermon on the Mount: if we hunger and thirst for righteousness, we will be fulfilled.

> Blessed [joyful, nourished by God's goodness] are those who hunger and thirst for righteousness [those who actively seek right standing with God], for they will be [completely] satisfied. (Matt. 5:6, AMP)

All that David spoke of regarding the source of delight, Jesus demonstrated. The Scriptures tell us that Jesus loved righteousness and hated wickedness. As a result, He was anointed with gladness (Heb. 1:9). Following His ways will produce joy and all manner of goodness. If our delight is in the things of the Lord, we will find ourselves a very happy people—guaranteed.

> Happy are the people whose God is the LORD! (Ps. 144:15, NKJV)

Keep reading: 2 Samuel 15:37; 16:15

The Measure of Our Days

TODAY'S READING: Psalms 28; 39; 41–43; 2 Samuel 16:16–17:23

LORD, make me to know my end. *Psalm 39:4,* NKJV

Life is short. David spoke of our human frailty and of our days being numbered.

> LORD, make me to know my end, and what is the measure of
> my days, that I may know how frail I am. Indeed, You have
> made my days as handbreadths, and my age is as nothing
> before You; certainly every man at his best state is but vapor.
> (Ps. 39:4–5, NKJV)

Regardless of the miracles of modern medicine, we are here on earth for such a short amount of time compared to eternity. That's why Jesus told us to store up eternal treasure rather than earthly riches.

> Do not lay up for yourselves treasures on earth, where moth
> and rust destroy and where thieves break in and steal; but lay
> up for yourselves treasures in heaven, where neither moth nor
> rust destroys and where thieves do not break in and steal.
> (Matt. 6:19–20, NKJV)

Here's the beautiful thing, my friend: the things we choose to do here and now can last an eternity. What an encouraging truth! God, in His grace, made a way for us to invest in heaven. So how do we send our treasure ahead to heaven? We live for His glory and not our own. We love Him. We obey Him. We share the truth of His Word with the lost and dying world around us because we cannot take earthly possessions into eternity, but we can take people. And since Jesus Himself died for those people, what a terrific treasure to store up (Prov. 11:30)!

Since we know our time is short, let's redeem it. Like David, let's ask the Lord for an eternal perspective and set our sights on things above, storing up treasure in heaven—which is right around the corner.

Unharmed

TODAY'S READING: Psalms 55; 58; 61–63; 2 Samuel 18

> He ransoms me unharmed from the battle waged against me.
> *Psalm 55:18,* NIV

Psalm 55:18 supernaturally summarizes the testimony of those who know the Lord. God has rescued us, just as He rescued the psalmist. The Bible itself says that the Old Testament saints were given to us as examples to follow (1 Cor. 10:11). The things they experienced are written down to show us how God works in our lives and how He fulfilled all His promises through His Son, Jesus Christ. In David's time we see God delivering His people from their enemies and rescuing them unharmed. Today, you and I find the perfect fulfillment of this same truth in and through Jesus!

Once held captive to the power of sin and death, we have been fully ransomed. Jesus Christ paid the price to buy us out of slavery to our Enemy, and in so doing, He has crushed our Adversary. He not only rescues but is able to deliver us totally unharmed.

We see the New Testament fulfillment of this Old Testament picture when Jesus delivered the demoniac from a legion of darkness (Mark 5:3–5). The man lived among the dead and was possessed by demons more powerful than any human could tame (v. 9). But Jesus rescued him from the power of darkness and completely restored his well-being.

> Then they came to Jesus, and saw the one who had been demon-possessed . . . sitting and clothed and in his right mind. (v. 15, NKJV)

Only through Jesus can those dead in sin be made alive. Only by His grace can those burdened by sin be freed from the chains of guilt (Rom. 8:1). You are free from sin, my friend.

Keep reading: 2 Samuel 17:24–29; 1 Chronicles 2:17

A Father's Love

May 13

TODAY'S READING: 2 Samuel 19; Psalms 64; 70; 84; 141; 143

The king weepeth and mourneth for Absalom. *2 Samuel 19:1*

David deeply loved his son Absalom. Yet Absalom wreaked havoc on David's family. To say he was the center of family drama would be an understatement. Absalom murdered his half brother, was banned from Jerusalem, and desired to dethrone his father.

So what can we learn from this heartbreaking and horrible situation? In Jesus we find meaning for the experiences of the Old Testament saints, even David's wayward son Absalom.

Consider how Jesus spoke directly of another father's love for his prodigal son.

> When he was yet a great way off, his father saw him, and had compassion, and ran, and fell on his neck, and kissed him. . . . For this my son was dead, and is alive again; he was lost, and is found. (Luke 15:20, 24)

David's grief over Absalom gives us a glimpse of our heavenly Father's unfailing love for us, which is perfectly described in Jesus's parable about the prodigal son. You and I were prodigals, yet the Father ran to receive us and rejoiced when we came home.

> Likewise, I say unto you, there is joy in the presence of the angels of God over one sinner that repenteth. (v. 10)

Regardless of whether you empathize with David or the prodigal in today's reading, may you stand amazed at the Father's unfailing love, which is always ready to receive a wayward son or daughter.

May 14

Standing with the King

TODAY'S READING: 2 Samuel 20; 1 Chronicles 22; Psalms 29–30; 140

> Give unto the LORD the glory due unto his name; worship the LORD in the beauty of holiness. *Psalm 29:2*

Praise for our King is a crucial part of the Christian life. It keeps our hearts soft, our attitudes in check, and our perspectives proper. On David's long road back home after Absalom's rebellion, the king encountered still more opposition, this time from a troublemaker named Sheba (2 Sam. 20:1). As a result, all the men of Israel deserted David—except the men of Judah (v. 2).

The name Judah means "praised." How fitting that the men of Judah stayed close to their king all the way from the Jordan to Jerusalem. David is a powerful picture of King Jesus, and Judah demonstrates the power of praise. Praise keeps us loyal and our hearts close to our King!

Just as the men of Judah followed David all the way to Jerusalem, we will follow Jesus all the way to Zion with songs of gladness and crowned with "everlasting joy" (Isa. 35:10; Rev. 7:17).

> I heard as it were the voice of a great multitude . . . and as the voice of mighty thunderings, saying, Alleluia: for the Lord God omnipotent reigneth. (19:6)

Regardless of the naysayers, critics, trouble makers, or abandoners, may we be like the men of Judah, staying close to the King and knowing that soon we will stand with Him in heaven. From now until eternity, let's stay close to our King through praise.

Morning and Evening

TODAY'S READING: 1 Chronicles 23–24

Four thousand praised the Lord with musical instruments.
1 Chronicles 23:5, NKJV

We've seen from the beginning that Jesus is the very essence of the Scriptures. He is the perfect fulfillment of all the Old Testament rules and regulations. Jesus fulfilled the law (Matt. 5:17) so that we might experience a better way (Heb. 8:6), enjoy abundant life (John 10:10), and be called heirs with Christ (Rom. 8:17). Part of our inheritance is colaboring with Christ (1 Cor. 3:9), and as colaborers, God calls us to be a nation of priests and kings (1 Pet. 2:9; Rev. 5:10).

The Old Testament tells us that the priests had the responsibility of offering thanksgiving and praise.

> . . . to stand every morning to thank and praise the Lord, and likewise at evening. (1 Chron. 23:30, NKJV)

Just as the Levitical priests had responsibilities, so do we. As a nation of priests under the direction of our great high priest, Jesus Christ, we are to give thanks continually, offering praise without end. Like the Old Testament priests, we have a duty to praise Him every morning and evening. What a privilege!

> Rejoice evermore. Pray without ceasing. In every thing give thanks: for this is the will of God in Christ Jesus concerning you. (1 Thess. 5:16–18)

Start and end your day by filling your mind with His Word and praising Him for who He is and what He has called you to do. It's the best job you'll ever have!

Keep reading: 1 Chronicles 6:16–30

A Job from God

TODAY'S READING: 1 Chronicles 6:31–55; 25–26

They performed their duties according to the regulations laid down for them. *1 Chronicles 6:32,* NIV

In what may appear to be mundane chapters in 1 Chronicles, we find a wonderful glimpse into the heart of God. He called individuals to specific tasks and roles. He appointed men by name, set their hands to specific callings, and established their occupation with defined lines and specificity. To some He appointed the ministry of music (25:7) and to others prophecy (v. 1). Still others were the maintenance men, caretakers, and priests (6:48). Some were financial folks (26:20), and others were assigned to be leaders (v. 6). In addition we read that some "were assigned duties away from the temple, as officials and judges" (v. 29, NIV). So we see that God was not just interested in the "ministry" roles. The jobs outside the temple were ordained by the Lord just as clearly as those inside.

Whatever God has called you to do, know that it is a holy calling. There is no such thing as a secular job when the Lord Himself has appointed you to it.

> It is God which worketh in you both to will and to do of his good pleasure. (Phil. 2:13)

Jesus used Peter's occupation as a fisherman to make him a fisher of men (Matt. 4:19). He used Luke, a doctor, to record Jesus's life from a physician's perspective, bringing healing to our souls (Luke 1:1–3; Col. 4:14). He used Zacchaeus, a tax collector, to demonstrate ethical repentance and fair practices even in such a secular job as his (Luke 19:1–10)!

Jesus calls us His temples, living stones, His workmanship—which means we are part of His work. He has a plan and purpose for the things He has called us to do. Your talents, your gifts, the personality He gave you, and the people around you are all part of His calling on your life.

From Solomon to Jesus

May 17

TODAY'S READING: 1 Chronicles 27:1–29:22; 1 Kings 1:1–27

The LORD, the God of Israel, chose me. *1 Chronicles 28:4,* NASB

Just think, the God of the entire universe, the master creator, looked on all His creation and uniquely knit you together for a divine purpose. King David understood this and acknowledged God's grace in the giving of His gifts and callings.

> The LORD, the God of Israel, chose me from all the house of my father to be king over Israel forever. . . . And among the sons of my father He took pleasure in me to make me king over all Israel. (1 Chron. 28:4, NASB)

In genuine humility David recognized it was not his own efforts that made him king; rather, it was a holy calling and solely God's doing. Out of this humble recognition, King David spoke these words to his son Solomon.

> As for you, my son Solomon, know the God of your father, and serve Him with a whole heart and a willing mind; for the LORD searches all hearts, and understands every intent of the thoughts. If you seek Him, He will let you find Him. . . . Consider now, for the LORD has chosen you to build a house for the sanctuary; be courageous and act. (vv. 9–10, NASB)

We have seen how David's life in many ways foreshadowed Christ, and as I read this passage, I cannot help but think of God the Father blessing His Son, Jesus, and admonishing Him in the work He was given to do (Matt. 3:17; John 12:49; 17:4). Like Solomon, Jesus was chosen to build a house, a sanctuary in which God would dwell—us! We are the temple of the living God (1 Cor. 3:16), purchased by the blood of Jesus, being built up for His glory (1 Pet. 2:5).

May 18

Teach Me, O Lord

TODAY'S READING: 1 Kings 1:28–2:12; Psalm 25

> Good and upright is the LORD: therefore will he teach sinners in the way. The meek will he guide in judgment: and the meek will he teach his way. *Psalm 25:8–9*

God is faithful and keeps all His promises. Right here in today's reading, He promises to teach us. We find that same promise made by Jesus in the New Testament. Jesus personally promised to give us the Holy Spirit to guide us!

> The Spirit of truth, has come, He will guide you into all truth. (John 16:13, NKJV)

He promised to teach us.

> But the Helper, the Holy Spirit, whom the Father will send in My name, He will teach you all things. (14:26, NKJV)

And by the inspiration of His Spirit, He promises to give us wisdom.

> If any of you lacks wisdom, let him ask of God . . . and it will be given to him. (James 1:5, NKJV)

We need God's wisdom—Jesus. We need His direction and instruction. Therefore, we need His Word.

As you cry out to your Creator to teach you His ways today, know that you can start by simply doing what you already know to do and are doing. Look for Jesus in His Word. Abide in Him and let His Word abide in you.

Keep reading: 2 Samuel 23:1–7; 1 Chronicles 29:23–30

King Eternal

TODAY'S READING: 1 Kings 2:13–3:28; Psalm 72

His name shall endure for ever: his name shall be continued as long as the sun: and men shall be blessed in him: all nations shall call him blessed. *Psalm 72:17*

Throughout the Old Testament we've plumbed the prophecies concerning the coming redeemer. Back in the Garden of Eden, salvation was promised to Adam and Eve (Gen. 3:15); in Job a living redeemer was said to stand on the earth (Job 19:25); in the land of Egypt, Christ's atoning sacrifice was pictured as Israel applied the Passover blood (Exod. 12); and throughout the Psalms Jesus is spoken of as our everlasting king.

The nation of Israel was in turmoil as David's sons fought one another for the throne. This seems to be the destiny of earthly kingdoms ruled by earthly kings. David understood his mortality and the frailty of his earthly kingdom, so he worshipped God as king and prophesied of a day when God would reign in righteousness.

> Endow the king with your justice, O God, the royal son with your righteousness. He will judge your people in righteousness. . . . He will endure as long as the sun . . . through all generations. (Ps. 72:1–2, 5, NIV)

Amazing! Just as prophesied here in Psalms, God sent His royal Son, perfectly righteous. He is coming again, and His kingdom will endure forever. It's true! Despite the nations of this world being at each other's throats, we know how the story ends: God will reign victorious. At the name of Jesus every knee will bow and every tongue from every nation will confess that Jesus Christ is Lord (Rom. 14:11).

> There were great voices in heaven, saying, The kingdoms of this world are become the kingdoms of our Lord, and of his Christ; and he shall reign for ever and ever. (Rev. 11:15)

Keep reading: 2 Chronicles 1:1–13

The Song of Songs

TODAY'S READING: Song of Solomon 1–4; Psalm 50

My beloved spake, and said unto me, Rise up, my love, my fair one, and come away. *Song of Solomon 2:10*

The Song of Solomon, written in youthful passion, is a set of poems penned as Solomon recalled the emotions of his first love. From a practical, literal viewpoint, this love song focuses on the Master Designer's intent for romantic marital love. However, if we peer into the stanzas from a heavenly perspective, we will discover an outpouring of our heavenly Bridegroom's desire and love for us, His bride, as illustrated through the institution of marriage.

C. H. Spurgeon said, "This Book stands like the tree of life in the midst of the garden, and no man shall ever be able to pluck its fruit, and eat thereof, until first he has been brought by Christ past the sword of the cherubim, and led to rejoice in the love which hath delivered him from death."[53]

As a follower of Jesus, you are His bride and can experience love and fellowship with your Lord, the groom of heaven.

As you read, look for Jesus. His name is ointment or a priceless fragrance (Song of Sol. 1:3; Phil. 2:9–11); He will rejoice and be glad in you (Song of Sol 1:4; Zeph. 3:17); He is the good shepherd (Song of Sol. 1:7; John 10:11); His feast awaits you (Song of Sol. 1:12; Rev. 3:20); and one day soon, He will raise you up and take you away to be with Him (Song of Sol. 2:10; 1 Cor. 15:52).

The Groom Knocks

May 21

TODAY'S READING: Song of Solomon 5–8; Psalm 45

It is the voice of my beloved that knocketh, saying, Open to me, my sister, my love, my dove, my undefiled. *Song of Solomon 5:2*

Today we continue through the Song of Solomon, essentially an album comprised of snapshots capturing the courtship and marriage of the king and his young bride. Like any relationship, heights of passion are countered with moments of daily life.

In one scene the voice of the beloved groom is met with something close to indifference and is certainly taken for granted by his bride. Solomon stands at the door, calling in affection to his maiden.

> Open to me, my sister, my love, my dove, my undefiled. (5:2)

But she is already settled in for the night. Although she expresses her love for his voice, she does not rise and meet him (v. 3).

This should remind us of another Groom standing at the door, knocking. Jesus, in His letter to the seven churches, His bride, wrote similar words.

> Behold, I stand at the door, and knock: if any man hear my voice, and open the door, I will come in to him, and will sup with him, and he with me. (Rev. 3:20)

Jesus could not love you any more than He does. His passion and desire to fellowship with you drove Him to the Cross (Heb. 12:2). Like Solomon, Jesus sees His bride as undefiled and perfect (Song of Sol. 4:7) because we are clothed in His righteousness. As He calls to you today, answer His knock and find sweet fellowship with your Groom.

Keep reading: 1 Kings 5:1–12; 2 Chronicles 2:1–16

A Magnificent Temple

TODAY'S READING: 1 Kings 5:13–7:12; 2 Chronicles 3; Psalm 127

Solomon built the temple and finished it. *1 Kings 6:14,* NKJV

Consider the vastness of Solomon's building project for the temple: thirty thousand men were sent to Lebanon to gather building materials—great cedars and exquisite stone. It took eighty thousand stonecutters to cut and prepare the massive stones to be used throughout the temple. With the absence of modern transportation, seventy thousand men were tasked to carry those enormous materials from the quarry site to the job site. All in all, it was an unimaginably huge undertaking.

Still, every detail was carefully considered. The result was spectacular—man's best effort to provide the Creator of the universe a dwelling place here on earth.

God is oh so gracious to inhabit a dwelling made of trees and stone. He filled that temple with His presence in Old Testament times. But consider this! God would later become a man and dwell among His people, walking in another temple built in that same place.

Jesus loved God's house. His heart was there as a child (Luke 2:46–49). The Bible tells us that zeal for His Father's house consumed Him, as evidenced when He cleansed it from the defilement of merchandising (John 2:16–17). In the temple Jesus healed the broken, restored the hurting (Matt. 21:14), and spoke truth to whoever would listen (John 2:18–23). On the temple mount Jesus offered salvation.

> Jesus stood and cried, saying . . . He that believeth on me, as the scripture hath said, out of his belly shall flow rivers of living water. (7:37–38)

We are now temples of the living God (1 Cor. 3:16). Just as Solomon built the temple and finished it, God promises to finish the work He has begun in you (Phil. 1:6). Just as God delighted in Solomon's temple, He delights in you. And just as Jesus loved the temple, He loves you! He is zealous for you.

Keep reading: 1 Kings 9:15–16, 20–23; 2 Chronicles 2:17–18; 8:7–10

The Master Designer

May 23

TODAY'S READING: 1 Kings 7:13–8:21; 2 Chronicles 4–5

The glory of the LORD had filled the house of God.
2 Chronicles 5:14

Solomon carefully constructed the temple with great detail according to God's precise instructions. Clearly, God cares about details. And what God builds, He builds so beautifully.

> He hath made every thing beautiful in his time. (Eccles. 3:11)

God had a purpose in giving Israel such precise instructions for the temple. It was meant to be a picture of our relationship with Him and a symbol of what God would accomplish thousands of years later through His Son, Jesus.

Jesus compared the temple to His own physical body (John 2:19), as well as to us, the church. We are now temples of the Holy Spirit, being built as living stones—Christ's workmanship (1 Cor. 6:19–20; Eph. 2:10). We can take great encouragement in knowing that He cares just as much about the details now as He did in Solomon's time. As Christians, we are His sanctuaries, living temples built with careful design and great purpose!

> You also, as living stones, are being built up a spiritual house, a holy priesthood, to offer up spiritual sacrifices acceptable to God through Jesus Christ. (1 Pet. 2:5, NKJV)

God gave Solomon a blueprint to follow, and it all pointed to Jesus—a glorious outcome. What details is God laying on your heart today? Follow His Word and those things that the Spirit lays on your heart; they will lead to magnificent beauty.

May 24

Filled with His Presence

TODAY'S READING: 2 Chronicles 6; 1 Kings 8:22–61

Arise, O Lord God, into thy resting place. *2 Chronicles 6:41*

Today's reading shows Solomon standing in the newly constructed temple into which he'd poured everything he had, asking the Lord to now fill it with His presence.

> Will God really dwell on earth with men? The heavens, even the highest heavens, cannot contain you. How much less this temple I have built! (2 Chron. 6:18, NIV)

No ordinary building, the temple was the size of about two football fields and contained approximately one thirtieth of all the gold ever mined in all of human history.[54] No wonder some have called it the Eighth Wonder of the World.

Despite the temple's grandeur, this was merely a building made by human hands. Solomon must have realized that man's works simply cannot compare to the handiwork of the Creator of the universe.

Nevertheless, like a loving parent who joyfully displays his child's masterpiece on the fridge, God answered Solomon's prayer and filled the temple with His presence (7:1).

In God's gracious choice to inhabit the temple made of wood and stone, we get a glimpse of another time when God would willingly accept a dwelling place far below His inestimable, eternal worth. Jesus came and dwelt among us, "and we beheld his glory, the glory as of the only begotten of the Father . . . full of grace and truth" (John 1:14). The good news of Jesus Christ crescendos in the reality that He now lives in us because of His love for us!

May Solomon's prayer of dedication be the prayer for your life today.

Repentance Brings Refreshment

May 25

TODAY'S READING: 1 Kings 8:62–9:28; 2 Chronicles 7–8; Psalm 132

He is good; for his mercy endureth for ever. *2 Chronicles 7:3*

As we saw yesterday, after Solomon built a magnificent temple, he petitioned the Lord to inhabit it. God graciously answered Solomon's prayer, and Israel saw fire come down from heaven and the glory of the Lord fill the temple (2 Chron. 7:1–3).

Despite God's people having the indescribable privilege of a front-row seat to this spectacular demonstration of God's glory, the memory of the moment would eventually fade. God knew that His people would one day have a desperate need for repentance and reassurance. In His grace He instructed Solomon in what to do when dry times came.

> When I shut up heaven and there is no rain, or command the locusts to devour the land, or send pestilence among My people, if My people who are called by My name will humble themselves, and pray and seek My face, and turn from their wicked ways, then I will hear from heaven, and will forgive their sin and heal their land. (vv. 13–14, NKJV)

Although you and I are living temples, filled with Jesus's Spirit (John 14:26), dry times will come. As with Israel, God graciously has given us the solution: humble ourselves, pray, seek His face, and repent from sin. If your life needs a touch from God, consider whether repentance is in order.

> Repent ye therefore, and be converted, that your sins may be blotted out, when the times of refreshing shall come from the presence of the Lord. (Acts 3:19)

Just as Jesus cleansed His earthly temple (Matt. 21:12–13; John 2:13–17), He desires to cleanse our hearts (1 John 1:7). Take Him at His Word, keep following His instructions, and watch as He brings refreshment and healing to the soil of your soul.

Keep reading: 1 Kings 10:22; 2 Chronicles 9:21

May 26

The Reflection of True Wisdom

TODAY'S READING: 1 Kings 10:1–13; 2 Chronicles 9:1–12; Proverbs 1

> When the queen of Sheba heard of the fame of Solomon concerning the name of the LORD, she came to prove him with hard questions. *1 Kings 10:1*

Surely the queen of Sheba had wise men in her kingdom with whom she could have conferred. But the connection between Solomon's fame and the name of the Lord drew her all the way to Israel. The queen was particularly intrigued by the fact that it was the Lord who gave Solomon his wisdom and whoever heard him inevitably got a glimpse of the true and living God.

What a marvelous picture of how the world can be drawn to God through His people. Christians, through Jesus Christ, are filled with the knowledge of the Holy One, and those who see us should get a glimpse of Him who saved us.

I love what the queen of Sheba said to King Solomon when she saw with her own eyes how God's hand was on Israel.

> The report I heard in my own country about your achievements and your wisdom is true. But I did not believe these things until I came and saw with my own eyes. . . . How happy your men must be! How happy your officials, who continually stand before you and hear your wisdom! Praise be to the LORD your God, who has delighted in you. (1 Kings 10:6–9, NIV)

Oh, that these same words would be used to describe us! This sort of response comes only from the fruit of the Spirit in people who allow Him to rule and reign in their lives so that they reflect the Son (James 3:17).

In His eternal love, grace, and mercy, Jesus has called you to Himself and filled you with His Spirit. May you walk in wisdom, shining forth His righteousness so that others will praise Him.

Keep reading: 1 Kings 4:1–19, 29–34

Wisdom Personified

TODAY'S READING: Proverbs 2–4

You will understand righteousness and justice and equity,
every good path. *Proverbs 2:9,* ESV

We are now diving headlong into the book of Proverbs, which is packed full of proven and profound advice. If you are looking for a course in leadership, this is your book. If you are looking for comfort in a difficult situation, this is your book. If you are in over your head at work, this is your book. If something is burdening your heart and you don't know what to do or even how to seek direction, this is your book. Above all, if you want wisdom, this is most definitely your book!

As we have seen throughout our journey in the Old Testament, Jesus is on every page. The Bible says about Him, "Lo, I come: in the volume of the book it is written of me" (Ps. 40:7). God gave His people Israel the law to point them to the Messiah (Gal. 3:24). He gives us the Old Testament so we can look back and see His plan from the beginning, perfectly fulfilled in and through Jesus Christ.

The book of Proverbs is no exception, because Jesus is wisdom personified. We read in Colossians 2:3 that in Christ are "hid all the treasures of wisdom and knowledge."

When you find the word *wisdom* in Proverbs, you can confidently replace it with *Jesus Christ,* and you will gain a deeper description of our Savior and the depth of the riches we find in Him.

Happy is the man that findeth wisdom, and the man that
getteth understanding. (3:13)

Truly, whoever has the Son has life (Prov. 3:18; 1 John 5:12)!

The Wise Son

TODAY'S READING: Proverbs 5–7

My son, attend unto my wisdom. *Proverbs 5:1*

Memorizing, meditating on, delighting in, and studying God's Word has an effect on our lives! It cleanses our minds (Rom. 12:2; Eph. 4:23), restores our hearts (1 John 3:20), and brings our perspectives back in line with the truth as revealed in God's Word (Phil. 2:5). We all need that, and the book of Proverbs provides a concentrated dose of wisdom.

Proverbs can be divided into six parts: (1) chapters 1–7 speak to us as the people of God; (2) chapters 8–9 praise wisdom; (3) chapters 10–19 describe the deceitfulness of sin; (4) chapters 20–29 warn and instruct those seeking wisdom; (5) chapter 30 is simply titled "the words of Agur"; and (6) chapter 31 sings the praise of a virtuous woman.

Today's chapters are addressed to the wise son, the son who listens and obeys. Here, as if to say, "Listen up, kids," the father gives lessons for life.

> My son, attend unto my wisdom, and bow thine ear to my understanding: that thou mayest regard discretion, and that thy lips may keep knowledge. (5:1–2)

Try as we may, you and I are not always the wise son or daughter, listening to and obeying our heavenly Father's instructions. But where we fail, Jesus has triumphed! Jesus was the wise son personified (Col 2:3). In all Jesus did, He pleased His Father (Matt. 3:17). Jesus listened to and knew His Father's instructions. He rightly understood God's Word as He faced temptation (4:1–11) and correctly applied wisdom as He spoke truth (Luke 4:32). Jesus demonstrated wisdom in every area of life (Heb. 4:15).

May you take in God's Word today and listen to His instructions. Bind them around your heart as though they were reins directing your steps. And as you grow in wisdom, may you continually look to Jesus, the wise son.

Jesus Is True Wisdom

TODAY'S READING: Proverbs 8–10

Whoso findeth me findeth life, and shall obtain favour of the LORD. *Proverbs 8:35*

God's Word is divine revelation. By it He instructs, guides, and defines principles for governing our lives. Through obedience to it, blessings abound. God's ways are good and right. His Word is a sure foundation and contains the wisdom necessary to navigate life successfully.

> Hear; for I will speak of excellent things; and the opening of my lips shall be right things. . . . Counsel is mine, and sound wisdom: I am understanding; I have strength. By me kings reign, and princes decree justice. By me princes rule, and nobles, even all the judges of the earth. (Prov. 8:6, 14–16)

Our redeemer, Jesus Christ, is the Word and wisdom of God made flesh (John 1:14; Col. 2:3). He is the wisdom that calls out to all humankind (Prov. 8:4; John 3:17). He opens His lips to speak what is right (Prov. 8:6).

> . . . who committed no sin, nor was deceit found in His mouth. (1 Pet. 2:22, NKJV)

Jesus is the way, the truth, and the life. In Him we find "all the treasures of wisdom and knowledge" (Col. 2:3, ESV).

As you read the Scriptures today, recognize Jesus as wisdom personified in the pages of Proverbs. In wisdom Christ's character is revealed and His nature meticulously described.

> He is the image of the invisible God, the firstborn of all creation. For by him all things were created. . . . And he is before all things, and in him all things hold together. (Col. 1:15–17, ESV)

When you seek wisdom, you seek Jesus.

May 30 The Wise Soul Winner

TODAY'S READING: Proverbs 11:1–13:25

> The fruit of the righteous is a tree of life; and he that winneth souls is wise. *Proverbs 11:30*

The book of Proverbs is packed with powerful pictures and practical pointers for godly living. God's Word is a road map for life, making the simple wise. If we simply keep reading each and every day, we're sure to reap a bountiful harvest of goodness and godliness. And the Bible tells us that such goodness and godliness lead to great gain and are a blessing to all around us.

> The fruit of the [consistently] righteous is a tree of life, and he who is wise captures and wins souls [for God—he gathers them for eternity]. (11:30, AMP)

This verse highlights what a wonderful blessing wise men and women are to those around them because their lives are fruitful. However, this same glorious verse poses a problem: it declares the "consistently righteous" as a tree of life. There is only one who is consistently, completely, uncompromisingly righteous—Jesus Christ. Through the fruit of His life, He has given us "the tree of life" (Rev. 2:7; 22:2, 14).

Jesus is the righteous one (1 John 2:1), and in Him we can bear much fruit (John 15:5–8; Gal. 5:22–25).

> I am the vine, ye are the branches: He that abideth in me, and I in him, the same bringeth forth much fruit: for without me ye can do nothing. (John 15:5)

As you abide in Him and He in you, may you reflect His fruit of righteousness, winning souls and being wise.

Debt-Free

TODAY'S READING: Proverbs 14–15

Fools mock at making amends for sin. *Proverbs 14:9,* NIV

God's Word shines light on the motives of the heart. Here in Proverbs we're taught that the fool mocks at making amends for sin or, as another translation says, makes light of guilt. God's Word tells us that sin cannot be ignored, and it certainly is no laughing matter. In fact, we're warned that the price tag for sin is death (Rom. 6:23). Since we're all sinners, that's bad news. But as Christians, we know the good news: Jesus paid that price for us on the cross (4:25; 5:9).

Through the blood of Jesus Christ, God forgives us and declares us not guilty; we can live debt-free (Isa. 61:10; Acts 13:39; Rom. 3:24–26).

Because of Jesus . . .

- You are cleansed from all sin (1 John 1:7).
- God remembers your sin no more (Heb. 10:17).
- You're freed from the power of sin (1 Cor. 10:13).
- You have peace with God (Rom. 5:1).
- You have a clean conscience (Heb. 9:14).
- God has justified you by His grace (Rom. 3:24; 6:18).
- You're made new (Rom. 6:6; 2 Cor. 5:17).
- You're born again (John 3:3; Acts 26:18; Eph. 4:24; 1 Pet. 1:23).
- You have eternal life (John 3:16).

The fool mocks at his or her need for atonement. But you know the precious price that was paid for your shortcomings (1 Pet. 1:18–19). Your account has been satisfied, and now you are debt-free indeed!

June 1

Mercy and Truth

TODAY'S READING: Proverbs 16–18

> By mercy and truth iniquity is purged: and by the fear of the LORD men depart from evil. *Proverbs 16:6*

The Old Testament saints looked forward to the Redeemer. As the New Testament church, we have the privilege of looking back and seeing Jesus Christ woven throughout the pages of Scripture. Long after Solomon spoke of mercy and truth exonerating sins, God's ultimate act of mercy was fulfilled as the Way, the Truth, and the Life came and walked among us.

> The Word was made flesh, and dwelt among us, (and we beheld his glory, the glory as of the only begotten of the Father,) full of grace and truth. (John 1:14)

Jesus is God's mercy and truth made flesh. By His mercy He shed His blood and forgave our sin. Our transgressions are forgiven!

> Who is a God like You, pardoning iniquity and passing over the transgression of the remnant of His heritage? He does not retain His anger forever, because He delights in mercy. (Mic. 7:18, NKJV)

And by His truth He sets men free.

> Ye shall know the truth, and the truth shall make you free. (John 8:32)

Just as Solomon penned in Proverbs thousands of years ago, mercy and truth perfectly purge our iniquities here and now. God brought salvation on the earth and showed His unfailing love and faithfulness in and through His Son, Jesus Christ—the way, the truth, and the life!

Perspective

TODAY'S READING: Proverbs 19–21

He that getteth wisdom loveth his own soul: he that keepeth understanding shall find good. *Proverbs 19:8*

Being born again begins the process of sanctification—being transformed, day by day, into the likeness of Christ. As we've seen throughout the book of Proverbs, when we read the word *wisdom,* we can with certainty replace it with *Jesus.* So here, *He that getteth Jesus loveth his own soul.* How true that is! For "he who has the Son has life" (1 John 5:12, NKJV).

And herein lies the importance of feasting on God's Word daily! Jesus is the eternal Word of God, and as we take in God's Word, we are filled with wisdom (Jesus) and learn to view life through His divine perspective. Through His Word Jesus cleanses our minds, transforms our hearts, and provides a divinely inspired moral compass—all vital to the process of sanctification.

Sanctify them through thy truth: thy word is truth. (John 17:17)

Today's reading contains God's perspective on a plethora of real-life issues. Just consider these few chapters in Proverbs and the vast array of topics they address: family relationships (19:26), disciplining children (v. 18), civil justice (vv. 28–29; 21:28), political realities (20:26; 21:1), military strategies (20:18), what to look for in a friend (v. 19), good business practices (v. 10; 21:5), the danger of a get-rich-quick scheme (20:21), the end result of alcohol (v. 1), God's view on crass speech (19:1), and even aging gracefully (20:29).

Jesus calls us to abide in Him and allow His Word to abide in us (John 15:7). So keep on taking it in! Keep reading, keep listening, and keep growing in the grace of His perspective.

Heavenly Treasure

TODAY'S READING: Proverbs 22–24

> A good name is rather to be chosen than great riches, and loving favour rather than silver and gold. *Proverbs 22:1*

Can you imagine being the richest person in the world? Where would you go, and what would you do? King Solomon knew a thing or two about riches. Israel's greatest wealth and grandeur took place during his reign (1 Kings 10:23; 2 Chron. 9:13–14, 22).

But Solomon, having experienced the splendor of incalculable amounts of gold and extravagance, said something deeply profound when he observed that a good name is more valuable than a ton of treasure.

You see, Solomon, through his own experience, understood the deceptiveness of riches and their inherent instability. He knew that his earthly treasures were temporary.

> Cast but a glance at riches, and they are gone, for they will surely sprout wings and fly off to the sky like an eagle. (Prov. 23:5, NIV)

We see this same principle propounded in the New Testament by Jesus.

> Lay up for yourselves treasures in heaven, where neither moth nor rust doth corrupt, and where thieves do not break through nor steal: for where your treasure is, there will your heart be also. (Matt. 6:20–21)

> What shall it profit a man, if he shall gain the whole world, and lose his own soul? (Mark 8:36)

There is a heavenly storehouse where we can make deposits and pay true riches forward for ourselves for all eternity! So turn your attention to your eternal destination and seek the things of His kingdom. For where your treasure is, there will your heart be also.

The Whys Make the Wise

TODAY'S READING: Proverbs 25–27

> It is the glory of God to conceal a thing: but the honour of kings is to search out a matter. *Proverbs 25:2*

Were you ever told as a kid, "Don't ask why"? Proverbs suggests quite the opposite approach to life, implying by its very nature that the whys are precisely what make us wise. Wisdom comes from understanding, and understanding comes from examination and comprehension. A person can have a knowledge of God's ways and honor those standards—which is good—but as we take up God's Word, search the Scriptures, and ask the Holy Spirit to reveal the whys, we become wise.

> Through [skillful and godly] wisdom a house [a life, a home, a family] is built, and by understanding it is established [on a sound and good foundation]. (24:3, AMP)

Jesus often taught in parables that required His disciples to probe to discern their meanings. This provoked deeper thinking and sparked further questions (Matt. 15:15; Luke 8:9). The disciples would sit and listen as Jesus gave them a full explanation in private (Mark 4:33–34).

What rich fellowship the disciples experienced as a result of their questions! And their answers came straight from Jesus, wisdom Himself.

Dear friend, if you're anything like me, you might be thinking you could stand to be a bit wiser. Well, I have good news for both of us: our Lord promises to answer when we call and to give wisdom to those who ask.

> If any of you lack wisdom, let him ask of God, that giveth to all men liberally, and upbraideth not; and it shall be given him. (James 1:5)

The whys make us wise, so keep reading, keep studying, keep contemplating, and keep digging into this divine truth we're so privileged to explore. As you do, you'll gain wisdom anew—I guarantee you!

June 5

The Power of His Word

TODAY'S READING: Proverbs 28:1–30:33

> Every word of God is pure: he is a shield unto them that put their trust in him. *Proverbs 30:5*

The orb of God's spoken Word is incomprehensible to our finite minds. Through the Word He spoke the worlds into existence. He speaks and the earth trembles. And in these last days, God has spoken to us through His Son, Jesus (Heb. 1:2). For the Word, who was from the beginning and by whom the worlds were created, became flesh and lived among us (John 1:1–5, 14).

> And thus the second person in the Trinity is fitly called the Word; for he is the first-begotten of the Father, that eternal essential Wisdom which the Lord possessed.[55]

Jesus demonstrated the power of His spoken Word as the dead came to life (11:43–44), the lame walked (5:8–9), and the blind could see (9:25). That same power works in us as we take in His written Word.

> The word of God is quick, and powerful, and sharper than any twoedged sword, piercing even to the dividing asunder of soul and spirit, and of the joints and marrow, and is a discerner of the thoughts and intents of the heart. (Heb. 4:12)

Jesus prayed that the Father would sanctify us through His Word (John 17:17). Jesus is truth, and His Word contains His truth (14:6). When we are faithful and diligent to devour God's Word, it accomplishes His purpose of transforming our hearts and minds (Isa. 55:11; 1 Thess. 2:13).

May we take in the Word of God and prove true what Solomon knew: "Every word of God is pure: he is a shield unto them that put their trust in him" (Prov. 30:5).

Aishet Chayil

TODAY'S READING: Proverbs 31

Who can find a virtuous woman? for her price is far above rubies. *Proverbs 31:10*

Every Friday evening, as the Jews enter Shabbat, their feast of rest, they sing a special song over their women. Husbands praise their wives, sons rejoice over their mothers, grandsons honor the matriarch, and brothers show respect to their sisters. It's a beautiful scene. And it still happens the world over. The song they sing is titled *"Aishet Chayil,"* translated "a woman of valor." The song is Proverbs 31.

As originally penned, this chapter was a poem sung over a beloved woman from the perspective of an adoring son.

As Christians, we've written volumes on this chapter, all with good intentions, geared toward helping women to be more virtuous. I'm glad for those materials, but permit me to challenge you today with this thought: you are the bride of Christ. This is the song He sings over you as you rest in Him, as you enter into His Shabbat. Rest in this: He sings over you not because you possess all these attributes but because Christ sees you as clothed in His righteousness.

The purpose of the entire Bible is to point our gaze upward, to Jesus. If we fail to find Him here in Proverbs 31, then we are focusing on the wrong person. Proverbs 31 is not about us. Like the rest of the Scriptures, it's all about Him! It's all about His grace to see you and me as virtuous.

So consider each attribute highlighted in this grand and glorious chapter of God's amazing grace, and look to Jesus—the person who possesses them all. He is virtuous and clothes us in strength and honor, and it's He who considers our value to be far beyond rubies (Prov. 31:25; Isa. 61:10).

Keep reading: 1 Kings 4:20–28; 10:14–21, 23–29; 2 Chronicles 9:13–20, 22–28; 1:14–17

June 7

Purpose and Perspective

TODAY'S READING: **1 Kings 11:1–40; Ecclesiastes 1–2**

> When Solomon was old, . . . his wives turned away his heart after other gods: and his heart was not perfect with the LORD his God. *1 Kings 11:4*

Solomon disregarded God's dire warning to not choose a wife from the godless nations around him (1 Kings 11:1–4). This turned his heart away from the true and living God and, in fact, led him to depression. This is the setting for the book of Ecclesiastes: Solomon, sitting in his own despondency and soaking in the sorrow he reaped from sowing in sin.

> "Meaningless! Meaningless!" says the Teacher. "Utterly meaningless! Everything is meaningless." (1:2, NIV)

Truly, there is nothing new under the sun! God's ways lead to peace and joy, but we have an Enemy whose entire goal is to rob our lives of all godliness, contentment, and the good gifts God gives us. Jesus, by contrast, came to give us purpose and abundant life.

> The thief cometh not, but for to steal, and to kill, and to destroy: I am come that they might have life, and that they might have it more abundantly. (John 10:10)

We can learn from Solomon's experience. Compromise leads to a purposeless life. But in Christ we find the meaning of life itself. Only He can make the old new, give life to the dead, restore the brokenhearted, and bring hope to the hopeless and purpose to the lost. Only life in Jesus gives meaning to life on earth.

Seasons Change

TODAY'S READING: Ecclesiastes 3–6

To every thing there is a season, and a time to every purpose under the heaven. *Ecclesiastes 3:1*

Seasons come and go, but one truth remains: God is in control. He is the creator of seasons, in nature as well as in life. Some of those seasons are certainly more enjoyable than others, but it's important for us to understand that seasons won't last forever. Like the weather throughout the year, seasons in life come and go, but for every one of them, God has appointed a set time and a specific purpose, and we know His plans are good.

Jesus spoke of seasons, saying that the harvest is great and admonishing us to spread the gospel (Matt. 9:37; Mark 16:15). He told us that we are in a season of watching and waiting for His return (Matt. 25:1–13). He also noted that there's a time to feast and a time to fast (9:15).

Whatever your circumstances today, know that there are treasures to be gathered in every season.

> Our light affliction, which is but for a moment, worketh for us a far more exceeding and eternal weight of glory; while we look not at the things which are seen, but at the things which are not seen: for the things which are seen are temporal; but the things which are not seen are eternal. (2 Cor. 4:17–18)

Whether in summer, when it's warm and fruit is bountiful, or in the dead of winter, when everything is cold and still, the season is not outside God's divine plan. Rest assured, you are in His hand. His times and seasons for you have been appointed in love (Ps. 74:16–17). He is mighty and able to do according to all He has promised (Eph. 3:20)!

June 9 The Best Is Yet to Come

TODAY'S READING: Ecclesiastes 7–10

> Do not say, "Why were the old days better than these?" For it is not wise to ask such questions. *Ecclesiastes 7:10,* NIV

Solomon had reason to long for the good ole days. As a result of compromise, his later years were full of discouragement and regret. But even in his despair, he recognized that longingly looking back bears little benefit.

Solomon's words offer sound advice for us today. Even if, like him, we have reason for regret, we have a remedy in Jesus (Heb. 9:14).

> There is therefore now no condemnation for those who are in Christ Jesus. (Rom. 8:1, ESV)

With our faith placed in Jesus Christ, the best is yet to come. As the apostle Paul notes,

> Brothers, I do not consider that I have made it my own. But one thing I do: forgetting what lies behind and straining forward to what lies ahead, I press on toward the goal for the prize of the upward call of God in Christ Jesus. (Phil. 3:13–14, ESV)

Praise the Lord, we can always move in a forward motion to fulfill God's mission for us. No matter how good (or bad) the old days were, what is yet to come is better. Why? Because God promises that we're headed for heaven!

> God shall wipe away all tears from their eyes; and there shall be no more death, neither sorrow, nor crying, neither shall there be any more pain: for the former things are passed away. (Rev. 21:4)

We may never see the finished tapestry of divine design this side of heaven, but our God is good! Let's arrive having trusted Him along the way, looking forward—not backward—and confidently declaring to the world around us that in Christ the best is yet to come!

Christ in Ecclesiastes

June 10

TODAY'S READING: Ecclesiastes 11–12; Psalms 73; 88

Remember now thy Creator in the days of thy youth.
Ecclesiastes 12:1

The influential English preacher C. H. Spurgeon affirmed our goal of seeking Jesus on every page of Scripture.

> Don't you know, young man, that from every town and every village and every hamlet in England, wherever it may be, there is a road to London? So from every text of Scripture there is a road to Christ. And my dear brother, your business is, when you get to a text, to say, now, what is the road to Christ? I have never found a text that had not got a road to Christ in it.[56]

Like all of Scripture, Ecclesiastes turns our gaze upward and points to Jesus Christ. At the end of his contemplating, Solomon concluded that all of life was vanity and any philosophy that did not rise above man himself was utterly worthless. Therefore, he noted, it is best if one finds God in his or her youth (11:9–10; 12:1–2) and continues to fear God throughout life (vv. 13–14).

Christ shines bright in contrast to all that man "under the sun" (1:3) can obtain, as we look at Ecclesiastes.[57] Only by following Jesus can we find the source of life and all things pertaining to life. All other paths lead to vanity—to utter meaninglessness.

Solomon strove to find the meaning of life, but Jesus tells us that He is "the way, the truth, and the life" (John 14:6). When we believe in Him, our lives take on rich purpose and everlasting joy!

Keep reading: 1 Kings 11:41–43; 2 Chronicles 9:29–31;
1 Kings 14:21; 2 Chronicles 12:13–14

June 11

Faithful Redeemer

TODAY'S READING: 1 Kings 12–13; 2 Chronicles 10:1–11:4

This was the sin of the house of Jeroboam that led to its downfall. *1 Kings 13:34,* NIV

Today we head back into the history of Israel, where we read about an oppressive king, a divided nation, and counterfeit worship. What a mess! But as we consider the situation through the tunnel of time, we see the full picture from the proper perspective and, ultimately, the final outcome. During this time the nation of Israel was divided. King Jeroboam now ruled the ten northern tribes of Israel. Rehoboam, Solomon's son, ruled the two remaining tribes of Judah and Benjamin. Neither Jeroboam nor Rehoboam was righteous, and both kingdoms were fraught with wickedness.

In the north Jeroboam was filled with jealousy. In a deliberate attempt to keep the people's hearts far from the Lord and from his rival King Rehoboam, he created a false religion with a distorted form of worship (1 Kings 12:27–28).

In the south Rehoboam was filled with pride and arrogance. He refused the wise counsel of the elders and followed the advice of haughty young men (vv. 13–15).

You might expect God to move on and choose another nation to receive His blessing. But despite their idolatry, pride, and rebellion, God remained faithful to His chosen people and to the promises He had made to them. God honored the covenants He had made with both Abram (Gen. 15) and David (Jer. 33:17). God used Israel, and through Judah He sent His redeemer, Jesus Christ.

We, too, can look back and see God's faithfulness, regardless of our faults or failures. God kept His covenant with David and sent the redeemer, Jesus Christ, who covered all our sins on the cross. He is the perfect fulfillment of God's faithfulness—to Israel and to you and me as well!

Keep reading: 2 Chronicles 11:13–17

And There Was Calm

TODAY'S READING: 1 Kings 14:1–18; Psalm 89

> You rule over the surging sea; when its waves mount up, you still them. *Psalm 89:9,* NIV

What can withstand the force of rushing water? In a flood, water demonstrates its power to re-create landscapes and crush man's creations, washing them away as though they were nothing. Water is both life sustaining and awesomely powerful. Yet God, who created water, rules over its power and governs its boundaries (Ps. 93:4). Jesus demonstrated this very truth as He spoke to the wind and waves.

> He arose, and rebuked the wind, and said unto the sea, Peace, be still. And the wind ceased, and there was a great calm. (Mark 4:39)

God's spoken Word created the water, the wind, and the waves—and His spoken Word calmed them. So, too, in your life His written Word brings peace. Just as the psalmist recounts God's promises and faithfulness despite outward circumstances, we can fill our hearts with His Word and experience His voice quieting the tempest (Isa. 26:3). No matter how fierce the storm, like the disciples in the boat, we can recognize His divine power and control. Jesus told the disciples they were going to the other side—and they arrived safely. Our Lord has promised to take us from glory to greater glory (2 Cor. 3:18).

If God has led you in a certain direction or given you a promise, don't be rattled by the storm you encounter along the way. Call on Jesus, who rules the seas (Mark 4:41). Let His Word rule in your heart and mind, and let there be calm amid the storm.

Keep reading: 2 Chronicles 11:5–12, 18–23; 12:1–12

June
13

Follow Him Wholeheartedly

TODAY'S READING: 2 Chronicles 13–15

> They . . . sought him with their whole desire; and he was found of them: and the LORD gave them rest round about.
> *2 Chronicles 15:15*

Nothing can give us rest quite like seeking the Lord and finding Him. God desperately desired ancient Israel to follow Him, to love Him, and to be fully devoted to Him. And He desires the same for you and me, here and now.

> Love the Lord thy God with all thy heart, and with all thy soul, and with all thy strength, and with all thy mind. (Luke 10:27)

In today's reading King Asa shows us what it means to follow the Lord wholeheartedly.

> He also removed the high places and the incense altars from all the cities of Judah, and the kingdom was quiet under him. (2 Chron. 14:4–5, NKJV)

King Asa accepted God's commands as his convictions, and they shaped how he governed Israel. He removed the false gods and the places that were devoted to false worship. As a result, there was peace in the land. If you're a believer in the true and living God, then you, too, are governed by Him and can experience that same peace.

> You, however, are not in the flesh but in the Spirit, if in fact the Spirit of God dwells in you. (Rom. 8:9, ESV)

Our lives are no longer our own, but we belong to Jesus Christ (1 Cor. 3:23). Therefore, our entire beings ought to glorify our Lord (6:20).

May we follow King Asa's example and remove any "high places" in the land of our lives—anything that competes for our affections and tempts us away from our love for the Lord. May you, like King Asa, find peace as your life is governed by God alone.

Keep reading: 1 Kings 14:29–15:34; 2 Chronicles 12:15–16

His Searching Eyes

June 14

TODAY'S READING: 2 Chronicles 16:1–18:1; 1 Kings 16

The eyes of the LORD run to and fro throughout the whole earth, to show Himself strong on behalf of those whose heart is loyal to Him. *2 Chronicles 16:9,* NKJV

Do you truly believe what this verse reveals about our Lord? When we grasp the fact that God really is looking for those whose hearts are loyal to Him and that He shows Himself strong on their behalf, it will change the way we live. Don't you want His searching eyes to stop and stare at you? I sure do!

Merriam-Webster defines the word *loyal* as "unswerving in allegiance."[58] None of us can claim to be unswerving in our faithfulness to the Lord (Rom. 3:10). None of us show complete and constant support. But Jesus Christ remains unswerving in His faithfulness to us; He proved it on the cross. Jesus shows us complete and constant support; He gave us the comforter, His Holy Spirit, to guide us and lead us along life's way.

When we read that God searches the earth for those who are loyal, we might think, *Well, He won't, He can't, stop and stare at me.* That is completely, 100 percent wrong! Why? Because when God looks at us, the unfaithful, the disloyal, He sees us covered in Christ, the most faithful and most loyal of all.

> For He made Him who knew no sin to be sin for us, that we might become the righteousness of God in Him. (2 Cor. 5:21, NKJV)

As God searches the earth, His eyes stop and stare at you. Because you have received His Son's gift of grace, you are the apple of His searching eyes.

Keep reading: 1 Kings 22:41–46; 2 Chronicles 20:31–34

A Still, Small Voice

TODAY'S READING: 1 Kings 17–19

Behold, there came a voice unto him. *1 Kings 19:13*

God, who speaks in a gentle whisper, with His Word spoke the world into existence (Gen. 1:3), commands the sun and the stars (Job 9:7), sets the oceans' limits (38:11), moves mountains (9:5–6), calms the raging sea (Ps. 65:7; Matt. 8:26), humbles hearts (17:5–6), heals the blind (John 9:6), makes the lame leap for joy (Matt. 11:5; 21:14), raises the dead (John 11:43), and brings eternal life (5:24).

In today's reading God stops the dew and rain, commands ravens to feed His prophet, and miraculously provides for a widow in the midst of a famine. Truly the spoken Word of God is powerful but never overbearing. Think ahead to the raging demoniac we find in the gospel of Mark. No chain was able to constrain him, but the voice of Jesus freed him (5:2–8).

Elijah experienced firsthand the power of God's voice.

> The LORD passed by, and a great and strong wind rent the mountains, and brake in pieces the rocks before the LORD; but the LORD was not in the wind: and after the wind an earthquake; but the LORD was not in the earthquake: and after the earthquake a fire; but LORD was not in the fire: and after the fire a still small voice. (1 Kings 19:11–12)

Did you know that we have the same opportunity to hear our Lord speak? Each and every day that we choose to open His Word, we get to hear from Him and experience the power of His still, small voice.

Jesus prayed to the Father that we would be sanctified through His Word (John 17:17). And the apostle Paul tells us that Christ washes us in the water of His Word (Eph. 5:25–26).

The world around us can get quite noisy and distract us from hearing God. So keep digging into God's Word today and every day and listen to what His still, small voice would say to you.

His Magnificent Work

TODAY'S READING: Psalms 104; 114–115; 1 Kings 20

> Bless the LORD, O my soul. O LORD my God, thou art very great; thou art clothed with honour and majesty. *Psalm 104:1*

We serve an awesome God! His ways are higher than our ways and His thoughts beyond our comprehension (Isa. 55:9). Today's passages should compel us to stop and consider the greatness of our God, His amazing majesty, and His awesome authority.

In His wisdom He created all things (Ps. 104:24). He rules creation (vv. 2–4) and sets boundaries that cannot be crossed (v. 9). His glory endures forever (v. 31), He brings water out of solid rock (114:8), and the earth trembles at His presence (v. 7).

> Our God is in heaven; he does whatever pleases him. (115:3, NIV)

In view of such majesty, consider that what pleased Him most was to humble Himself by becoming a man and enduring the Cross for the joy of redeeming us.

> Looking unto Jesus the author and finisher of our faith; who for the joy that was set before him endured the cross, despising the shame, and is set down at the right hand of the throne of God. (Heb. 12:2)

He created all things, and yet He chose to die in order to redeem the very things He created. Amazing love! What a magnificent work He wrought on the cross. And now He calls you His masterpiece, the work of His hands (Eph. 2:10). What does Jesus, who loves you to death, desire to create in you today? His works are magnificent, and you are one of them.

June 17

He Will Accomplish His Plan

TODAY'S READING: 1 Kings 21:1–22:40

Mark my words, all you people! *1 Kings 22:28,* NIV

Today's reading highlights our humanity and vulnerability in the context of God's steadfast plans and purposes. God, through the prophet Micaiah, warned King Ahab that he would be killed in combat. Ahab, thinking he could hide from the Maker of heaven and earth, disguised himself and hid in the middle of the battle.

> Now a certain man drew a bow at random, and struck the king of Israel between the joints of his armor. (1 Kings 22:34, NKJV)

What appeared to be a random act was, in reality, God at work, accomplishing exactly what He had decreed would be Ahab's fate.

> I know that you [God] can do all things; no plan of yours can be thwarted. (Job 42:2, NIV)

For the wicked king, God's resolve was anything but a comfort. By contrast, you and I have passed from death to life. Because of Jesus Christ we are not cursed but blessed with God's favor.

> God sent not his Son into the world to condemn the world; but that the world through him might be saved. (John 3:17)

Ahab covered himself hoping to disguise his identity. But we are covered in Jesus's blood (Eph. 1:7) and clothed in His righteousness (Isa. 61:10), and our identity is in Christ (Rom. 8:17).

As certain as God's plan was for Ahab, so, too, is His plan for you. He promises to complete the work He's begun in you (Phil. 1:6). And He promises that He will work all things together for His good purposes (Rom. 8:28). Even if you never see that good this side of heaven, the promise remains true. Best of all, His plan is to one day take you home to live with Him for all eternity (John 14:3). What a wonderful plan He has, and He will accomplish it (Jude 24)!

Keep reading: 1 Kings 22:51–53; 2 Chronicles 18:2–34

Trust and Stand Firm

TODAY'S READING: 2 Chronicles 19:1–20:30; Psalms 46–48

> You will not need to fight in this battle. Stand firm, hold your position, and see the salvation of the LORD on your behalf.
> *2 Chronicles 20:17,* ESV

The Old Testament records a plethora of war and military exploits. Nations rise up to conquer other nations, then fall as stronger ones take their place. Conflict between kings is a constant theme throughout the Scriptures. The Bible tells us there's nothing new under the sun. As long as this world carries on, the pattern of war will continue (Matt. 24:6–13). It's the result of sin and man's fallen nature.

Yet God promised to be with His people amid their battles. In fact, He promised to fight the battle for them.

> Do not be afraid and do not be dismayed . . . for the battle is not yours but God's. . . . You will not need to fight in this battle. Stand firm, hold your position, and see the salvation of the LORD on your behalf. (2 Chron. 20:15, 17, ESV)

God promised King Jehoshaphat that Israel wouldn't have to fight against the Moabites and Ammonites this time. His instruction to Israel was to simply trust and stand firm.

Sound familiar? Old Testament examples reveal New Testament principles. While Israel's battles were physical, ours are spiritual. Through Jesus's death and resurrection, He has triumphed over this fallen, fractured, fighting world. Just like Israel, we have to put on our armor (Eph. 6:13–17), trust in the Lord, and stand firm.

> You are of God, little children, and have overcome them, because He who is in you is greater than he who is in the world. (1 John 4:4, NKJV)

Whether you hear of physical wars raging around the world or sense the very real spiritual battles around you, know this: God is mighty to save. Stand firm in Jesus's name!

June 19

A Costly Ransom

TODAY'S READING: Psalms 49; 83; 91; 2 Kings 1

> The redemption of their souls is costly . . .
> That he should continue to live eternally,
> And not see the Pit. *Psalm 49:8–9,* NKJV

If we're looking with eyes open for the presence of the Savior, we'll see that Psalm 49:8–9 speaks directly of the costly sacrifice of Jesus Christ. The psalmist was well aware of his sinful condition and knew of his need for redemption.

> Wash me thoroughly from mine iniquity, and cleanse me from my sin. For I acknowledge my transgressions: and my sin is ever before me. (51:2–3)

The Old Testament saints relied on sacrifices to atone for sin (Lev. 16:15). But as you know, these sacrifices pointed ahead to the ultimate sacrifice that would cover over all sin for all time.

> God presented him as an atoning sacrifice in his blood, received through faith, to demonstrate his righteousness, because in his restraint God passed over the sins previously committed. (Rom. 3:25, CSB)

As New Testament believers, we look to Jesus, the one who redeemed our lives by way of a costly sacrifice—all so we could live with Him eternally. We owed a debt we could not pay (6:18–20). But God, who loves us, sent His only Son to die for us.

> I give them eternal life, and they will never perish. No one will snatch them out of my hand. (John 10:28, CSB)

Jesus, your redeemer, paid your debt. I encourage you to read today's passage and see Jesus, remembering the price He paid and rejoicing in His gift of salvation.

Keep reading: 1 Kings 22:47–49; 2 Chronicles 20:35–37

Our Fickle Faith

TODAY'S READING: 2 Kings 2–3; 8:16–29; 2 Chronicles 21:4–20

The word of the LORD is with him. *2 Kings 3:12*

God is faithful to keep His promises. He graciously reassures our often doubting hearts. He demonstrates His power so our trust is renewed. And He is merciful to hear and answer our prayers. We find examples of all these attributes in today's reading, which recounts God's power, faithfulness, provision, and unfailing love—exactly the reminders we need to reenergize our fickle faith.

For example, God had promised that David's descendants would remain on the throne of Israel. Despite Judah turning away from their Lord, He did not turn away from them. God remembered His promise and, with supernatural patience, preserved Judah.

> Nevertheless, for the sake of his servant David, the LORD was not willing to destroy Judah. (2 Kings 8:19, NIV)

Consider next the prophets Elijah and Elisha. God used these two miracle workers to minister to those in Israel who loved the Lord—and to warn those who did not. Both provision and admonition are blessings. This principle is confirmed in Jesus, who is a blessing and provision for those who believe but a stumbling block for those who do not (2 Cor. 2:15–16).

Finally, we see the power of praise when seeking God's will (2 Kings 3:15). Perhaps this is where Paul and Silas got the idea to praise the Lord while patiently awaiting their release from prison (Acts 16:16–40).

There's so much to glean from today's reading. God's Word speaks to every situation and gives us wisdom for every circumstance in life. All we have to do is read it, cover to cover. Keep reading, my friend, and let your faith be renewed.

Keep reading: 1 Kings 22:50; 2 Chronicles 21:1–3; 22:1–6

June 21

The King's Highway

TODAY'S READING: 2 Kings 9:1–10:27

> He answered, What peace, so long as the lewd acts of thy mother Jezebel and her witchcrafts are so many? *2 Kings 9:22,* WBT

Jehu was a godly man whose heart leaned toward the Lord. The prophet Elisha sent one of his servants undercover to anoint Jehu as king and to give him a secret mission. As Jehu rode out on this assignment, he was met by the current king. When the wicked King Joram saw Jehu coming, he asked, "Have you come in peace, Jehu?" Jehu's poignant reply is appropriate for all people, but especially for us as Christians.

Jehu knew that lewdness, idolatry, and witchcraft (also translated as "rebellion") rob a nation of peace.

We may not be able to rid the world of sin, but we can sanctify (or set apart) our hearts and homes and experience the peace that comes by consecration to the Lord. Don't be deceived. You may think that a little lewdness in entertainment, in conversation, or in thought has minimal effect, but God's Word tells us that such things rob us of peace (Isa. 57:20–21; Ps. 38:3–4). On the other hand, filling our hearts and homes with worship, the Word, and God's ways brings gladness (Heb. 1:9).

There is a way of peace, joy, and abundant life—it is the King's highway.

> A highway shall be there, and a road, and it shall be called the Highway of Holiness. (Isa. 35:8, NKJV)

Jesus said His path is narrow and marked by a small gate that leads to life (Matt. 7:14). Through Jesus we can enter that gate and walk the King's highway.

> I am the door: by me if any man enter in, he shall be saved, and shall go in and out, and find pasture. (John 10:9)

May you walk with Jesus today, be led by His Spirit, and enjoy fellowship with the Father as you walk the King's highway.

Keep reading: 2 Chronicles 22:7–12

Cast Down Those Idols

June 22

TODAY'S READING: 2 Kings 11:1–12:16; 2 Chronicles 23:1–24:16

> Jehoiada made a covenant between himself, the people, and the king, that they should be the LORD's people. And all the people went to the temple of Baal, and tore it down. They broke in pieces its altars and images. *2 Chronicles 23:16–17,* NKJV

Israel's repentance and renewed love for the Lord ushered in a disdain for idolatry. This pattern remains true today: devotion to God leads directly to the destruction of idols.

> No man can serve two masters: for either he will hate the one, and love the other; or else he will hold to the one, and despise the other. Ye cannot serve God and mammon. (Matt. 6:24)

Picture the scene: the Israelites, caught up in zeal for the Lord, must have stormed the temple in a righteous rage to tear down those idols and finally be freed from their bondage to false gods. Their righteous anger mirrors the zeal of Jesus as He turned over the tables in the temple.

> He drove them all out of the temple . . . and overthrew the tables. . . . And his disciples remembered that it was written, The zeal of thine house hath eaten me up. (John 2:15, 17)

So, too, should you and I be zealous for our Lord to the point that we rush to tear down every idol, anything that distracts us from true worship. Like Jehoiada and Joash, let's commit our hearts to be zealous and fully devoted to the Lord.

> Casting down imaginations, and every high thing that exalteth itself against the knowledge of God, and bringing into captivity every thought to the obedience of Christ. (2 Cor. 10:5)

We've been redeemed, bought with the precious blood of Christ. We're new creations, free to walk as imitators of Him. So let's cast down all idols and lift up the Lord in our lives.

Keep reading: 2 Kings 10:28–36; 13:1–3

June 23

The Right Plan

TODAY'S READING: 2 Chronicles 24:17–25:10; 2 Kings 4

> The LORD is able to give thee much more than this.
> *2 Chronicles 25:9*

Have you ever realized at the last minute that you have committed yourself to the wrong plan? Excuses begin to flood the mind once we see our mistake: *What about the money I spent? What about the relationships I built? I'll look like a fool if I change my mind now!* And on and on. That's exactly what happened to King Amaziah of Judah.

He had a battle plan he was convinced was right. He enlisted and paid one hundred thousand men from Israel to help in his attack. But God sent a prophet to warn Amaziah that his plan was wrong and would not be blessed by the Lord. Can't you hear Amaziah respond, "But what about the money I paid for these troops?" (2 Chron. 25:9). The prophet's response reflects God's goodness, mercy, patience, and grace.

> The man of God answered, The LORD is able to give thee much more than this. (2 Chron. 25:9)

Although we may have invested precious time, energy, and money, if God isn't in our plan, the waste is in going through with it! God blesses obedience and is able to give "abundantly above all that we ask or think" (Eph. 3:20).

Think of the rich young ruler. When Jesus told him to sell what he had and to follow Him, the young man went away sad (Mark 10:17–22). He had accumulated great wealth and was unwilling to let it go for the sake of Christ.

If the Lord has laid it on your heart that your plan or your focus is wrong, be courageous today and obey! What may seem now an impossible change in direction will bring great blessing in the end. God's Word is true, and His plans are always the right ones.

Keep reading: 2 Kings 12:17–18; 13:4–11; 8:1–6; 12:19–21; 14:1–6

Wash in the Water

June 24

TODAY'S READING: 2 Kings 14:7–14; 2 Chronicles 25:11–24; 2 Kings 5:1–7:2

Wash, and be clean. *2 Kings 5:13*

The story of Naaman, whose flesh was diseased with leprosy, offers a powerful visual of salvation through faith. Naaman was a commander in a foreign army, yet he asked the Jewish prophet Elisha to heal him. A seemingly impossible request! But God is in the business of answering the seemingly impossible. Through Elisha the Lord offered Naaman an unexpected path to restoration and healing: wash in the Jordan River seven times (2 Kings 5:10).

Naaman, angered and humiliated by the simplicity of the instruction, reluctantly obeyed. But God wanted to paint a picture of the power of His plan of salvation, a plan that reached beyond the Jewish people. Naaman's obedience to the simple instructions led to his complete healing.

Leprosy, as you'll recall, represents sin. Every one of us is afflicted with this disease that ravages our souls. But, like Naaman, we have been offered a simple way to be restored, healed, and brought near to the family of God.

> Believe on the Lord Jesus Christ, and thou shalt be saved.
> (Acts 16:31)

Close to nine hundred years after Naaman's healing, Jesus would be baptized in those same waters, a symbol of giving His will up to His Father and the beginning of His earthly ministry (Matt. 3:13). Because of Jesus's submission, we, like Naaman, can be washed and cleansed from our condition of sin.

You have been redeemed, and you are being washed—sanctified and cleansed—in the water of the Word and made whole (Eph. 5:26).

Believing in Jesus and reading your Bible may seem too simple, but they lead to restoration, healing, and cleansing—guaranteed!

June 25

Good News to Share

TODAY'S READING: 2 Kings 7:3–20; 8:7–15; 2 Chronicles 26:1–21; Amos 1

> This is a day of good news and we are keeping it to ourselves.
> *2 Kings 7:9,* NIV

Imagine stumbling upon a massive treasure, totally yours for the taking. Today's reading contains a similar situation, but one far more dramatic because it deals with life and death. In 2 Kings 7 we find four leprous men ready to die of hunger because Israel was in the midst of a terrible famine. Then these men stumbled upon a "treasure" that could save the nation.

> The LORD had made the host of the Syrians to hear a noise of chariots. . . . Wherefore they arose . . . and fled for their life. And when these lepers came . . . they went into one tent, and did eat and drink, and carried thence silver, and gold, and raiment, and went and hid it. (vv. 6–8)

As they were snatching up all the spoils the Syrians had so hastily deserted, the four lepers realized it wasn't right to keep it all to themselves. They had good news to share with their countrymen, who were also starving from the famine!

> Then they said to each other, "We're not doing right. This is a day of good news and we are keeping it to ourselves. . . . Let's go at once and report this." (v. 9, NIV)

Like these men, we were sick with sin and condemned to spiritual death (Eph. 2:1). But God, in His goodness, gave us a treasure that saved us. We, too, have good news, and it's wrong to keep it to ourselves!

Salvation and forgiveness are available through Jesus. He died and rose again to pay the debt we owed and to free us from the bondage of sin. In a world experiencing a spiritual famine, this is news worth sharing.

Keep reading: 2 Kings 13:12–25; 14:15–23; 2 Chronicles 25:25–28; 2 Kings 15:1–5

Amazing Grace!

June 26

TODAY'S READING: Amos 2–6

Prepare to meet your God. *Amos 4:12,* NIV

The prophet Amos arrived on the scene shortly before Isaiah and was a contemporary of another prophet named Hosea. Amos was a simple country farmer, called by the Lord to deliver a challenging message. In the midst of his people experiencing a period of prosperity, strength, and security, Amos was directed to warn of God's coming judgment for Israel's sin. Of course, with things moving along swimmingly for the Israelites, Amos's message was not welcomed or widely embraced. The idea of Israel being completely destroyed seemed unbelievable. Yet within fifty years of Amos's prophecy, God's warnings were perfectly fulfilled.

God's message to Amos wasn't just for the ancient Jews. The apostle Paul tells us that everything that happened to the Old Testament saints was given to us as an example (1 Cor. 10:6, 11; Rom. 15:4). We can look at the lessons and the message in Amos and find instruction for today.

The book of Amos begins with pointing out the sin and the subsequent judgment that was to fall on Jerusalem. But after judgment comes restoration. Hundreds of years later, a young disciple named Stephen would reach back to the book of Amos as he proclaimed to the Jewish leaders that the Righteous One had indeed come. But just as their ancestors rejected the prophets, they had crucified the Christ (Acts 7:42, 52).

God's message to Israel (and us) through Amos ends with the glory of the Davidic covenant (9:11–15)—God's promise to send the Righteous One. Jesus came, died, and rose again—just as prophesied. And this, my friend, is where we see Jesus in Amos!

June 27

A Faithful Husband

TODAY'S READING: Amos 7:1–9:15; Hosea 1:1–3:5

> I will even betroth thee unto me in faithfulness: and thou shalt know the LORD. *Hosea 2:20*

The Lord Jesus Christ has taken as His bride all of us who put our trust in Him. It's true! His promise to you and me is that we will know Him (1 Cor. 13:12) and He will be faithful (Rev. 19:6–11). And as we've seen throughout the entire Old Testament, God, in His infinite goodness, gave us a picture of this principle. We find it confirmed here through the prophet Hosea. God's word to Hosea was that he was to take an unfaithful wife, love her, and, despite her whoredom, remain faithful to her.

Hosea's wife, Gomer, failed to recognize what her husband, Hosea, had done for her. Despite his commitment to cover her in love and protection, she continued to be unfaithful. Yet God told Hosea to remain faithful nonetheless. Why? Because God wanted to give us a picture of Jesus's love and faithfulness toward us, the bride of Christ.

> Go, show your love to your wife again, though she is loved by another and is an adulteress. Love her as the LORD loves the Israelites. (Hosea 3:1, NIV)

Just think about that grace and mercy! Hosea's constant love toward unfaithful Gomer shows us the depth of love and forgiveness our heavenly groom, Jesus, has toward us.

> I will betroth you to Me forever; yes, I will betroth you to Me in righteousness and justice, in lovingkindness and mercy; I will betroth you to Me in faithfulness, and you shall know the LORD. (2:19–20, NKJV)

In loving-kindness, in mercy, in righteousness, Jesus has betrothed you to Himself. And His love is forever faithful.

A Whale of a Tale

June 28

TODAY'S READING: Hosea 4:1–5:7; Jonah 1–4

Salvation is of the LORD. *Jonah 2:9*

Today we dive into the book of Jonah—a great big whale of a tale that portrays God's patience, perseverance, and relentless pursuit of lost sinners. Through Jonah's incredible journey we witness just how right the apostle Peter was when he wrote that God is "not willing that any should perish" (2 Pet. 3:9). As you read the book of Jonah, contrast God's character with that of the prophet.

Jonah didn't agree with God's decision to give Nineveh a chance to repent. After all, the capital city of Assyria was populated with wicked, cruel people who were a perpetual thorn in Israel's side. We know from the biblical account that it was a large city of at least six hundred thousand people, none of whom Jonah wanted to see saved (Jon. 3:3; 3:10–4:2).

In protest of God's call to preach a message of repentance to the Ninevites, Jonah instead jumped on a boat headed for Joppa, sailed straight into a storm, and got himself tossed into the sea, where he was swallowed by a great fish. After the fish finally spit him out, Jonah begrudgingly took God's message to the Ninevites, and God brought about a great revival. Why? Because He's not willing that any should perish. Our Lord loves us so much that in the story of the Cross we basically hear Him say, *You can perish, but only over My dead body.* And in Christ's death and resurrection, we can look back and see how Jonah pictured Jesus centuries before the Savior's birth:

> For as Jonah was three days and three nights in the belly of the great fish, so will the Son of Man be three days and three nights in the heart of the earth. (Matt. 12:40, NKJV)

Jonah would have left the Ninevites on their path toward death, but his three days in the "grave" of the fish brought them life. In a similar way, we were headed for death, but Jesus spent three days in the grave to bring us life. Rejoice today in the whale of a tale that is the gospel of grace!

Keep reading: 2 Kings 14:24–29; 15:8–16

June 29 Cleansed and Ready to Serve

TODAY'S READING: 2 Kings 15:17–29; Isaiah 6; 2 Chronicles 26:22–28:21

> I saw also the LORD sitting upon a throne, high and lifted up, and his train filled the temple. *Isaiah 6:1*

A glimpse of God cannot help but leave a person completely humbled. When Isaiah saw the Lord, "high and lifted up" (Isa. 6:1), his reaction was complete humility.

> Then said I, Woe is me! for I am undone; because I am a man of unclean lips, and I dwell in the midst of a people of unclean lips: for mine eyes have seen the King, the LORD of hosts. (v. 5)

Isaiah acknowledged his total unworthiness in light of God's great glory. He knew his guilt, in that moment, as a palpable reality. Placing himself at the mercy of God Almighty, Isaiah confessed his sin and the sin of his people, after which God touched and cleansed him.

> Then flew one of the seraphims unto me, having a live coal in his hand . . . and he laid it upon my mouth, and said, Lo, this hath touched thy lips; and thine iniquity is taken away, and thy sin purged. (vv. 6–7)

Have you felt the weight of sin? Did it lead you to confess and, like Isaiah, place yourself humbly at the mercy of God? Jesus came that we could be cleansed from our sin—not via the purging effect of a live coal but by the Lord Jesus Himself (Col. 2:14; 1 John 1:7).

Today, like Isaiah, you can see God's glory. Jesus Christ is the glory of God made manifest in human form (John 1:14). And as Isaiah's mouth was cleansed by the coal, the Bible tells us that if our mouths confess our sins, He is faithful to forgive us and "cleanse us from all unrighteousness" (1 John 1:9). Then we're ready to respond, like Isaiah, "Here am I; send me" (Isa. 6:8).

Keep reading: 1 Chronicles 5:23–26; 2 Kings 15:6–7; 15:32–16:9; 1 Chronicles 5:11–17

Unto Us a Son Is Given

TODAY'S READING: Isaiah 7:1–10:4; 17

Unto us a child is born, unto us a son is given: and the government shall be upon his shoulder: and his name shall be called Wonderful, Counsellor, The mighty God, The everlasting Father, The Prince of Peace. *Isaiah 9:6*

We find in Isaiah 9 one of the most recognizable prophecies of Christ in the entire Old Testament. Isaiah prophesied more than seven hundred years before Jesus was born as the babe of Bethlehem. Isaiah was referred to as the "prophet of redemption"; in fact, his very name means "Yahweh is salvation."[59] He warned the people of Israel of their need for repentance and told of Yahweh's salvation through the coming redeemer.

Although Isaiah did not know Jesus's name, he did know that Yahweh would send Israel a savior. Inspired by the Holy Spirit, he prophesied details of future events. Let's look at just a few of the riches in Isaiah 7 and 9.

Jesus is the son born of a virgin (Isa. 7:14; Luke 1:35; Matt. 1:23). Jesus is the one who bears our sin, who carries the governments upon His shoulder, and whose kingdom has no end (Isa. 9:6; Rev. 1:5; 19:16). Jesus's name is wonderful, and He is the only wise counselor (Isa. 9:6; Phil. 2:9–11; 1 Cor. 1:30). Jesus is the mighty God (John 1:14; Rev. 1:8), the everlasting Father, and the prince of peace whose peace passes understanding (John 16:33; Phil. 4:7). Jesus is the light of the world who gave light to those who walked in darkness (Isa. 9:2; John 1:4–5; 3:19; Luke 1:77, 79).

Truly, it is all about Jesus, the son who was given to make a way for us!

July 1

On the Third Day

TODAY'S READING: Hosea 5–9; 2 Kings 16:10–18; 2 Chronicles 28:22–25

> After two days will he revive us: in the third day he will raise us up, and we shall live in his sight. *Hosea 6:2*

In Hosea 6 we read God's message to rebellious Israel. Since we know that the Old Testament sets the stage for the truth of Jesus Christ in the New Testament, we should not be surprised to find that God's message through Hosea previews His message through His Son.

In response to God's chastisement, Hosea's humble prayer acknowledged God's love and care, even in the midst of correction. Hosea's prayer pictures God's tender love, as his words foreshadow Jesus, who would take their chastisement upon Himself.

> Come, and let us return unto the LORD: for he hath torn, and he will heal us; he hath smitten, and he will bind us up. After two days will he revive us: in the third day he will raise us up, and we shall live in his sight. (vv. 1–2)

Jesus was torn and stricken that we might be made whole (Isa. 53:5; 2 Cor. 5:21; 1 Pet. 2:24). Yet God gloriously raised Him up on the third day.

Only through Jesus can those who are dead in sin be made alive (Eph. 2:1). Only by His grace can those burdened by sin be free from the chains of guilt (Rom. 8:1). Hosea reminded Israel that the Lord raises us up, the Lord makes us right in His sight, and the Lord gives us life!

> He will restore us, that we may live in his presence. Let us acknowledge the LORD; let us press on to acknowledge him. (6:2–3, NIV)

Press on to acknowledge your Lord today (Phil. 3:14). Sin brought you death, but praise be to Jesus Christ, who has raised you to life!

Keep reading: 2 Kings 15:30–31

Ransomed and Redeemed

July 2

TODAY'S READING: Hosea 10–14; Micah 1

I will ransom them from the power of the grave; I will redeem them from death: . . . O grave, I will be thy destruction. *Hosea 13:14*

The message of ransom and redemption from death, here in Hosea, sounds a lot like something Jesus would have said, doesn't it? Because that's exactly what He came to do! Yet these words were spoken by the prophet Hosea more than seven hundred years before Christ. This is exactly why I love reading the Bible looking for Jesus all the way through.

Though Hosea, along with his contemporary Micah, prophesied God's impending judgment on Israel, he knew God would send a redeemer. And just as the beloved storyteller Paul Harvey gave us the "rest of the story," the great preacher Paul the apostle tells us that the rest of Hosea's story is found in Jesus.

> O death, where is thy sting? O grave, where is thy victory? The sting of death is sin; and the strength of sin is the law. But thanks be to God, which giveth us the victory through our Lord Jesus Christ. (1 Cor. 15:55–57)

Today we can look back and see exactly how God kept all His promises through His Son. Jesus fulfilled Hosea's prophecy and paid our ransom (Matt. 20:28). He redeemed us and freed us from the power of the grave (Heb. 2:15).

> Ye know that ye were not redeemed with corruptible things, as silver and gold . . . but with the precious blood of Christ, as of a lamb without blemish and without spot. (1 Pet. 1:18–19)

We have reason to rejoice today, for we have been ransomed and redeemed!

July 3

Sound Opinions

TODAY'S READING: **2 Kings 17; Isaiah 5**

> Woe to those who call evil good, and good evil; . . . Woe to those who are wise in their own eyes. *Isaiah 5:20–21,* NKJV

It's surprisingly easy to base our views of right and wrong on popular opinion, especially in these days when depravity abounds and God's law has been replaced with mankind's beliefs. Even in the church the truth of God's Word is often replaced with emotionally stimulating sound bites that are easier for us to accept.

Today's reading warns us against measuring right and wrong by anything other than God's Word.

> Woe unto them that are wise in their own eyes, and prudent in their own sight! (Isa. 5:21)

Do you hear the similarity to Jesus's words of rebuke to the religious rulers of His day?

> Woe unto you, scribes and Pharisees, hypocrites! for ye pay tithe of mint and anise and cummin, and have omitted the weightier matters of the law, judgment, mercy, and faith: these ought ye to have done, and not to leave the other undone. . . . Even so ye also outwardly appear righteous unto men, but within ye are full of hypocrisy and iniquity. (Matt. 23:23, 28)

They were twisting the Scriptures to fit their own agenda. They wanted to look good to those around them, but their hearts were far from God. Both Isaiah and Jesus said "Woe," meaning "judgment is coming" (Isa. 5:20–21, AMP), to those who misuse the Word of God.

You see, Jesus is the Word of God made flesh (John 1:1–5, 14). When we misrepresent the standard of Scripture, we misrepresent God Almighty and distort the truth of Christ.

So today, hold fast to His truth, as written in His Word.

Keep reading: 2 Kings 16:19–20; 2 Chronicles 28:26–27; 1 Chronicles 4:34–43

King of Kings

TODAY'S READING: Isaiah 13–16

In mercy the throne will be established;
And One will sit on it in truth, in the tabernacle of David,
Judging and seeking justice and hastening righteousness.
Isaiah 16:5, NKJV

When reflecting on kings and kingdoms, the Bible says that righteousness exalts a nation (Prov. 14:34). Today's reading gives us a glorious glimpse of God reigning in righteousness. What a majestic day it will be when the Lord establishes His kingdom to reign forever!

> Unto the Son he saith, Thy throne, O God, is for ever and ever: a sceptre of righteousness is the sceptre of thy kingdom. Thou hast loved righteousness, and hated iniquity; therefore God, even thy God, hath anointed thee with the oil of gladness above thy fellows. (Heb. 1:8–9)

Much of the Old Testament's revelation of the Messiah relates to Jesus's earthly ministry. But the beauty of this particular prophecy in Isaiah is that it gives us a glimpse of Christ's second coming—when He will reign on earth as King of kings and Lord of lords (Rev. 19:16). For His rule will be established in mercy, truth, justice, and righteousness.

> There were great voices in heaven, saying, The kingdoms of this world are become the kingdoms of our Lord, and of his Christ; and he shall reign for ever and ever. (11:15)

As certain as the prophecies were concerning Jesus's first coming, they are just as firm concerning His return.

> He which testifieth these things saith, Surely I come quickly. Amen. Even so, come, Lord Jesus. (22:20)

July 5

Come and See

TODAY'S READING: Psalms 66–67; Isaiah 18–21

> Come and see what God has done, how awesome his works in man's behalf! *Psalm 66:5,* NIV

Throughout the Old Testament we read about those who loved God, faithfully proclaiming His forgiveness and redemption—His "awesome . . . works in man's behalf." They urge us to "come and see what God has done" (Ps. 66:5, NIV).

> Come and listen, all you who fear God; let me tell you what he has done for me. (v. 16, NIV)

We see the same "song" echoed in the gospel of John when those who heard and saw Jesus called others to "come and see."

> Nathanael said unto him, Can there any good thing come out of Nazareth? Philip saith unto him, Come and see. (1:46)

> The woman then left her waterpot, and went . . . and saith to the men, Come, see a man, which told me all things that ever I did: is not this the Christ? (4:28–29)

There's no greater news to be told than simply "Your sins are forgiven!" Everyone has sinned and fallen short of God's standard (Rom. 3:23). We cannot work our way to heaven (Isa. 64:6; Eph. 2:8). We need someone to plead our case, and that someone is Jesus.

> He is able also to save them to the uttermost that come unto God by him, seeing he ever liveth to make intercession for them. (Heb. 7:25)

Consider Jesus's goodness, His great love, and His saving grace. What are some ways Jesus has worked in your life? Take time today to invite those around you to "come and see" what He's done for you!

His Cleansing Work

July 6

TODAY'S READING: 2 Chronicles 29–31

Hezekiah appointed . . . the priests and Levites for burnt offerings and for peace offerings, to minister, and to give thanks, and to praise in the gates of the tents of the Lord.
2 Chronicles 31:2

Hezekiah was only twenty-five years old when he was appointed king of Israel (2 Chron. 29:1). He inherited nothing but devastation and wickedness from his father, King Ahaz, who was the ruin of all Israel (28:19–20, 22–23). But upon becoming king, Hezekiah immediately began to undo the blasphemous work of his father (29:2–11).

Where Ahaz found fellowship with false gods and wicked Assyrian kings (28:16), Hezekiah turned to the prophet Isaiah and listened to what the Lord was saying. There is no doubt that his relationship with Isaiah is one of the reasons Hezekiah was such a good king.

Now Hezekiah found the temple in ruins. The doors had been shut, the lights had burned out, and it was filled with a bunch of junk and debris. The priests were not fulfilling their role, daily offerings were not being made, and there were no songs of praise filling its gates.

Hezekiah made it his purpose to reestablish the temple and turn the people back to the true and living God. He reinstated the priests, had the temple walls cleansed, and ordered that the piles of junk be hauled away. Finally, praise and worship filled God's temple once again.

The picture here mirrors Jesus Christ's work in the believer's life and heart. Being born again begins the beautiful work of sanctification—the rebuilding of one's life, the establishment of praise, and the cleansing work by the Word of God (John 17:17).

Take a look around your heart. Is it in need of some cleansing or repair? Is there junk that needs to be taken out? Is praise filling the gates of your life? This is the work Jesus desires to do in you.

July 7

Remember to Give Thanks

TODAY'S READING: Isaiah 22–23; Micah 2–3

> You did not look to him who did it, or see him who planned it long ago. *Isaiah 22:11,* ESV

As life unfolds and plans take shape, we want to remember to give the Lord the glory for all things! Isaiah pointed out how Israel forgot to give God thanks. In essence, he said, "You built all these things, but you didn't remember to look to the One who did it or regard the One who planned it long ago" (Isa. 22:11).

Israel's lack of gratitude reminds me of a scene in the life of Jesus. As He traveled through Samaria and Galilee, ten lepers met Him. They cried out to Jesus and begged to be healed. Full of compassion, Jesus told them to go and show themselves to the priests. Immediately they took off down the road. Only one of those lepers, when he realized he'd been healed, turned back to thank the Lord.

> One of them, when he saw that he was healed, turned back, and with a loud voice glorified God. . . . And Jesus answering said, Were there not ten cleansed? but where are the nine? (Luke 17:15, 17)

Can't you relate to this leper? Jesus touched and healed you when you were born again. Through faith in Him you were given new life—and this He planned from long ago. It was God's plan to redeem you through His Son, Jesus, before the foundations of the earth (1 Pet. 1:20).

Let's be sure to pause and say "Thank You, Jesus" today!

Little Town of Bethlehem

TODAY'S READING: Micah 4–7

You, O Bethlehem . . .
from you shall come forth for me
one who is to be ruler in Israel. *Micah 5:2,* ESV

Despite being the hometown of King David, Bethlehem remained small and insignificant. And yet God chose Bethlehem as the birthplace of His greatest promise—the Son of David, the Messiah. Seven hundred years later, this prophecy rang in Herod's ears when the Magi came seeking the King of the Jews.

> When Herod the king heard this, he was troubled, . . . and assembling all the chief priests and scribes of the people, he inquired of them where the Christ was to be born. They told him, "In Bethlehem of Judea, for so it is written by the prophet: 'And you, O Bethlehem, in the land of Judah, are by no means least among the rulers of Judah; for from you shall come a ruler who will shepherd my people Israel.'" (Matt. 2:3–6, ESV)

How appropriate that Bethlehem means "House of Bread."[60] For Jesus, born in Bethlehem, is "the bread of life" (John 6:35). Just as prophesied, Jesus is the King of kings, the ruler "whose goings forth have been from of old, from everlasting" (Mic. 5:2). Jesus is the "Alpha and Omega, the beginning and the end" (Rev. 22:13). He has been from the beginning and will be forevermore.[61]

Truly, Jesus is our eternal ruler, the King of kings and Lord of lords. The glory of all eternity belonged to that babe born in Bethlehem.

Take the Taunts to the Temple

TODAY'S READING: 2 Kings 18–19; 2 Chronicles 32:1–23; Isaiah 36–37

> Be strong and courageous; do not be afraid nor dismayed before the king of Assyria. . . . With him is an arm of flesh; but with us is the LORD our God, to help us and to fight our battles. *2 Chronicles 32:7–8,* NKJV

King Hezekiah and his countrymen were being taunted for their faith by the ferocious Assyrians. Their story is tremendously encouraging for anyone who's been mocked for trusting God.

The king of Assyria had sent messengers to stand at the gate of Jerusalem to mock and call into question Israel's faith in God's protection. The people of Israel stood and listened, but they did not respond, even though their hearts were heavy and their spirits severely troubled. The king of Assyria then delivered a death threat directly to King Hezekiah. Rather than panic, King Hezekiah took the letter to the temple and "spread it before the LORD" (2 Kings 19:14).

We often hear mocking from the world around us as our culture continually calls into question God's ways, His power, and His authority. Jesus told us this would happen.

> They will lay their hands on you and persecute you, delivering you up to the synagogues and prisons, and you will be brought before kings and governors for my name's sake. This will be your opportunity to bear witness. . . . You will be hated by all for my name's sake. But not a hair of your head will perish. (Luke 21:12–13, 17–18, ESV)

We have a chance to take Jesus at His word and to learn a lesson from Hezekiah. When the king laid his fears before the Lord, God showed Himself strong on Israel's behalf (2 Kings 19:35). Jesus also promises to be our defender. So the next time you face a frightful situation, take the taunts to the temple, lay them before the Lord at His throne of grace, and watch Him come through for you!

Remember His Redeeming Arm

TODAY'S READING: Psalms 75–77; 80

In the day of my trouble I sought the Lord. *Psalm 77:2*

Discouragement strikes most of us at some point in our lives. Maybe you're feeling low today. If so, take heart, my friend, remembering what your great God has done for you.

> I will remember the works of the LORD: surely I will remember thy wonders of old. I will meditate also of all thy work, and talk of thy doings. Thy way, O God, is in the sanctuary: who is so great a God as our God? (Ps. 77:11–13)

The psalmist here was in the middle of a brutal battle for his mind's focus. Dogged by doubt and questioning God's faithfulness, he wrote these words of wisdom to his weary soul:

> "This is my anguish; but I will remember the years of the right hand of the Most High." I will remember the works of the LORD; surely I will remember Your wonders of old. (vv. 10–11, NKJV)

The psalmist was wise enough to separate the eternal truth of who God is from his present bummed-out feelings. He recounted the deeds of the Lord as proof of God's character (v. 11). Finding hope in the midst of feeling down, the psalmist both historically and prophetically declared, "Thou hast with thine arm redeemed thy people" (v. 15).

Truly with arms outstretched, Jesus redeemed His people by and through Himself.

As the psalmist laid his cares before the Lord, he wonderfully foreshadowed Jesus's invitation to you and me: "Humble yourselves therefore under the mighty hand of God, that he may exalt you in due time: casting all your care upon him; for he careth for you" (1 Pet. 5:6–7).

Like the psalmist, fix your eyes on Him and remember His great love. With His arm He redeemed you.

White as Snow

TODAY'S READING: Psalms 87; 125; Isaiah 1–4

> Come now, and let us reason together, saith the LORD: though your sins be as scarlet, they shall be as white as snow; though they be red like crimson, they shall be as wool. *Isaiah 1:18*

The Creator of the entire universe loves us individually and invites us to accept His provision and remedy for our sinful condition. He stands ready to "bind up the brokenhearted" (Isa. 61:1), heal the wounded, and give new life and a fresh start to sinners (2 Cor. 5:17).

Who wouldn't want to grab hold of such a tremendous opportunity? God challenged His people through Isaiah, "Why do you keep on rebelling?" (Isa. 1:5, CSB). "If you consent and obey, you will eat the best of the land" (v. 19, NASB). "Stop sinning! Learn to do what is right!" (vv. 16–17, NET). Forgiveness is available! Though your sins are as scarlet, they can be white as snow (v. 18).

This is the gospel message. Consider that classic set of verses we refer to as the Romans Road to Salvation: We have all sinned and fallen short of God's glory (Rom. 3:10, 23). The penalty of this sin is spiritual death (5:12; 6:23). But God demonstrated His love toward us in that "while we were yet sinners, Christ died for us" (5:8). The way to this eternal life is by calling on the name of the Lord Jesus Christ (10:13). For "if you confess with your mouth the Lord Jesus and believe in your heart that God has raised Him from the dead, you will be saved" (10:9, NKJV).

> With the heart man believeth unto righteousness; and with the mouth confession is made unto salvation. (10:10)

God saw Israel drenched in the filth of sin, but in His grace He offered cleansing and new life (Isa. 1:18). He offers the same to us today. Forgiveness of sins is ours for the asking!

The Coming Messiah

July 12

TODAY'S READING: Isaiah 10:5–12:6; 28

The spirit of the Lord shall rest upon him, the spirit of wisdom and understanding, the spirit of counsel and might, the spirit of knowledge and of the fear of the Lord. *Isaiah 11:2*

Isaiah, of course, did not know how God's plan about the Messiah would manifest itself, but inspired by the Holy Spirit, he wrote of Christ seven hundred years before Jesus's birth. Amazing! We see incredibly detailed descriptions of Christ in Isaiah's writings.

In Isaiah 11:1 the prophet wrote that the Redeemer would come from Jesse's descendants (King David's line). Matthew 1:6 tells us that Jesus was, in fact, descended directly from the line of David.

Isaiah 11:2 says that "the spirit of the Lord shall rest upon him, the spirit of wisdom and understanding, the spirit of counsel and might, the spirit of knowledge and of the fear of the Lord." Indeed, the Scriptures tell us that Jesus was the very fulfilment of all these (Luke 4:18–21).

Isaiah 11:4 declares that the Messiah will judge in truth. In John 5:22 we find the Father giving all judgment to His Son, Jesus.

Isaiah 11:5 reveals to us that righteousness would be His girdle. In Revelation 1:13–16 the apostle John describes Jesus in heaven clothed in a golden girdle of righteousness.

Isaiah 11:10 says that the Gentiles will seek Him. In Luke 24:47 Jesus proclaims "that repentance and remission of sins should be preached in his name among all nations."

Isaiah 28:16 speaks of God's foundation stone, "a tried stone," a sure foundation. Jesus, of course, is that cornerstone (Matt. 21:42; 1 Pet. 2:6–8).

These are just a few examples of the insight Isaiah had into the coming of the promised messiah. So remember to look for Jesus throughout today's reading. After all, He is the Word made flesh (John 1:14).

July 13

His Marvelous Work

TODAY'S READING: Isaiah 29–32

> I will proceed to do a marvellous work . . . for the wisdom of their wise men shall perish, and the understanding of their prudent men shall be hid. *Isaiah 29:14*

God promised to do a marvelous work among His people. Through the prophet Isaiah God spoke of His coming Son, who would confound the wisdom of this world. Indeed, Jesus does just that!

> Hath not God made foolish the wisdom of this world? . . . But we preach Christ crucified, unto the Jews a stumblingblock, and unto the Greeks foolishness; but unto them which are called . . . Christ the power of God, and the wisdom of God. Because the foolishness of God is wiser than men; and the weakness of God is stronger than men. (1 Cor. 1:20, 23–25)

Isaiah also prophesied of One who would bring refreshment, like the shade of a rock and rivers of water in a dry land (Isa. 32:2).

Jesus is our rock, the stone that the builders rejected, the rock from which Israel drank in the wilderness (Matt. 21:42; Acts 4:11; 1 Cor. 10:4).

> In the last day, that great day of the feast, Jesus stood and cried, saying, If any man thirst, let him come unto me, and drink. He that believeth on me, as the scripture hath said, out of his belly shall flow rivers of living water. (John 7:37–38)

Jesus is our wisdom. He is our refreshment in this dry and weary land. Jesus is God's marvelous work, and He does marvelous things!

He Came to Save

TODAY'S READING: Isaiah 33–35

He will come and save you. *Isaiah 35:4*

In today's Bible reading Isaiah proclaims the promise of a redeemer and gives us a grand glimpse into Jesus's future ministry.

> Say to those who are fearful-hearted, "Be strong, do not fear! Behold, your God will come. . . . He will come and save you." Then the eyes of the blind shall be opened, and the ears of the deaf shall be unstopped. (Isa. 35:4–5, NKJV)

We know that God kept His promise! While Jesus walked through this world, He healed the sick, gave sight to the blind, caused the deaf to hear, and promised everlasting life to those who would forsake theirs to follow Him (Luke 7:22). But Isaiah also prophesied of the Lord Jesus as the judge, the lawgiver, and the king.

> The LORD is our judge, the LORD is our lawgiver, the LORD is our king; he will save us. (33:22)

Jesus is the judge of the whole earth and the fulfillment of the law, and He will reign as King of kings forevermore (John 5:22–23; Matt. 5:17–20; Rev. 19:16).

> In the wilderness shall waters break out, and streams in the desert. . . . And the ransomed of the LORD shall return, and come to Zion with songs and everlasting joy upon their heads: they shall obtain joy and gladness, and sorrow and sighing shall flee away. (Isa. 35:6, 10)

As certainly as Jesus fulfilled the promises of His first coming, He will fulfill those regarding His return. In the Gospels we read of Jesus's miracles and the fulfillment of Isaiah 35:4–5, but in Revelation we look forward to the perfect fulfillment of Isaiah 35:10, when Jesus will cause waters to break forth and we, the ransomed of the Lord, will rejoice forevermore (Rev. 22:1–8).

He Hears Your Prayers

TODAY'S READING: Isaiah 38–39; 2 Kings 20; 2 Chronicles 32:24–33

I have heard thy prayer, I have seen thy tears. *Isaiah 38:5*

God really does hear our prayers and listen to our cares. King Hezekiah was seriously sick, and the Lord informed him he was going to die. Hezekiah responded in fervent prayer, petitioning the Lord to spare his life.

> Hezekiah turned his face . . . and prayed unto the LORD, and said, Remember now, O LORD, I beseech thee. . . . And Hezekiah wept sore. (Isa. 38:2–3)

God answered Hezekiah's prayer and extended his life. But this encouraging story doesn't stop there. After telling Hezekiah that his life would be spared, God knew that the king's heart was still filled with fear, so God gave Hezekiah a miraculous sign to reassure him.

> And this shall be a sign unto thee from the LORD. . . . The sun returned ten degrees, by which degrees it was gone down. (vv. 7–8)

This wonderful story confirms that God meets us where we are and with what we need. Each of us was in need of restoration and new life. Jesus came, died for our sins, offers us eternal life, and reassures our doubting hearts (John 14:1; 1 John 3:20). Throughout the Gospels we find examples of Jesus healing and restoring lives, and that remains His desire for us.

For Hezekiah, God literally restored time—a physical sign of His spiritual work. In Christ we are born again as a new creation; old things are passed away and all things are made new (2 Cor. 5:17). The believer's way of life becomes a physical sign of Christ's miraculous work.

Just as God heard Hezekiah's cry for help, Jesus hears our every prayer. So take all your concerns to the Lord in confidence and find mercy and grace in times of need (Heb. 4:16).

Perfect Peace

July 16

TODAY'S READING: **Isaiah 24–27**

> You will keep him in perfect peace, whose mind is stayed on You, because he trusts in You. *Isaiah 26:3,* NKJV

God's Word is our anchor in the storms of life. It's where we learn the truth about who God is and what His will is. Just imagine Isaiah's situation: he spent sixty-two years warning a people who never listened. Despite what the world would consider a failed ministry, Isaiah was filled with peace because his mind was fixed on God's Word and the promises in it. The same is true for you and me. Fixing our minds on Jesus and His Word brings peace to our hearts and minds.

> Blessed (happy, fortunate, prosperous, and enviable) is the man . . . [whose] delight and desire are in the law of the Lord, and on His law (the precepts, the instructions, the teachings of God) he habitually meditates (ponders and studies) by day and by night. (Ps. 1:1–2, AMPC)

At any given point throughout any given day, our minds will be focused on something. If we choose to focus on Jesus, we will have peace. If we don't, we won't. Pretty simple, right?

> Let this mind be in you, which was also in Christ Jesus. (Phil. 2:5)

The choice is yours, my friend. If you want peace—real peace—heed the Word that tells us to take every thought captive under the authority of Christ (2 Cor. 10:5), and think as Paul instructed the church at Philippi to think: "Whatsoever things are true, whatsoever things are honest, whatsoever things are just, whatsoever things are pure, whatsoever things are lovely, whatsoever things are of good report; if there be any virtue, and if there be any praise, think on these things" (Phil. 4:8).

July 17

Prophecy Fulfilled Perfectly

TODAY'S READING: Isaiah 40–42

Comfort ye, comfort ye my people, saith your God. *Isaiah 40:1*

Has looking for Jesus on every page of the Bible reinvigorated your interest in God's Word? When our focus is the Savior, what may have seemed boring and bland suddenly comes to life. And today's reading is filled with Jesus!

> The glory of the LORD will be revealed, and all mankind together will see it. (Isa. 40:5, NIV)

This was the word of the Lord to the prophet Isaiah seven hundred years before the Word became flesh. And as you know, Jesus came and fulfilled every single prophecy absolutely perfectly!

- He is the good shepherd (Isa. 40:11; John 10:11).
- His wisdom is unsearchable (Isa. 40:13; Col. 2:3).
- His greatness is incomprehensible (Isa. 40:18; Col. 2:9).
- He is the creator of the universe (Isa. 40:28; Col. 1:16).
- He sustains and strengthens the weak (Isa. 40:29; Matt. 11:5).
- He takes hold of our hand and leads us (Isa. 41:13; John 16:13).
- He is our redeemer (Isa. 41:14; Acts 4:12).
- He is the living water and makes water flow in the dry desert (Isa. 41:18; John 4:14).
- He opens the eyes of the blind (Isa. 42:7, 18; John 9:11).
- He frees the captives (Isa. 42:7; Mark 5:1–20).
- He is the light of the world (Isa. 42:16; John 8:12).

Jesus of Nazareth was the glory of the Lord in human form. He came so we could see and touch God Himself as He dwelt among us, instructing us through word and deed and offering forgiveness to all who believe and receive Him.

A Beloved Bride

TODAY'S READING: Isaiah 43–46

Since you are precious in My sight, since you are honored and I love you . . . *Isaiah 43:4,* NASB

God created love and marriage between a man and a woman to paint a powerful picture of His love for us (Eph. 5:22–33). Like a groom who watches his bride walk down the aisle, God fixes His eyes on the ones He has chosen. The Bible makes it oh so clear that He is the bridegroom and we, the church, are His bride.

Today's reading gives a glimpse into God's heart for His bride. It begins with redemption and restoration as He lavishes us with love and a future filled with hope.

Take special note today of how Jesus sees you:

- You are Christ's (Isa. 43:1; 1 John 4:4).
- He calls you by name (Isa. 43:1; John 10:3).
- You are precious in Jesus's sight (Isa. 43:4; Matt. 13:45–46).
- Because of Christ, you are honorable (Isa. 43:4; Eph. 5:27).
- You are loved (Isa. 43:4; John 15:9).
- You are chosen (Isa. 43:10; Rom. 8:30).
- You are redeemed (Isa. 44:22; 1 Pet. 1:18–19).

> Thus saith the LORD that created thee, O Jacob, and he that formed thee, O Israel, Fear not: for I have redeemed thee, I have called thee by thy name; thou art mine. (Isa. 43:1)

As God spoke to His people, He was pointing ahead to His plan of salvation. In Christ you are made righteous and honorable. You are precious in His sight, and it was for the joy of having you as His own that He bore the Cross (Heb. 12:2). You are a deeply beloved bride.

July 19

Redeemer and King

TODAY'S READING: Isaiah 47–50

As for our redeemer, the LORD of hosts is his name, the Holy One of Israel. *Isaiah 47:4*

To find a national ruler who possesses all power and all authority yet is filled with perfect humility would be an impossibility, given our fallen nature. Yet this is our God! Today's reading foreshadows Christ our Savior, both in His humility and in His authority—as redeemer and king. The prophet Isaiah, inspired by the Holy Spirit, penned descriptions of both the babe born in Bethlehem and the King of kings reigning in heaven.

The LORD hath called me from the womb. . . . The LORD . . . formed me from the womb to be his servant, to bring Jacob again to him. (49:1, 5)

Humbling Himself, Christ became a man in order to bring us to Himself (Phil. 2:8).

I will also give thee for a light to the Gentiles. (Isa. 49:6)

He came as the light of the world, illuminating our path both spiritually and physically as we see Him restore sight to those who walked in darkness (John 9:25; Matt. 4:16; Eph. 2:1–2).

And as Isaiah proclaimed, He will come again to reign eternally, and the whole world will submit to His glory (Phil. 2:10–11).

Unto me every knee shall bow, every tongue shall swear. (Isa. 45:23)

What a majestic God we serve! He lights the stars in the sky yet sees fit to light the path of His people. He is both redeemer and king.

Looking for the Messiah

TODAY'S READING: Isaiah 51–54

Surely he hath borne our griefs, and carried our sorrows.
Isaiah 53:4

Today's reading provides one of the most obvious and poignant prophecies about the coming of the Christ in the entire Old Testament! Let's compare a few of these prophecies with the gospel accounts of Christ's crucifixion:

- He was "despised and rejected of men" (Isa. 53:3), for "he came unto his own, and his own received him not" (John 1:11).
- He was led like "a lamb to the slaughter" (Isa. 53:7), for He was "the Lamb of God" who came to be sacrificed for our sin (John 1:29).
- "Yet he opened not his mouth" (Isa. 53:7). He remained silent, not answering His accusers a word (Matt. 26:63; Mark 15:2–5).
- Having been stricken for the transgressions of the people (Isa. 53:8), He did not spare Himself; rather, He died for the sins of the world (John 11:51–52).
- He died with the wicked (Isa. 53:9), for He hung on the cross between two criminals (Matt. 27:38).
- Just as the prophecy declared, He was buried with the rich (Isa. 53:9), for Joseph of Arimathaea, a rich man, buried Christ in his tomb (Mark 15:43, 46).

With these as your starting point, dig into Isaiah 53 once more. Let yourself be awed by Isaiah's Holy Spirit–inspired prophecies, which offer a detailed description of Christ's crucifixion, a foreshadowing of His suffering, and a proclamation of His perfect love.

A Glorious Invitation

TODAY'S READING: Isaiah 55–59

> Come, everyone who thirsts,
> come to the waters;
> and he who has no money,
> come, buy and eat! *Isaiah 55:1,* ESV

The prophet Isaiah boldly proclaimed God's invitation to those who had nothing to offer. That is our story in Christ! Jesus offered living water to the thirsty, bread to the hungry, and everlasting life to those who were dead in sin.

> Incline your ear, and come to me; hear, that your soul may live; and I will make with you an everlasting covenant, my steadfast, sure love for David. (Isa. 55:3, ESV)

> Behold, I stand at the door and knock. If anyone hears my voice and opens the door, I will come in to him and eat with him, and he with me. (Rev. 3:20, ESV)

Jesus is God's everlasting covenant, the ultimate demonstration of His steadfast love.

> Verily, verily, I say unto you, He that heareth my word, and believeth on him that sent me, hath everlasting life, and shall not come into condemnation; but is passed from death unto life. (John 5:24)

A more glorious invitation has never been written! May you read the divine details today and see all His glorious benefits extended to you through Jesus.

Good Tidings

TODAY'S READING: Isaiah 60–63

> The Spirit of the Lord GOD is upon me; because the LORD hath anointed me to preach good tidings. *Isaiah 61:1*

The subject of this prophecy is clearly Jesus, the coming redeemer. Isaiah specifically spoke of One who was anointed to "preach good tidings." And the truth of Christ's substitutionary death and subsequent resurrection is absolutely good, in every way. Isaiah prophesied of God's only begotten Son bringing good tidings, and the angel confirmed the fulfillment, proclaiming Christ's birth and declaring, "I bring you good tidings of great joy" (Luke 2:10–11).

Seven hundred years before the birth of Christ, Isaiah wrote these words:

> He hath sent me to bind up the brokenhearted, to proclaim liberty to the captives, and the opening of the prison to them that are bound; to proclaim the acceptable year of the LORD, and the day of vengeance of our God; to comfort all that mourn; to appoint unto them that mourn in Zion, to give unto them beauty for ashes, the oil of joy for mourning, the garment of praise for the spirit of heaviness; that they might be called trees of righteousness, the planting of the LORD, that he might be glorified. (61:1–3)

In Luke 4:18–21 Jesus declared Himself the fulfillment of these words. Truly, Jesus binds up the brokenhearted, proclaims freedom for those bound in sin, comforts those who mourn, and fills us with joy. He has set us free, anoints us with the oil of joy, and clothes us in His robes of righteousness. These are good tidings indeed!

Keep reading: Psalm 82

July 23

He Came Down

TODAY'S READING: Isaiah 64–66; 2 Kings 21

> Oh, that You would rend the heavens! That You would come down! *Isaiah 64:1,* NKJV

Here Isaiah prophesied of the incarnation of Jesus Christ. Indeed, He did come down.

> The Word became flesh and dwelt among us, and we beheld His glory, the glory as of the only begotten of the Father, full of grace and truth. (John 1:14, NKJV)

Jesus is the glorious manifestation of the Father, "the image of the invisible God" (Col. 1:15).

Isaiah also prophesied that the Messiah would seek those who did not seek Him and would save nations outside of Israel.

> I am sought of them that asked not for me; I am found of them that sought me not: I said, Behold me, behold me, unto a nation that was not called by my name. (65:1)

To all of us, regardless of heritage or nationality, Jesus extends the offer of salvation, making us His people.

> There is neither Jew nor Greek . . . for ye are all one in Christ Jesus. And if ye be Christ's, then are ye Abraham's seed, and heirs according to the promise. (Gal. 3:28–29)

Isaiah contrasted Israel's rebellion with God's grace.

> I have spread out my hands all the day unto a rebellious people, which walketh in a way that was not good. (65:2)

While we were enemies of God, Jesus spread out His hands on the cross and offered us salvation (Rom. 5:7–8). By His grace we are saved!

Certainly, from promise to fulfillment, the Bible is one story pointing to one person: Jesus.

Keep reading: 2 Chronicles 33

Zephaniah and the Messiah

TODAY'S READING: Zephaniah 1–3; Jeremiah 1

The LORD thy God in the midst of thee is mighty; he will save, he will rejoice over thee with joy; he will rest in his love, he will joy over thee with singing. *Zephaniah 3:17*

The brief book of Zephaniah records the words of a minor prophet with a major message: God is in your midst and He will save you! Zephaniah's message might seem limited to ancient Israel, but in reality he provided what's called a double prophecy—it was relevant then and it's relevant now. It both proclaimed Jesus's coming and foreshadowed the end times and Jesus's return.

Consider it through the lens of this simple outline: the decree of the Lord (1:1–6), the day of the Lord (1:7–3:8), and the deliverance of the Lord (3:9–20). As you read Zephaniah, see it both through the lens of history as applied to Israel and through the lens of contemporary reality as applied to us today.

Just as prophesied by Zephaniah, Jesus is mighty to save (Matt. 19:25–26). He rejoices over you with joy (Luke 15:5–6), and His love is everlasting (Jer. 31:3; John 13:1).

God did not redeem us because of our great goodness. He redeemed us out of His great love.

> God, who is rich in mercy, for his great love wherewith he loved us, even when we were dead in sins, hath quickened us together with Christ, (by grace ye are saved;) and hath raised us up together, and made us sit together in heavenly places in Christ Jesus. (Eph. 2:4–6)

Zephaniah prophesied of the coming messiah. Jesus is the one in our midst (Matt. 18:20) and the one who keeps us (Jude 1:24). Jesus rests in His love for us, not in ours for Him (John 2:23–25). "We love him, because he first loved us" (1 John 4:19). It is all about Jesus, because of Jesus, and dependent on Jesus.

July 25 Reformation Versus Regeneration

TODAY'S READING: Jeremiah 2–4

> Although you wash yourself with soda and use an abundance of soap, the stain of your guilt is still before me. *Jeremiah 2:22,* NIV

Do you know the difference between reformation and regeneration? The distinction between the two offers an important insight for our spiritual development. Reformation is obedience that flows from outward imitation. It's fine, but it's fleeting. On the contrary, regeneration is obedience that flows from inward dedication—and that's what brings a lasting transformation. Reformation touches the mind and the will, at least for a season. But regeneration touches the heart, which gives our obedience a reason to last.

The book of Jeremiah begins with King Josiah reigning from Jerusalem. He was one of the few kings who followed God wholeheartedly. And the people of Israel loved King Josiah, so they followed his lead. But theirs was an outward act of imitation rather than an inward heart of dedication. In truth, their hearts were far from God. They used the "soap" of obedience to clean themselves on the outside, but that couldn't remove the ugly stain of sin on the inside. What they experienced was reformation, but what they needed was regeneration.

This was the precise message Jesus gave regarding the Pharisees.

> Woe to you, scribes and Pharisees, hypocrites! For you clean the outside . . . but inside they are full of greed and self-indulgence. (Matt. 23:25, ESV)

But praise the Lord! Through the power of Jesus's atoning blood (1 John 1:9), our spirits can be reborn (John 3:3; 1 Pet. 1:23) and our minds and lives transformed (Rom. 12:2). This is regeneration from the inside out!

A Good Path

July 26

TODAY'S READING: Jeremiah 5–6; 13

> To whom shall I speak, and give warning, that they may hear?
> *Jeremiah 6:10*

The Lord stands ready to guide and lead His people with perfect wisdom, just as God offered direction and peace to the nation of Israel, if they would only listen.

> Stand ye in the ways, and see, and ask for the old paths, where is the good way. . . . But they said, We will not walk therein. (Jer. 6:16)

So, too, Jesus told us to enter by the narrow gate and walk the path to righteousness.

> Enter by the narrow gate. For the gate is wide and the way is easy that leads to destruction, and those who enter by it are many. For the gate is narrow and the way is hard that leads to life, and those who find it are few. (Matt. 7:13–14, ESV)

In Jeremiah's time the people asked which way they should go, but then they foolishly refused to follow the directions the Lord revealed. Jesus extends the same guidance to us, inviting us to follow Him. But we must decide if we will listen.

> If anyone is a hearer of the word and not a doer, he is like a man who looks intently at his natural face in a mirror . . . and at once forgets what he was like. (James 1:23–24, ESV)

Today, ask the Lord to reveal His path to you. When you hear Him answer, listen. For His way is a good way!

July 27

Heart Healing

TODAY'S READING: Jeremiah 16–17; 2 Kings 22; 2 Chronicles 34

> The heart is deceitful above all things, and desperately wicked: who can know it? I the LORD search the heart. *Jeremiah 17:9–10*

Each and every human heart is sick with sin. But there's a cure! It's Jesus and washing in the water of His Word (Eph. 5:26). One sin that attacks the heart and is desperately wicked is pride. Pride is dangerous in part because it's so subtle. It can easily be overlooked and grow to a point where the pain it causes is disastrous.

So how do we seek out and destroy such sin? Simple—by applying God's Word. Jesus, being the Word made flesh, prayed that God would cleanse us and sanctify us through His Word.

> Sanctify them through thy truth: thy word is truth. (John 17:17)

We cannot decipher our own motives and intentions, but Jesus knows our hearts (2:24; 1 John 3:20) and reveals our thoughts and intentions to us through His Word.

> The word of God is living and active, sharper than any two-edged sword, piercing to the division of soul and of spirit, of joints and of marrow, and discerning the thoughts and intentions of the heart. (Heb. 4:12, ESV)

When I was growing up, we raised sheep. Those woolly sheep looked clean and white when standing against the backdrop of bright-green spring grass. But against a different backdrop—that of freshly fallen snow—all their dirt was visible.

That's how it is as we look to Jesus. The more we see Him, the more we're humbled and realize our need for His grace. Outside of Him we are filthy (Isa. 64:6), but in Christ we are washed completely clean (John 15:3).

So keep looking to Jesus and let Him cleanse your heart through His Word.

Useful Revival

TODAY'S READING: Nahum 1–3; 2 Kings 23:1–28; 2 Chronicles 35:1–19

> Before him there was no king like him, who turned to the LORD with all his heart, with all his soul, and with all his might. *2 Kings 23:25,* NKJV

One look around us confirms that the world needs one thing more than any other: revival. We need men and women who, like King Josiah, will turn to the Lord with all their hearts, souls, and minds. The word *revival* is defined as "restoration to life" and "restoration to use."[62] True revival includes not only restoration to life in God but also restoration to use for God.

> If anyone cleanses himself from these things, he will be a vessel for honor, sanctified, useful . . . , prepared for every good work. (2 Tim. 2:21, NASB)

Jesus desires to reveal Himself through us. But this often requires us to undergo revival. A perfect example of this New Testament principle is revealed in today's Old Testament reading. King Josiah's response after experiencing God's tug on his heart gives us a picture of true revival.

It all started with Josiah reading God's law. As a result, repentance was experienced, evangelism practiced, the temple repaired, God's instruction sought, the law studied, and sin dealt with. Josiah's love for God was infectious. He implemented righteousness, and all Israel benefited.

We often think of revival as times when the Lord's presence is experienced in a fresh way or there is an overwhelming response to an altar call. These times are precious indeed, but they are just part—or really the start—of being truly revived. As we can see from Josiah's story, God intends revival to include both restoration to life in Him and restoration to use for Him!

Jesus wants our lives to be used for His glory (Matt. 5:16; 2 Thess. 1:11–12; Phil. 1:9–11; 1 Pet. 2:12). Oh, that He would revive our hearts today, restoring us to life in Him and to use for Him.

He Removed Our Burden

TODAY'S READING: Psalm 81; Jeremiah 47–48

> I removed his shoulder from the burden;
> His hands were freed from the baskets.
> You called in trouble, and I delivered you. *Psalm 81:6–7,* NKJV

Not only do we live in a fallen world that is steeped in stress and dishes out difficulties, but our own sin also adds to the burden. But there's good news for those who come to Christ. Jesus said,

> Come to Me, all you who labor and are heavy laden, and I will give you rest. Take My yoke upon you and learn from Me, for I am gentle and lowly in heart, and you will find rest for your souls. For My yoke is easy and My burden is light. (Matt. 11:28–30, NKJV)

In Psalm 81 God reminded His people that He lifts their burdens and frees them from toil. Jesus carried our burdens as He bore His cross (Isa. 53:4; 1 Pet. 2:24). Just as Psalm 81 proclaims, He has removed the burden of sin from our shoulders and freed us from striving under the law (Rom. 6:14).

Now, in Christ, we can cast all our cares upon Jesus.

> Humble yourselves therefore under the mighty hand of God, that he may exalt you in due time: casting all your care upon him; for he careth for you. . . . But the God of all grace, who hath called us unto his eternal glory by Christ Jesus, after that ye have suffered a while, make you perfect, stablish, strengthen, settle you. (1 Pet. 5:6–7, 10)

Take Him at His word today and cast your cares on Jesus, for He cares for you. He has removed your burden and delivers you when you call.

Keep reading: 2 Kings 23:29–30; 2 Chronicles 35:20–36:1

Wait for It

TODAY'S READING: Jeremiah 22; Habakkuk 1–3

The earth shall be filled with the knowledge of the glory of the LORD, as the waters cover the sea. *Habakkuk 2:14*

One day, not too long from now, the earth will be filled with the knowledge of the glory of the Lord. As in Habakkuk's time, the evils of the world cause us to eagerly look forward to that day, when King Jesus will reign forever and set right all that's wrong in this world.

But until Jesus returns, remember that God's timing is absolutely perfect. He remains faithful to His Word and the promises in it. So even if the days feel long and it seems as though the Lord is delaying His coming, don't grow weary (Gal. 6:9). Think back to Habakkuk's time. The people of Israel were waiting . . . and waiting . . . and waiting for the promised messiah. That promise was made way back in Genesis 3:15, reiterated to their father Abraham (22:18), and pictured throughout the law and sacrifices. Yet it was only in God's perfect timing that His glory walked among us in human form, perfectly fulfilling His promise (John 1:14–16).

> The vision is yet for an appointed time; but at the end it will speak, and it will not lie. Though it tarries, wait for it; because it will surely come, it will not tarry. (Hab. 2:3, NKJV)

If God was faithful to come the first time, He will be faithful to come again.

> We which are alive and remain shall be caught up together with them in the clouds, to meet the Lord in the air: and so shall we ever be with the Lord. Wherefore comfort one another with these words. (1 Thess. 4:17–18)

So wait for it . . . and watch in eager anticipation, for He *is* coming back soon!

Keep reading: 2 Kings 23:31–37; 2 Chronicles 36:2–5

July 31

Glory in the Lord

TODAY'S READING: Jeremiah 7–10

> Let not the wise man glory in his wisdom, neither let the mighty man glory in his might. *Jeremiah 9:23*

Jeremiah spoke in compelling terms of our nature apart from God's Word. He put human wisdom in perspective when he compared it to the Lord's. You see, God's Word anchors our minds in a world that wants to toss us to and fro. Without God's Word—without a biblical worldview—we're left only with our own thoughts and theories, which are faulty at best. Think with me for a minute. If we're forming our own theories about the world and our place in it, either we are creating a god of our own, apart from the God revealed in the Scriptures, or we're setting ourselves up as our own god.

> Thus saith the LORD, Let not the wise man glory in his wisdom, neither let the mighty man glory in his might . . . : But let him that glorieth glory in this, that he understandeth and knoweth me, that I am the LORD which exercise lovingkindness, judgment, and righteousness, in the earth. (Jer. 9:23–24)

As Jeremiah penned these words, he prophesied of the Lord Jesus Christ. Jesus alone holds all wisdom (Col. 2:3), for in Him dwells all the fullness of God (v. 9). His strength is made perfect in our weakness (2 Cor. 12:9). He has made us coheirs with His inheritance, and our riches are in Him (Rom. 8:17). Through His loving-kindness He has made us the righteousness of Christ (2 Cor. 5:21), and we are His delight (Eph. 5:2).

> As it is written, He that glorieth, let him glory in the Lord. (1 Cor. 1:31)

The Lord alone exercises loving-kindness, judgment, and righteousness in the earth. May our view of the world and all that is in it be a biblical one, and may our glory be solely in Him.

Feed Your Hungry Soul

TODAY'S READING: Jeremiah 15; 26; 35

Thy words were found, and I did eat them; and thy word was unto me the joy and rejoicing of mine heart: for I am called by thy name, O LORD God of hosts. *Jeremiah 15:16*

I love how Jeremiah 15:16 compares God's Word to a sumptuous serving of joy and rejoicing. God often likens His Word to food or drink. Why? Because throughout the Bible God is communicating majestic eternal truths in tangible terms we can wrap our minds around. He wants us to see that, like our bodies, our souls need to be nourished, sustained, and satisfied. His Word should be both what sustains your days and what gives joy to your feasts. Let's see what else He says about our soul food today:

I have esteemed the words of his mouth more than my necessary food. (Job 23:12)

As newborn babes, desire the sincere milk of the word, that ye may grow thereby. (1 Pet. 2:2)

But remember, all Scripture points to Jesus. As Jeremiah wrote these words, he was also describing God's living Word, Jesus, who said this of Himself:

I am the living bread which came down from heaven: if any man eat of this bread, he shall live for ever: and the bread that I will give is my flesh, which I will give for the life of the world. (John 6:51)

Jesus, the Word of God in human form, gave us His body, the bread of life. Feed your hungry soul today, my friend. Take in His Word, the nourishment you really need!

August 2

The Whole Message

TODAY'S READING: Jeremiah 36; 45

> Whenever Jehudi had read three or four columns of the scroll, the king cut them off with a scribe's knife and threw them into the firepot, until the entire scroll was burned. *Jeremiah 36:23,* NIV

In today's reading we see King Jehoiakim rebel in response to the Word of the Lord. God had told Jeremiah to write a message on a scroll specifically for the king. As that message was read by one of the king's men named Jehudi, King Jehoiakim cut it up and tossed it piece by piece into the fire. None of the king's officials showed any concern that God's words were being cut up and burned up.

> The king and all his attendants who heard all these words showed no fear, nor did they tear their clothes. (Jer. 36:24, NIV)

We might be inclined to think we would never engage in such brazen behavior. Yet we live in a culture that consistently compels the church to cut out portions of Scripture that make people uncomfortable. Jesus gave us insight as to why this is.

> Everyone who does wicked things hates the light and does not come to the light, lest his works should be exposed. (John 3:20, ESV)

Just as Jesus calls people to repentance, God's Word exposes darkness—and many people do not want their sin exposed.

Jesus rebuked the scribes and Pharisees for partitioning out portions of Scripture and misusing them in order to elevate themselves (Matt. 23:23–28).

> He said, Yea rather, blessed are they that hear the word of God, and keep it. (Luke 11:28)

May we be people who listen to the whole Bible, take in the full counsel of God, and hear all His Words—even the difficult parts.

Keep reading: 2 Kings 24:1–4; 2 Chronicles 36:3–7; Jeremiah 25

Ask for Wisdom

August 3

TODAY'S READING: Jeremiah 46; Daniel 1–2

There is a God in heaven that revealeth secrets. *Daniel 2:28*

I love the book of Daniel for the simple fact that Daniel sought the Lord, and God answered him. Daniel beseeched God for wisdom, and God bestowed it. Daniel inquired of God for insight, and God enlightened him. Daniel asked God for favor with the king, and God granted it.

Just as God answered Daniel, He answers us too. His Word tells us that we have not because we ask not (James 4:2); that if we ask according to His will, He hears us; and that if He hears us, we have what we ask (1 John 5:14–15).

But lest we forget, only through the blood of Jesus do we have the ability to ask and the favor to receive (Rom. 5:2; Eph. 2:18; 3:12). And Jesus is here in the book of Daniel! We will see Him prophesied of as the stone (2:45). He is the fourth man walking in the fiery furnace (3:25). He is seen in the clouds of heaven and is referred to as "the Son of man" (7:13) and "the Messiah" (9:25–26).

Only because of Jesus are we, like Daniel, given what we ask, according to His will, in His name (Matt. 7:7–11; James 4:2). And one thing we know: He desires for us to grow in wisdom!

> Daniel answered and said . . . for wisdom and might are his: and he changeth the times and the seasons: he removeth kings, and setteth up kings: he giveth wisdom unto the wise, and knowledge to them that know understanding: he revealeth the deep and secret things. (Dan. 2:20–22)

In Jesus are hidden "all the treasures of wisdom and knowledge" (Col. 2:3). So today, look to Jesus and ask Him for wisdom! He promises to give it freely (James 1:5; Jer. 33:3).

August 4 — Jesus Is with Us in the Fiery Trials

TODAY'S READING: Daniel 3

> Our God whom we serve is able to deliver us from the burning fiery furnace. *Daniel 3:17*

At various points in life, all of us will find ourselves in the middle of a fiery trial. If that's you today, take heart! There's hope, even in the furnace of your stressful situation. The account of Shadrach, Meshach, and Abednego describes three brave young men who refused to bow before an idol and, as a result, were thrown into the hottest of fires. But their unyielding faith was rewarded with a literal walk with the Lord. Jesus Himself walked and talked with them in the midst of the fire!

> Then Nebuchadnezzar the king was astonished. . . . Did not we cast three men bound into the midst of the fire? . . . Lo, I see four men loose, walking in the midst of the fire, and they have no hurt; and the form of the fourth is like the Son of God. (Dan. 3:24–25)

Just as Jesus walked with Shadrach, Meshach, and Abednego, so He stands with you in your fiery trial (1 Pet. 4:12–13). *But if God loves us so much, why do we even have to endure such hardships?* you may wonder when you're feeling the heat. The apostle Peter gives us a hope-filled answer:

> . . . that the trial of your faith, being much more precious than of gold . . . though it be tried with fire, might be found unto praise and honour and glory at the appearing of Jesus Christ. (1 Pet. 1:7)

The Lord promises to never leave you or forsake you (Heb. 13:5). In fact, Jesus is a friend who sticks "closer than a brother" (Prov. 18:24), even in the fire.

Keep reading: Jeremiah 9:16–21; 19:14–20:18; 2 Kings 24:5–9

A Righteous Branch

August 5

TODAY'S READING: Jeremiah 23:1–8; 49; Obadiah 1

I will raise unto David a righteous Branch. *Jeremiah 23:5*

Have you ever looked at a branch in the winter and thought, *That thing is dead! It'll be a miracle if it comes back in the spring*? Then, after the cold of winter passes and the warmth and water of spring come, that seemingly dead thing suddenly buds into something green. That's the picture we find in today's reading.

The situation appeared dismal indeed. The Jewish priests were like wayward shepherds (Jer. 23:1), the flock was scattered and afraid (vv. 2, 4), the house of David seemed dead (22:30), and the promised savior was nowhere in sight. Was God abandoning His promises to Israel? Was God through with the bloodline of David? Was the world without hope? No way! It's our privilege today to read how God confirmed His covenant with Israel, with King David, and with the world.

> I will raise unto David a righteous Branch, and a King shall reign and prosper, and shall execute judgment and justice in the earth. . . . And this is his name whereby he shall be called, THE LORD OUR RIGHTEOUSNESS. (23:5–6)

And then God did just as He promised! Jesus Himself came to be the shepherd His people needed (John 10:11–29). He became that branch—a righteous branch—from the line of David (Matt. 1:1). The world was lost, but "God so loved the world, that He gave His only begotten Son" (John 3:16, NASB).

God is faithful to fulfill every word He speaks. Keep reading your Bible, my friend, and see God's promises fully fulfilled in Jesus—God Himself!

Keep reading: 2 Kings 24:10–17

August 6 — Clay in the Potter's Hand

TODAY'S READING: **Jeremiah 14; 18:1–19:13; 24**

> Go down to the potter's house, and there I will give you my message. *Jeremiah 18:2,* NIV

Do you remember going on a field trip as a schoolkid? God sent Jeremiah on a field trip of sorts, instructing him to go to the potter's house, where he would be schooled in how God molds us into His image.

> O house of Israel, cannot I do with you as this potter? . . . Behold, as the clay is in the potter's hand, so are ye in mine hand. (Jer. 18:5–6)

Clay represents you and me, while the potter represents the Lord (Isa. 64:8). Clay is just squishy, sticky mud. It's earthy and it's dirty—a great illustration of our human nature (Gen. 2:7; Ps. 103:14). There's nothing special about clay until the potter begins to work with it. And that's exactly what God does with us.

Consider how Jesus worked with clay. His first miracle involved clay pots. He miraculously turned their ordinary contents into extraordinary joy (John 2:1–11). Jesus also applied clay to a blind man's eyes, and when the man opened his eyes, he saw Jesus (9:6–7).

Today, Jesus is still working with clay. He fills these earthen vessels, you and me, with His Holy Spirit and opens our eyes to see His face. He is the potter, and we are the work of His hands (Eph. 2:10). Like the clay on the wheel, we may feel dizzy and pressed, but all the while our Master Potter is molding us into the image of Christ (Rom. 8:29).

> We have this treasure in jars of clay, to show that the surpassing power belongs to God and not to us. (2 Cor. 4:7, ESV)

Today, remember you're in the Potter's hands and He is making you into a vessel of honor, filled with joy, eyes fixed on Jesus, and ready to be used by Him (Rom. 5:3–5; 1 Pet. 4:12–13; 2 Tim. 2:20–22).

Jesus, God's Good Promise

TODAY'S READING: Jeremiah 29; 49:34–50:46

> I know the thoughts that I think toward you, saith the LORD.
> *Jeremiah 29:11*

Our compassionate God always offers His people hope. His grace is abundant and His mercy endless, even in the midst of His righteous punishment. The Israelites were suffering the disastrous consequences of their sin. Because of their idolatry and rebellion, God had allowed them to be conquered by the Babylonians. But God, in His infinite goodness and grace, gave them a message of hope in the middle of what seemed like a hopeless mess. The Lord told Jeremiah that Israel's captivity would last seventy years. But that was not their end.

> When seventy years are completed . . . , I will come to you and fulfill my gracious promise to bring you back to this place. (Jer. 29:10, NIV)

God has kept all His good promises! Not only did He bring the people of Israel back to their land, but through the nation Israel, He sent us His Son, Jesus. Indeed, His thoughts toward us are very good!

> Ye shall seek me, and find me, when ye shall search for me with all your heart. And I will be found of you, saith the LORD: and I will turn away your captivity, and I will gather you from all the nations. (vv. 13–14)

Jeremiah's message applied to both Israel and us. For in Jesus we have full access to God Almighty. He answers when we call and listens to our prayers (Eph. 2:18; Heb. 4:16). Jesus promised that if we seek Him, we will find Him (Matt. 7:7–8). He brought us out of our captivity and set us free from the law of sin and death (John 8:32; Rom. 8:2–4).

As you read Jeremiah's words, look for their fulfillment in Christ, God's good promise given to you!

Keep reading: 2 Kings 24:18–20; 2 Chronicles 36:9–14

Don't Let the News Panic You

TODAY'S READING: Jeremiah 11–12; 51

> Do not lose heart or be afraid when rumors are heard in the land. *Jeremiah 51:46,* NIV

Ever feel your blood pressure rise as you watch the news? I certainly have. But God tells us not to panic as we listen to the news. That was His message to His people thousands of years ago, and it's His message to us.

I am amazed at how this word of encouragement, given to Jeremiah long before modern media, is so applicable to and comforting for us today. God used the nation Israel as an example for us (1 Cor. 10:11). "In these last days he has spoken to us by his Son" (Heb. 1:2, ESV). And His Son, Jesus, encouraged us in this same way.

> You will hear of wars and rumors of wars. See that you are not alarmed, for this must take place, but the end is not yet. (Matt. 24:6, ESV)

In the book of Colossians, we're told that God holds all things together by the power of His Word (1:17). Nothing is out of His control. He kept Noah safe through the storm and brought His people unharmed through the plagues of Egypt. He shielded Shadrach, Meshach, and Abednego in the fire and protected Daniel in the lions' den. He is able to keep us safe through whatever may come.

We live in difficult and often distressing days, but Jesus prepared us for these days.

> These things I have spoken unto you, that in me ye might have peace. In the world ye shall have tribulation: but be of good cheer; I have overcome the world. (John 16:33)

The news around us is simply verification of His Word—but you have to be in His Word to recognize that! So keep reading and studying, and as you do, look to Jesus.

God's Omnipresence

August 9

TODAY'S READING: Jeremiah 23:9–40; 27–28

Am I a God near at hand . . .
And not a God afar off?
Can anyone hide himself in secret places,
So I shall not see him? *Jeremiah 23:23–24,* NKJV

God is everywhere, omnipresent. We cannot escape His presence or His watchful eye.

> If I ascend into heaven, You are there; if I make my bed in hell, behold, You are there. If I take the wings of the morning, and dwell in the uttermost parts of the sea, even there Your hand shall lead me, and Your right hand shall hold me. (Ps. 139:8–10, NKJV)

In today's reading Jeremiah reflects on God's greatness and omnipresence. The prophet writes of God's power and our inability to thwart His plan. This truth will either comfort you or terrify you. Time and time again, David clung to God's omnipresence as his comfort (Ps. 139). On the other hand, Jonah experienced it the hard way when God sent a great fish as a literal course correction. But if you are born again, you are God's personal treasure, purchased with His own blood!

You see, in Jesus these words of Jeremiah find their perfect fulfillment. Through the redemptive work of the Savior, we can draw near to God. His Spirit is living in us, and He is always with us (1 Cor. 3:16). You are adopted by Him as one of His children. This means that, as it did for David, God's omnipresence should bring you great comfort! He watches over you with the eyes and nail-pierced hands of the Good Shepherd.

> He hath said, I will never leave thee, nor forsake thee. So that we may boldly say, The Lord is my helper, and I will not fear what man shall do unto me. (Heb. 13:5–6)

Wherever you find yourself today, may your heart be filled with God's presence and the knowledge that He is with you!

Raised for a Purpose

TODAY'S READING: Ezekiel 1–4

This was the appearance of the likeness of the glory of the LORD. And when I saw it, I fell upon my face. *Ezekiel 1:28*

Have you ever wondered about God's plan for your life or His purpose for you? You're not alone in your wondering. I bet even the prophet Ezekiel had similar questions. Then he received a mission directly from the Lord—and he got a glimpse of heaven at the same time!

As is so often the case, God prepared Ezekiel for his mission by taking him through a tough situation. He was captured by the brutal Babylonians and carried off to live as a foreigner in their land (Ezek. 1:1). But the Lord met him in that difficult spot. God opened Ezekiel's eyes, and Ezekiel saw the Lord seated on His throne. Consumed by God's glory, Ezekiel fell facedown (vv. 25, 28). Experiencing God's presence leaves a person humbled. But then God said to him, "Stand on your feet, and I will speak to you" (2:1, NKJV). Ezekiel discovered his purpose as he received his mission: to deliver a message to Israel straight from the Lord.

Like Ezekiel, we sinners fall flat on our faces when we get a glimpse of who God is, but through Jesus we've been raised to our feet and are able to stand before the Lord, robed in His righteousness (Isa. 61:10).

And just like Ezekiel, we've been given a purpose through our mission to take Jesus's message of salvation to this lost world, even if no one listens (Mark 16:15). Be encouraged today because Jesus has raised you up and has given you a purpose: to share the gospel with those around you.

On the Walls of Your Heart

TODAY'S READING: Ezekiel 5–9

> Have you seen what the elders of the house of Israel do in the dark, every man in the room of his idols? *Ezekiel 8:12,* NKJV

First God gave Ezekiel a glimpse into heaven, and then He gave him a glimpse into the heart of man. What a sad contrast. God instructed Ezekiel to dig a hole in the wall of the temple and look inside. Ezekiel couldn't believe what he saw! Idols were carved right into the walls, and each priest had a shrine set up for his individual idol and was holding on to a censer, one of the tools God had set aside for priestly use.

> When I dug into the wall, there was a door. And He said to me, "Go in, and see the wicked abominations which they are doing there." So I went in and saw, and there—every sort of creeping thing, abominable beasts, and all the idols of the house of Israel, portrayed all around on the walls. (Ezek. 8:8–10, NKJV)

This story should prompt us to pause and consider what might be seen on the walls of our hearts if someone were to peer inside. Even though Ezekiel was looking into a physical building, the principle as applied to our lives is the same.

> What? know ye not that your body is the temple of the Holy Ghost which is in you . . . ? For ye are bought with a price: therefore glorify God in your body, and in your spirit, which are God's. (1 Cor. 6:19–20)

Jesus ushered in the New Covenant, whereby He promised, "I will put my laws on their hearts, and write them on their minds" (Heb. 10:16, RSV).

God has made us priests and kings for His glory (Rev. 1:6). May you and I be the kind of priests who have His Word written on the walls of our hearts so that anyone who peers inside will see His glory reflected.

The Man Dressed in Linen

TODAY'S READING: Ezekiel 10–13

> He spake unto the man clothed with linen, and said, Go in between the wheels . . . and fill thine hand with coals of fire from between the cherubims. *Ezekiel 10:2*

How would you explain the beauty of the color blue to someone who cannot see? Or how do you describe the delightfully sweet sound of a songbird to someone who has never heard? You'd be hard-pressed to articulate the wonder of such experiences to a person who doesn't have a point of reference. I'm willing to bet this is how Ezekiel felt as he tried to convey his vision of heaven in the language of mortals. We lack the necessary frame of reference to comprehend the glory that awaits us (1 Cor. 2:9).

Nevertheless, Ezekiel aimed to describe the indescribable—a firmament and a throne of glory and the cherubim that shine as sapphires around the throne (10:1–2). His focus soon turned to a man dressed in linen (vv. 2–7). This same man is spoken of in Ezekiel 9, Daniel 10:5, and Revelation 1:12–20.

Consider this heavenly man's attributes and you will undoubtedly recognize our Savior! Ezekiel saw a wheel and coals that represented judgment. The man in linen, knowing He was to bring judgment using those coals, first took them in His own hands (Ezek. 10:7; 1 Pet. 2:24). The judgment that Christ was to give, He first received. He took our judgment through His nail-pierced hands.

The man in linen held an inkwell and used it to mark those who were protected from the coming judgment (Ezek. 9:3–6). That same Jesus is our protector and savior! The mark He gave speaks of those who have been sealed with the Holy Spirit, whose names are written in the Lamb's Book of Life and who have passed from death to life (Eph. 1:13; 4:30; 2 Cor. 1:21–22; 2 Tim. 2:19; Rev. 7:3–4).

This same Jesus, our blessed messiah who holds the writer's inkwell, has written your name in heaven. Because Jesus took our judgment and has written our names in His book, we, too, will one day see the indescribably beautiful glories of heaven.

The Heart of Discipline

August 13

TODAY'S READING: **Ezekiel 14–16**

I will do this to recapture the hearts of the people of Israel.
Ezekiel 14:5, NIV

The phrase *to recapture the hearts of the people* reassures my soul. For in those words God reveals His heart for our hearts. God told Ezekiel that He intended to discipline the people of Israel, but with one distinct purpose in mind: to bring their hearts back to Him (Ezek. 14:5–6).

Our heavenly Father never corrects or chastises us without good reason or godly purpose (v. 23). And here in Ezekiel God describes both the reason for Israel's discipline and what He would accomplish through it. The Israelites would emerge from this season of correction freed from their bondage to idolatry and restored to the Land of Promise.

Throughout His earthly ministry Jesus echoed the Father's emphasis on the heart of the matter. Consider how, after Peter had denied the Lord three times, Jesus asked Peter three times whether he loved the Lord (John 21:15–17). Jesus still desires that His disciples love Him (14:21).

May it be Jesus's love that drives us to obedience. But if needed, as God lovingly and purposefully disciplined Israel, He will do the same for you and me. And He graciously tells us what His purpose is:

> All discipline for the moment seems not to be joyful, but sorrowful; yet to those who have been trained by it, afterwards it yields the peaceful fruit of righteousness. (Heb. 12:11, NASB)

So if you feel a bit of correction today, know this, child of God: your heavenly Father wants you to be totally set free from anything that would keep you from serving Him wholeheartedly. He has a purpose, a plan, and a blessing in store for your life.

A New Heritage

TODAY'S READING: Ezekiel 17:1–20:29

You will no longer quote this proverb in Israel. *Ezekiel 18:3,* NIV

An old saying in Israel went something like this: "Don't blame me. I'm this way because of my parents!" Actually, the exact phrase was "The fathers have eaten sour grapes, and the children's teeth are set on edge" (Ezek. 18:2). But God essentially tells them, "Don't say that!"

> What do you mean when you use this proverb . . . ? As I live, . . . you shall no longer use this proverb in Israel. Behold, all souls are Mine; the soul of the father as well as the soul of the son is Mine. . . . The son shall not bear the guilt of the father, nor the father bear the guilt of the son. The righteousness of the righteous shall be upon himself, and the wickedness of the wicked shall be upon himself. (vv. 2–4, 20, NKJV)

Certainly we are all affected by our environments, but blaming other people for our difficulties, especially our parents (Exod. 20:12), sidesteps the biblical teaching of personal responsibility.

You see, just as this verse prophesied, Jesus is the righteousness of the righteous (1 Cor. 1:30; Phil. 3:9). Through Him we are released from old chains and given a new heritage.

> This is the heritage of the servants of the LORD, and their righteousness is of me, saith the LORD. (Isa. 54:17)

Jesus came to offer new life to *individuals,* and it is every individual's choice whether he or she will believe and receive and walk in that new life. Our righteousness is measured not by our parents, our upbringing, or our social status. Rather, it is based solely and completely on our acceptance of the gift of salvation and redemption offered to us by Jesus Christ.

> Therefore turn and live! (Ezek. 18:32, NKJV)

Divinely Different

August 15

TODAY'S READING: Ezekiel 20:30–22:31

> You say, "We want to be like the nations, like the peoples of the world, who serve wood and stone." But what you have in mind will never happen. *Ezekiel 20:32,* NIV

Israel was feeling out of place next to the cultures surrounding them. They watched their neighbors live lasciviously and worship all kinds of "interesting" gods, and they desired to be more like those nations. But God declared, "What you have in mind will never happen" (Ezek. 20:32, NIV).

Perhaps you, too, have felt like a misfit. As much as the culture may tempt us to conform, the Scriptures indicate that, as Jesus followers, we simply can't. We are called to be sanctified. You and I, just like Israel, are God's people. Not only are we called to reflect Jesus, but by His grace we *are* different!

> You are a chosen generation, a royal priesthood, a holy nation, His own special people, that you may proclaim the praises of Him who called you out of darkness into His marvelous light. (1 Pet. 2:9, NKJV)

As Ezekiel enumerated the sins of the priests, princes, prophets, and people (22:23–31), he shared God's message with the people, saying, "I searched for a man . . . who would build up the wall and stand in the gap before Me . . . so that I would not destroy it" (v. 30, NASB). That man is Jesus Christ! Jesus has taken our place on the cross (Rom. 3:21–31) and now stands before the Father, interceding on our behalf (Heb. 7:25). Because of Jesus we have passed from death to life (John 5:24) and are made into a new creation (2 Cor. 5:17).

God calls us a royal priesthood, a special people. May we show forth His praise, being conformed into Jesus's likeness (1 Pet. 2:9), for we are divinely different.

August 16

The Tale of Two Lewd Sisters

TODAY'S READING: Ezekiel 23–24; Jeremiah 21

> I the Lord have spoken. The time has come for me to act.
> *Ezekiel 24:14,* NIV

The Bible tells us that all the stories and testimonies in the Old Testament were given so that we could learn who God is and find hope in all the Scriptures (Rom. 15:4). This hope of the Scriptures has a name—Jesus—and His hope is evident in today's reading.

Ezekiel tells the story of two symbolic sisters, illustrating how Judah followed in the sinful steps of Israel, her sister (23:1–49). He described them as having "played the harlot" (16:28, NKJV), because both were unfaithful to Yahweh, loved the world, followed other gods, and were completely lewd. God determined to rid them of their gross idolatry through conquest and exile (23:46–49).

> Thus will I cause lewdness to cease out of the land, . . . and
> ye shall know that I am the Lord God. (vv. 48–49)

God's patience is one of His most encouraging attributes, but we should never mistake His patience as indifference toward sin. God is righteous and deals with all sin—Israel's and ours. But praise the Lord, for now we look to Jesus. Ezekiel's story reminds me of the woman caught in adultery (John 8:1–11).

> Jesus stood up and said to her, "Woman, where are they? Has no one condemned you?" She said, "No one, Lord." And Jesus said, "Neither do I condemn you; go, and from now on sin no more." (vv. 10–11, ESV)

Jesus has intervened on our behalf as well. We have been forgiven! Our gross sin, like Israel's, has been dealt with, paid for with the precious blood of Jesus. In Christ we are no longer condemned (Rom. 8:1). We are free to obey the words of Jesus: "Go, and sin no more."

Look to Jesus

August 17

TODAY'S READING: Ezekiel 25; Jeremiah 37–38; Ezekiel 29:1–16; 30:20–26

I have broken the arm of Pharaoh. . . . It has not been bound up for healing or put in a splint so as to become strong enough to hold a sword. *Ezekiel 30:21,* NIV

God continually told Israel not to look to Egypt for provisions, strength, or support (Deut. 17:16; Isa. 31:1). In human logic this makes no sense. The Egyptian empire was a powerhouse. For example, their engineering and irrigation systems provided a surplus of agricultural resources, they discovered ways to mine and exploit minerals, theirs was a land of culture and education, and their military strength and literal horsepower were unparalleled. But the Bible tells us that the Lord owns the cattle on a thousand hills, so Egypt's might meant nothing in His economy (Ps. 50:10).

God saw Egypt for what it was: a godless society that worshipped nearly everything other than the Creator. Their leader, Pharaoh, was so arrogant that he even took credit for the Nile River (Ezek. 29:3). But what is man compared to God Almighty? God pronounced utter destruction on Pharaoh and declared He would break both of Pharaoh's arms, rendering him helpless, unable to even hold a sword (30:20–22).

So what does God's judgment on Pharaoh have to do with you and me? Keeping in mind that Egypt is a picture of the world in Bible typology, consider that God told Israel not to turn to Egypt for provision, strength, and support. Jesus tells us not to look to the world for those things either (Matt. 6:25–34).

God delivered Israel from Pharaoh, king of Egypt, and Jesus has delivered us from the god of this world (Gal. 1:4; Col. 1:13). Pharaoh was rendered helpless, unable to wield his sword, and Jesus has likewise defeated the devil, our foe, and given us His Word, which is "sharper than any twoedged sword" (Heb. 2:14; 4:12).

Jesus is good, friend! His promises are true. Look to Jesus rather than the world and watch Him come through for you.

August 18

Death to Life

TODAY'S READING: Ezekiel 31; Jeremiah 32–33

> I will heal my people and will let them enjoy abundant peace and security. *Jeremiah 33:6,* NIV

What may, at first glance, seem like a gloom-and-doom passage from Jeremiah, the weeping prophet, is really a story filled with hope and purpose. That's so true of our own lives! What seems hopeless in the moment can be precisely what the Lord uses to bring us hope and purpose.

Israel was filled with and completely taken over by sin, resulting in Jerusalem's destruction and the nation's devastation. Yet God promised to renew and bring life back to His precious people Israel (Jer. 33:6). What a poignant picture of our redemption through Christ, after having previously been slaves to sin (Rom. 6:15–23). We were dead in our sins, but He made us alive in and through Him!

> You hath he quickened, who were dead in trespasses and sins; . . . and hath raised us up together, and made us sit together in heavenly places in Christ Jesus. (Eph. 2:1, 6)

Jesus suffered and died to bring us joy and life. But the apostle Paul instructed us that we, too, need to die (1 Cor. 15:31). Every day we are to die to our flesh and instead live for Christ, which brings abundant life. As Jesus said, unless a seed dies, it cannot bring forth fruit (John 12:24).

Israel needed to be purged from her idolatry. We also need to be cleansed from sin. Israel had to suffer the sword, but we're given the sword of the Spirit with which we fight and defend (Eph. 6:17; Heb. 4:12).

God promised to bring restoration to Israel (Jer. 3:12–14), and He has restored you to new life in Christ (2 Cor. 5:17). So die to yourself and to sin today and watch as real, abundant life comes your way—in Jesus's name!

Is the Bible Really Inerrant?

August 19

TODAY'S READING: Jeremiah 34; 2 Kings 25; 2 Chronicles 36:15–21; Jeremiah 39

Every word of God proves true. *Proverbs 30:5,* RSV

Have you ever read what initially appeared to be a contradiction in Scripture? Since we know that "all Scripture is given by inspiration of God" (2 Tim. 3:16), what might seem at first glance to be an inconsistency must have an explanation, something that God desires us to see.

God instructed Jeremiah to tell King Zedekiah, "You will see the king of Babylon with your own eyes, and he will speak with you face to face. And you will go to Babylon" (Jer. 34:3, NIV). But we read elsewhere, in Ezekiel 12:12–13, that Zedekiah wouldn't see Babylon. So what is going on? The answer underscores the importance of reading the entire Bible in context and cover to cover!

Zedekiah did see the king of Babylon with his own eyes and Zedekiah did go to Babylon, just as Jeremiah prophesied, but Zedekiah never saw Babylon. How does that work itself out?

When taking control of Jerusalem, King Nebuchadnezzar found Zedekiah trying to escape by digging his way out of the city. After Nebuchadnezzar caught him, Zedekiah spoke with the king of Babylon face to face (Jer. 39:5), so he saw him with his own eyes. But then Nebuchadnezzar had Zedekiah's eyes poked out before he was carried off to Babylon (39:7; 52:11). So Zedekiah went to Babylon, but he never saw Babylon because he was blinded by the king of Babylon—perfectly fulfilling Ezekiel 12:12–13!

God's Word is true, my friend! Every single thing He says has, or will, come to pass. The Bible is one book, with one theme—with Jesus at the center of it all. Jesus confirmed this in Luke 24:44 saying that "all things must be fulfilled, which were written in the law of Moses, and in the prophets, and in the psalms, concerning me." So as you read, may His testimonies be your delight and your counselors, even if at first glance they sometimes seem inconsistent. It all fits together perfectly, and it all points to Jesus.

August 20

Salvation on the Earth

TODAY'S READING: Jeremiah 52; Psalms 74; 79; 85

> You, O God, are my king from of old; you bring salvation upon the earth. *Psalm 74:12,* NIV

The year was 586 BC, and Jeremiah concluded his story with a heartbreaking account of Jerusalem's destruction by the Babylonians. Those fortunate enough to survive the devastating invasion were carried off to Babylon. One benefit to reading the Bible in chronological order is that the psalmist gives us insight into what those survivors experienced. In today's reading we find a series of songs written as a response to the Babylonian invasion and captivity.

Although these psalms were written about the destruction of Jerusalem, during which the Jews watched the temple burn to the ground, the words capture our thoughts at those times when everything in our lives is going up in smoke. The psalmist clung to God's promises and recounted His acts of old (Ps. 74:12–18). He pleaded with the Lord to remember His covenant (v. 20), and in faith he declared, "You, O God, are my king from of old; you bring salvation upon the earth" (v. 12, NIV).

The Lord did, of course, remember His covenant with the Israelites and, in His perfect time, restored them to their land (2 Chron. 36:22–23; Ezra 1:1–4). But God brought salvation to the rest of the world as well! He didn't forget His promise to bring salvation on the earth. Hundreds of years later, outside restored Jerusalem, John the Baptist would introduce the Savior and proclaim the fulfillment of God's promise.

> The next day John seeth Jesus coming unto him, and saith, Behold the Lamb of God, which taketh away the sin of the world. (John 1:29)

If things seem to be going up in smoke for you today, remember God's promises and look to your Savior, who brought salvation upon the earth!

The Weeping Prophet Weeps

TODAY'S READING: Psalms 102; 120; 137; Lamentations 1–2

Behold, O LORD; for I am in distress. *Lamentations 1:20*

The word *lamentation* means "the passionate expression of grief or sorrow; weeping."[63] And that is exactly what we find in the book of Lamentations, penned by Jeremiah, also known as the weeping prophet.

For forty years Jeremiah had prophesied to the people of Jerusalem. But in all those years, he never saw a single convert! Not one person repented in response to his message. When God finally brought judgment, you'd think Jeremiah would have been shouting, "I told you so!" Instead, Jeremiah passionately portrays our Father's grieving heart for His people.

The prophet Jeremiah's weeping should remind us of someone else who wept over Jerusalem: Jesus.

> As he approached Jerusalem and saw the city, he wept over it and said, "If you, even you, had only known on this day what would bring you peace." (Luke 19:41–42, NIV)

The prophet Jeremiah's compassion and suffering is a picture of Jesus's lament over Jerusalem and His suffering for the sins of the whole world.

> O Jerusalem, Jerusalem, thou that killest the prophets, and stonest them which are sent unto thee, how often would I have gathered thy children together, even as a hen gathereth her chickens under her wings, and ye would not! Behold, your house is left unto you desolate. For I say unto you, Ye shall not see me henceforth, till ye shall say, Blessed is he that cometh in the name of the Lord. (Matt. 23:37–39)

Jeremiah wept over the sins of the people, but Jesus bore them (1 Pet. 2:24). Both Jeremiah and Jesus prayed for Jerusalem, but Jesus continues to intercede on our behalf (Heb. 7:25). Jeremiah wrote with a heavy heart and tears, but Jesus provided a solution (John 11:25) and healing to the brokenhearted (Matt. 5:4). God sent a message of judgment through Jeremiah but sent the remedy through His Son, Jesus.

August 22

The Prophet's Purpose

TODAY'S READING: Lamentations 3–4

Wait for the salvation of the LORD. *Lamentations 3:26*

God gave Jeremiah a difficult message to share—a call to repentance. Despite his passion not one person responded to Jeremiah's prophecies. Jeremiah's tender heart caused him to weep over the punishment of the people and grieve over his beloved Jerusalem. Few of us can comprehend the devastation this poor man's heart and soul endured. And yet God's great purpose was fulfilled despite the pain! Every aspect of Jeremiah's ministry pointed to Jesus Christ, the perfect fulfillment of all the law and prophets.

- Jeremiah was consumed with grief, burdened by his people's sin (Lam. 3:14–18). Jesus carried our sin and bore all our iniquities in and on Himself (1 Pet. 2:24).
- Jeremiah wept over the sin of his people (Jer. 4:19–22). Jesus, who also wept over Jerusalem (Matt. 23:37; Luke 19:41–44), will one day wipe away every tear from our eyes (Rev. 21:4).
- Jeremiah preached repentance from sin (Jer. 7:2–3). Jesus took our sin, nailed it to His cross (Col. 2:14), and conquered sin and death (1 Cor. 15:55–57).

Jeremiah's heartache, burden, and lament over sin all pointed to Jesus.

You search the Scriptures because you think that in them you have eternal life; it is these that testify about Me. (John 5:39, NASB)

Remember, Repent, Praise, and Petition

August 23

TODAY'S READING: Lamentations 5; 2 Kings 25:22–26; Jeremiah 40–42

Restore us to yourself, O LORD, that we may return; renew our days as of old. *Lamentations 5:21,* NIV

Lamentations offers a great example of how we can pray when we, or those we love, are in need of refreshment, renewal, or restoration. But we find even greater insight when we compare Jeremiah's prayer to its perfect fulfillment in Jesus Christ and the prayer He taught us to pray.

Remember: Jeremiah begins by remembering God's faithfulness (Lam. 5:1–15, 19–21). Jesus taught us to remember who God is as He prayed, "Our Father which art in heaven, hallowed be thy name" (Matt. 6:9). We can remember who God is and how He sent His Son, Jesus, from heaven to die for us. Remember your first love for the Lord (Rev. 2:4), and remember all the trials He's so faithfully brought you through.

Repent: Taking the first step in remembering God's goodness leads us to repentance (Rom. 2:4). Jeremiah confessed the sins of Israel (Lam. 5:16), just as Jesus taught us to confess:

> Forgive us our debts, as we forgive our debtors. (Matt. 6:12)

Praise: Repentance brings refreshment (Acts 3:19), which prompts us to praise (Lam. 5:19). Jesus taught us the importance of praise in prayer.

> Thine is the kingdom, and the power, and the glory, for ever.
> Amen. (Matt. 6:13)

Petition: Finally, Jeremiah petitions the Lord (Lam. 5:21). In the same way, Jesus taught us to cast all our cares upon Him who so abundantly provides all that we need (Matt. 6:30; 1 Pet. 5:7; Eph. 3:20).

> Give us this day our daily bread. (Matt. 6:11)

Today, as you read this weeping prophet's prayer, look to Jesus and remember God's faithfulness. Repent from sin, praise Him for who He is, and petition Him in Jesus's name.

The Reason We Praise

TODAY'S READING: Psalms 71; 116

> Let my mouth be filled with thy praise and with thy honour all the day. *Psalm 71:8*

Is your mouth filled with praise all day long? If we're honest, I bet you and I both could use some help with that. Good news! The book of Psalms provides the instruction and inspiration we need.

In addition, we can prime the pump of praise by searching the Scriptures to see just some of what Jesus has done for you and me.

Praise the Lord, for in Jesus we are not given a spirit of confusion but of a sound mind.

> In thee, O LORD, do I put my trust: let me never be put to confusion. (Ps. 71:1)

> God hath not given us the spirit of fear; but of power, and of love, and of a sound mind. (2 Tim. 1:7)

Praise the Lord for hope in Christ.

> Thou art my hope, O Lord GOD. (Ps. 71:5)

> The God of hope fill you with all joy and peace in believing, that ye may abound in hope, through the power of the Holy Ghost. (Rom. 15:13)

Praise the Lord for salvation.

> I will take the cup of salvation, and call upon the name of the LORD. (Ps. 116:13)

> This cup is the new testament in my blood, which is shed for you. (Luke 22:20)

Let's do as the psalmists suggest and fill our mouths with praise and His honor all the day (Ps. 63:3)!

Keep reading: Jeremiah 43–44

The Glorious New Covenant

TODAY'S READING: Jeremiah 30–31

I will make a new covenant with the house of Israel.
Jeremiah 31:31

As we've seen, Jesus is the very essence of the Scriptures. After all, He is the Word made flesh (John 1:14). But in Jeremiah 31 we don't have a shadow or a colorfully painted picture of our prophesied Savior. Rather, this chapter speaks the words of God Himself, plainly giving us perhaps the most significant key to unlocking our understanding of the glorious New Covenant.

In the Old Testament God revealed His plan of redemption through a series of covenants: the Adamic Covenant, the Abrahamic Covenant, the Mosaic Covenant, and the Davidic Covenant—all of which pointed to the promised messiah.

In Jeremiah 31 we find the Lord spelling out His plans for a New Covenant, in which God's law would no longer be written on tablets of stone but instead on our hearts, by His Spirit!

> I will put my law in their minds and write it on their hearts. I will be their God, and they will be my people. . . . They will all know me. . . . I will forgive their wickedness and will remember their sins no more. (vv. 33–34, NIV)

Jesus Christ ushered in the New Covenant with His atoning sacrifice on the cross. He extended His covenant to us with the bread and cup, saying, "This cup is the new covenant in my blood, which is poured out for you" (Luke 22:20, NIV).

He has promised to write His law on our hearts. He is our God and we are His people. This is God's New Covenant with me and with you!

Keep reading: Ezekiel 26

August 26

Hear and Do!

TODAY'S READING: Ezekiel 27–28; 33:21–33

> They hear your words, but they do not do them. *Ezekiel 33:31,* NKJV

Did you know that as we take in God's Word each day, we have a huge choice to make? The choice I'm talking about is whether we'll let the Word of God do its work in our hearts, making us doers of the Word and not just hearers (James 1:22–25). If we decide to take it in and let it transform us, we will discover that God's Word is exactly what it says it is:

> . . . quick, and powerful, and sharper than any twoedged sword, piercing even to the dividing asunder of soul and spirit, and of the joints and marrow, and is a discerner of the thoughts and intents of the heart. (Heb. 4:12)

On the flip side, if we ignore the Holy Spirit's instruction, our hearts grow calloused and cold and eventually completely self-consumed. That's exactly what happened to Israel long ago. God's people had heard God's Word, but they chose not to do anything with it (Ezek. 33:31–32). What a picture of how Israel would respond six hundred years later to Jesus, the Word made flesh (John 1:14).

In the parable of the sower, Jesus gave us a gracious reminder to listen to His Word and allow it to do what it is intended to do: transform us, change us, cleanse us, and bear fruit in us.

> He that received seed into the good ground is he that heareth the word, and understandeth it; which also beareth fruit. (Matt. 13:23)

As you take in the Word today, may it fall on a soft heart, ready to listen and understand. And may you expect to see Jesus, the one who gives us abundant life.

A Good Shepherd Will Come

August 27

TODAY'S READING: Ezekiel 34–36

Indeed I Myself will search for My sheep and seek them out.
Ezekiel 34:11, NKJV

The realization that God revealed His character and demonstrated His nature through His relationship with Israel should breathe life into our reading of the Scriptures. Who God says He is to Israel is *exactly* who Jesus Christ says He is to you and to me!

Ezekiel 34 begins by detailing the failures of Israel's shepherds. But here is the good news! Where men fail, God provides. And we find in this chapter a glorious promise that God Himself would be the people's shepherd. Indeed, God sent His Son, Jesus Christ, the good shepherd, to perfectly fulfill these promises.

God promised the Israelites that He would seek His lost sheep and restore them (vv. 11–12). Jesus declared,

> I am the good shepherd. (John 10:11)

God promised the Israelites that He would feed His flock and they would find rest (Ezek. 34:14). Jesus, the good shepherd, says the same to His tired and hungry flock today.

> Come unto me, all ye that labour and are heavy laden, and I will give you rest. (Matt. 11:28)

Jesus is the good shepherd, God's promise in Ezekiel fulfilled! Jesus gave His life for us, His sheep (1 John 3:16). We were lost, but He found each of us. When you grow weary today, go to your Good Shepherd and find rest for your soul.

Dry Bones

TODAY'S READING: Ezekiel 37–39

Can these bones live? *Ezekiel 37:3*

God loves to use object lessons to demonstrate His truths, like when He led Jeremiah to the potter's house to see the shaping of clay (Jer. 18:1–11). Today's reading provides another example of the creativity the Lord uses to make His points and teach us about His character.

It all starts with a graveyard filled with dry bones, where the Lord tells Ezekiel to prophesy to them. As Ezekiel obeys, the bones begin to shake . . . and rattle . . . and roll! What a sight that must have been! But God isn't finished yet. The bones are still dry. They need to be made alive. So God tells Ezekiel to prophesy to the bones another time. When he does, God breathes life into them and they rise up as a great army, full of life.

> I prophesied as he commanded me, and the breath came into them, and they lived, and stood up upon their feet, an exceeding great army. (37:10)

What a glorious picture of our resurrected lives in Jesus Christ. We who were once dead have been made alive!

> You were dead in your trespasses and sins. . . . But God, being rich in mercy, because of His great love with which He loved us . . . raised us up with Him, and seated us with Him in the heavenly places in Christ Jesus. (Eph. 2:1, 4, 6, NASB)

We are born again, but like these dry bones in Ezekiel, we need God to breathe on us the fresh wind of His Spirit. Take for example the day of Pentecost, when God filled His disciples with His Holy Spirit. On that day God's church was brought to life and rose up as a great army that turned the world upside down for His glory (Acts 2:2, 4)!

Jesus has raised you up to new life, but if you feel like a pile of dead bones, ask the Holy Spirit to come and breathe life into you.

Watchmen

TODAY'S READING: Ezekiel 32–33

> I have made you a watchman for the house of Israel; therefore you shall hear a word from My mouth and warn them for Me.
> *Ezekiel 33:7,* NKJV

Have you ever awakened from a nightmare in a cold sweat, breathing heavily? Remember the sudden relief of realizing it was just a dream? As a young adult, I had a recurring nightmare of just this sort. The setting was usually somewhere dark, and I was always with a group of people who were totally oblivious to the approaching danger. I would try to warn them, but to no avail.

For Ezekiel, his nightmare was reality! God had revealed to him the danger that was coming, and like a watchman on a wall, the prophet had sounded the alarm, just as God directed. If the Israelites had listened, they would have heard the good news that God had provided a way of escape: repentance!

> If he turns from his sin . . . , none of his sins which he has committed shall be remembered . . . ; he shall surely live. (33:14, 16, NKJV)

God's message is the same today. He has provided a way of escape through His Son, Jesus. And as God called Ezekiel to herald His message, Jesus has given us the Great Commission.

> He said unto them, Go ye into all the world, and preach the gospel to every creature. (Mark 16:15)

God has given you good news to declare to your countrymen, to your family members, to your own soul. That good news is the gospel of Jesus Christ, which saves us from sin. So be that watchman on the wall for your people today, dear messenger from the Lord.

August 30

The Messiah in the Omissions

TODAY'S READING: Ezekiel 40–43

> Look with your eyes and hear with your ears, and fix your mind on everything I show you. *Ezekiel 40:4,* NKJV

The final few chapters of the beautiful book of Ezekiel deal primarily with the Millennium and the temple that will be built during the glorious thousand-year reign of Jesus Christ on earth. You might be thinking, *Can we skip these chapters and move on to something with more personal application for today?* Not so fast, my friend! For if we omit this amazing section of Scripture, we miss out on a glorious glimpse of Christ pictured in the temple to come.

In God's description of the millennial temple, four items from His temple in the Old Testament are missing, each of which points to our Messiah. The omitted items are the veil separating the holy of holies, the table of showbread, the golden lampstand, and the ark of the covenant.

I suggest these items are missing not due to oversight but as an indication of the finished work of Christ. There will be no veil because it was torn from top to bottom when Jesus died on the cross (Matt. 27:51). The veil separated us from the glory of God, but Jesus made a way for us to come boldly into His glorious presence (Heb. 4:16). There will be no table of showbread because Jesus declared that He is the bread of life and He, personally, will be in the temple (John 6:35). There will be no golden lampstand because the Light of the World will shine for all to see (8:12). Finally, there will be no ark of the covenant—that container of the law God gave Moses—because Jesus Christ perfectly fulfilled the law.[64]

When we look closely, we realize that in Scripture even what isn't seen can point to the Messiah.

The Eastern Gate

August 31

TODAY'S READING: Ezekiel 44–46

This gate shall be shut; it shall not be opened, and no one shall enter by it, for the LORD God of Israel has entered by it. *Ezekiel 44:2,* NASB

The Old City of Jerusalem was surrounded by a wall with eight main gates into the city. Each gate had a name with some significance. There was Herod's Gate, the Damascus Gate, the New Gate, Jaffa Gate, Zion Gate, the Dung Gate, the Lions' Gate, and the Eastern Gate. Today we read about the magnificent Eastern Gate.

The Eastern Gate is a marvelous arched structure that faces the Mount of Olives. It is also called the Golden Gate and the Beautiful Gate (Acts 3:2), and in Hebrew it is translated "the Mercy Gate." The prophet Ezekiel tells us that the "gate shall be shut" (44:2). Indeed, in AD 1540–1541 a Muslim ruler, in an attempt to thwart the prophecy that the Messiah would one day enter through the Eastern Gate, sealed it up. Today, nearly five hundred years later, it remains shut.[65] However, if we could pass through its splendid arches, we would find ourselves facing the old temple mount, where sacrifices were made for the sins of the people and where God's presence dwelt.

In 44:1–3 God told Ezekiel that when the Messiah returns, He will enter Jerusalem through the Eastern Gate. How appropriate that the Beautiful Gate will receive the Messiah once more.

Jesus first entered through this gate, the Mercy Gate, on a donkey as He rode through Jerusalem on His way to the Cross. Mercy personified passed through the gate and was offered to all (Matt. 21:1–11). His mercy removed the need for the Old Testament sacrifices. Jesus is coming again, and when He returns, this gate will welcome Him into the New Jerusalem.

Lift up your heads, O ye gates; even lift them up, ye everlasting doors; and the King of glory shall come in. Who is this King of glory? The LORD of hosts, he is the King of glory. Selah. (Ps. 24:9–10)

A Future Hope

TODAY'S READING: Ezekiel 47–48; 29:17–30:19

This is what the Sovereign LORD says . . . *Ezekiel 30:2,* NIV

Our God is a God of hope! He had given His prophet Ezekiel a message of warning before judgment came to Israel. Now, as the nation experienced the consequences of disobedience, God gave Ezekiel a different message, a vision of better days to come. That vision should give you and me great hope for today. The vision reveals a day when Jesus Christ will return and we will live with Him forever. What a day that will be!

> Along the bank of the river, on this side and that, will grow all kinds of trees used for food; their leaves will not wither, and their fruit will not fail. They will bear fruit every month, because their water flows from the sanctuary. Their fruit will be for food, and their leaves for medicine. (47:12, NKJV)

Jesus gave John a similar vision in Revelation.

> The angel showed me . . . on either side of the river, the tree of life with its twelve kinds of fruit, yielding its fruit each month. The leaves of the tree were for the healing of the nations. (22:1–2, ESV)

At the time Ezekiel received this vision, Israel was stuck in Babylon. Yet God, in His infinite compassion, told Israel the troubled times would pass. The pattern set in Ezekiel foreshadows the truth Jesus later declared.

> Let not your heart be troubled: ye believe in God, believe also in me. In my Father's house are many mansions: if it were not so, I would have told you. I go to prepare a place for you. And if I go and prepare a place for you, I will come again, and receive you unto myself; that where I am, there ye may be also. (John 14:1–3)

Perhaps you, too, have been carried away to a place of sorrow. Know this, my friend: the hope God gave Israel is your hope too. God is the God of deliverance. Jesus is coming again!

Nebuchadnezzar's Testimony

TODAY'S READING: **Daniel 4; 7**

It is my pleasure to tell you about the miraculous signs and wonders that the Most High God has performed for me.
Daniel 4:2, NIV

In case you're wondering what happened to Daniel 1–3, remember that we're reading chronologically, and we covered them about a month ago.

God is gracious, merciful, and slow to anger. As we've seen repeatedly, He warns His people when they go astray and gives them ample opportunity to repent. Daniel was given a message of repentance to share with the king of Babylon. But arrogant King Nebuchadnezzar did not respond to God's goodness, and God chastised him with instability and outright insanity (4:33).

I find Daniel 4 fascinating. Like a pastor opening the pulpit for testimonies, Daniel, inspired by the Holy Spirit, inserts this testimony of Nebuchadnezzar, who was humbled by God, brought to the end of himself, and lifted out of his desperate condition only after he lifted his eyes to heaven and confessed God as supreme (v. 34).

Like Nebuchadnezzar, we walked in darkness, our minds clouded by sin (Eph. 4:18; 5:8). But when we recognized our depravity and need for a savior, Jesus lifted us up and gave us sound minds (2 Tim. 1:7) that we might praise His name and confess Him as Lord of lords.

> I . . . lifted up mine eyes unto heaven, and mine understanding returned unto me, and I blessed the most High, and I praised and honoured him that liveth for ever. (Dan. 4:34)

Jesus is the "King of heaven," as declared by Nebuchadnezzar (v. 37). His works are truth (John 14:6), and He is the one who will judge all mankind (5:22). Nebuchadnezzar experienced God's judgment on the proud, but through Jesus we are able to humble ourselves under the mighty hand of God that He may exalt us in due time (1 Pet. 5:6; James 4:6).

Keep reading: 2 Kings 25:27–30; Jeremiah 52:31–34

September 3

Writing on the Wall

TODAY'S READING: Daniel 8; 5; 9

> Suddenly the fingers of a man's hand emerged and began writing opposite the lampstand on the plaster of the wall.
> *Daniel 5:5,* NASB

You've likely heard the figure of speech "the writing was on the wall," which alludes to an ominous warning about an inevitable disaster. But what if you didn't *hear* "the writing is on the wall" but instead *saw* the writing on your wall, mystically, magically, supernaturally?

Belshazzar, king of Babylon, was living large and in charge. But all that came crashing down on him one night in the middle of a blasphemous party (Dan. 5:3), when he saw a hand—just a hand—delivering a message he instinctively knew could not be good. Belshazzar sobered up and freaked out, understandably. God's message was delivered by His hand and translated by Daniel in unmistakable terms.

Sure enough, that very night Babylon was conquered by the Medes, and God's Word to the haughty king of Babylon came to pass. It always does!

Dear friend, God has written us a message too. He has told us how these earthly kingdoms, like Belshazzar's, will end. Throughout the book of Daniel, we see glimpses of Jesus as the promised messiah and returning King of kings (2:44–45; 7:13–14; 9:24–26).

Jesus announced the ushering in of God's everlasting kingdom (Mark 1:15; Dan. 2:44–45). Jesus revealed Himself as the prophesied "Son of man" (Mark 14:62; Luke 9:22; Dan. 7:13) and the anointed one, the long-awaited messiah (Matt. 1:16; 16:16; John 1:41; 4:25; Dan. 9:24–26). As you read through the book of Daniel, look for Jesus. As certain as the writing on the wall, He is there.

Keep reading: 2 Chronicles 36:22–23

A Toothless Lion

TODAY'S READING: Ezra 1:1–2:20; Daniel 6; Nehemiah 7:4–25

. . . who has delivered Daniel from the power of the lions.
Daniel 6:27, NKJV

Daniel in the lions' den. What a fantastic, classic Bible story! Not only is it an incredible account of God's deliverance of Daniel, but it's also a great example of God's deliverance of you and me, here and now. You see, the Bible tells us in 1 Peter 5:8, "Be sober, be vigilant; because your adversary the devil walks about like a roaring lion, seeking whom he may devour" (NKJV).

We might not ever face a real lion as Daniel did, but God has rescued each of us from a very real spiritual beast—a roaring lion. Perhaps you didn't see the vicious predator with your physical eyes, but he was there, and he was hungry for your soul!

But just as God saved Daniel from the powerful jaws of the real lions, He has rendered our Enemy completely powerless. For the Lord saved us from our sin and snatched us right out of the devil's den (Eph. 2:1–5). God has shut the mouth of our Adversary, and he no longer has any power over us!

God demonstrated to the entire nation of Babylon His authority over all creation when He saved Daniel from the lions' den. But He also demonstrated His authority over principalities, powers, and spiritual darkness to all creation when Jesus died and rose again.

> Having disarmed principalities and powers, He made a public spectacle of them, triumphing over them in it. (Col. 2:15, NKJV)

So remember today, dear Christian: Jesus has conquered the Enemy. If you feel as though you're stuck in the lions' den, know that you're safe from your foe because Jesus died and rose again!

Family Tree

TODAY'S READING: Ezra 2:21–70; Nehemiah 7:26–73

These searched for their family records, but they could not find them. *Ezra 2:62,* NIV

Researching ancestry is big business these days, for good reason. We want to know where we've come from. This was a serious question back in ancient Israel as well. In today's reading we see several families who had lost their genealogical records and, as a result, were excluded from the priesthood. What a sad story for these men who desired to serve the Lord. But the Bible makes it clear that all these things happened to those people back then as examples for you and me today (1 Cor. 10:11). So it shouldn't surprise us to see a picture of Jesus in Ezra 2!

God required any Israelite who wanted to serve as a priest to demonstrate his Levitical ancestry (Deut. 18:1). Maybe today you would say, "My family is not particularly special, and maybe even a bit dysfunctional." I have good news for you: God still keeps family records. And when you accepted His Son, He made you part of His family. He wrote your new heritage in Christ in His Book of Life. As believers in Jesus Christ, we are adopted as children of God and made heirs with His own Son.

> . . . having predestined us to adoption as sons by Jesus Christ to Himself, according to the good pleasure of His will. (Eph. 1:5, NKJV)

Our family record is engraved on our Savior's hands.

> Behold, I have graven thee upon the palms of my hands. (Isa. 49:16)

Unlike the folks in the book of Ezra who couldn't be priests due to lost records, God has declared us a chosen generation, a holy nation of kings and priests (1 Pet. 2:9; Rev. 1:6; 5:10). Who we are in Christ can never be lost, for it is recorded in heaven, on His heart, and on His hands!

Shout for Joy

TODAY'S READING: Ezra 3; Psalms 92; 126

The people shouted with a great shout, when they praised the LORD, because the foundation of the house of the LORD was laid. *Ezra 3:11*

The building of the second temple prompted some raw emotions. When the final stone was laid, the young men shouted for joy, but the old men wept because this second temple simply did not compare to the majesty of the first one.[66]

God promised the people through the prophet Haggai that the glory of the second temple would surpass the first. And despite the old men undoubtedly wondering how that could possibly be, God accomplished it through Jesus Christ, as we'll see!

> The glory of this latter house shall be greater than of the former . . . and in this place will I give peace. (2:9)

Exactly where Israel's shouts of joy echoed forth, our chief cornerstone, Jesus Christ, would declare salvation over four hundred years later (Luke 2:22–38; John 7:3–38; 2:13–22). Indeed, in that place God gave us the greatest peace known to man, for in Christ we are free from the law of sin and death.

> Behold, I lay in Zion a chief cornerstone, elect, precious, and he who believes on Him will by no means be put to shame. (1 Pet. 2:6, NKJV)

In the temple, sacrifices were made to atone for sin, but on Calvary the ultimate price was paid once and for all (Heb. 10:10). In the temple God's glory rested in the holy of holies, but through Jesus Christ we have full access to His presence.

Dear friend, if the Lord is building something new in your life, be like the young men in today's story and shout for joy!

Keep reading: Daniel 10:1–11:35

(Daniel's vision dates to around 536 BC, about the same time as Ezra.)

Seeing Jesus Produces Praise

TODAY'S READING: Daniel 11:36–12:13; Psalms 93–96

> Bless His name; proclaim the good news of His salvation from day to day. *Psalm 96:2,* NKJV

God Almighty is worthy of worship, regardless of our knowledge or comprehension of His majesty. Despite our inabilities, in His tender mercies He stirs our understanding and provides us with plenty of reason for praise. As we continue in Psalms, remember that these dynamic descriptions of God's divinity are also powerful poems picturing Jesus, who was a living demonstration of God's glory.

The psalmist declares God's eternal nature.

> Thy throne is established of old: thou art from everlasting. (93:2)

Likewise, we see Jesus, who was from the beginning (John 1:1) and whose kingdom is everlasting.

> Unto the Son he saith, Thy throne, O God, is for ever and ever: a sceptre of righteousness is the sceptre of thy kingdom. (Heb. 1:8)

The psalmist sang of God's power over the raging sea.

> The LORD on high is mightier than the noise of many waters,
> yea, than the mighty waves of the sea. (93:4)

Jesus, God in the flesh, demonstrated His power by calming the sea (Matt. 8:26).

The psalmist praised God for His tender mercies and care, comparing Him to a good shepherd (95:7). Jesus is "the good shepherd" (John 10:11).

The psalmist declared God as "the rock of our salvation" (95:1). Jesus is the rock from which flows rivers of living water (Rev. 7:17).

Consider God's attributes as described in Psalms, and then let your heart be filled with praise as you consider how our precious Jesus demonstrated those same attributes when He walked among us.

Poetry, Praise, and the Prince of Peace

September 8

TODAY'S READING: Psalms 97–100; Haggai 1–2

He has done marvelous things; his right hand and his holy arm have worked salvation. *Psalm 98:1,* NIV

The psalms we read today not only serve as beautiful pieces of poetry and powerful songs of praise but also provide pictures of the promised prince of peace, prophecies we see unmistakably fulfilled in Jesus!

Salvation was promised by His hand, and salvation was brought by His hand.

> His right hand and his holy arm have worked salvation. (Ps. 98:1, NIV)

> . . . blotting out the handwriting of ordinances that was against us, which was contrary to us, and took it out of the way, nailing it to his cross. (Col. 2:14)

Salvation was promised to the nations, and salvation came to the nations.

> The LORD has made known His salvation; His righteousness He has revealed in the sight of the nations. (Ps. 98:2, NKJV)

> He is the propitiation for our sins: and not for ours only, but also for the sins of the whole world. (1 John 2:2)

> Go ye into all the world, and preach the gospel to every creature. (Mark 16:15)

What a glorious picture of our Prince of Peace! Indeed, just as Jesus said, all Scripture points to Him.

> These are My words which I spoke to you while I was still with you, that all things which are written about Me in the Law of Moses and the Prophets and the Psalms must be fulfilled. (Luke 24:44, NASB)

September 9

Clean Clothes

TODAY'S READING: Zechariah 1–6

> See, I have removed your iniquity from you, and I will clothe you with rich robes. *Zechariah 3:4,* NKJV

I love the story of Joshua the high priest. This account in Zechariah 3 clearly demonstrates how God pardons and provides for those who are His. We find here a vision of Joshua standing before the Lord. The problem is that Satan is also there, and he's accusing the priest Joshua, no doubt bringing up his human faults and frailties and failures. That's what Satan does. The Bible calls him "the accuser of our brethren" for a reason (Rev. 12:10). In the vision Joshua was dressed in filthy, dirty clothes, and Satan, in his sliminess, made sure to point out that Joshua was robed in unrighteousness. But notice that God did not listen to Satan's accusations. Instead, He robed Joshua in clean garments and took away his sin.

> He answered . . . saying, Take away the filthy garments from him. And unto him he said, Behold, I have caused thine iniquity to pass from thee, and I will clothe thee with change of raiment. (Zech. 3:4)

Sound familiar? The vision of Joshua is a picture of you and me before we were cleansed by the blood of Jesus (Isa. 61:10; Rom. 5:10; 1 John 2:2; 4:10). But by God's grace we are robed in Christ's righteousness and made completely new!

> If any man be in Christ, he is a new creature: old things are passed away; behold, all things are become new. (2 Cor. 5:17)

Joshua did not defeat Satan by providing his own defense or change of clothes. He simply stood there and let God speak and act on his behalf, just as we can. Let the cleansing blood of Jesus be your righteousness and your defense.

Sanctification Leads to Joy

TODAY'S READING: Zechariah 7–8; Ezra 5–6

The Lord had made them joyful. *Ezra 6:22*

Who God is—His personality, His essence, His very nature—is never changing (Heb. 13:8). His character and attributes are eternal, which means the God we read about all through the Old Testament is the exact same God we read about in the New Testament (Mal. 3:6). His standards are the same, and His love and justice remain (Ps. 119:89; 33:11). I love that about our Lord! He was just and right when He purged Israel of sin, and He is just and right as He wipes away ours (Acts 3:19; 1 John 1:9).

In our chapters today we find God's people being set apart for His glory—sanctification. The process began with fasting and prayer (Zech. 8:19). The people sought the Lord, confessed their sin, and celebrated the Feast of Unleavened Bread (Ezra 6:21–22). As a result, the people shouted for joy!

All the law and the prophets were fulfilled in Jesus (Matt. 5:17–20), for they all spoke of Him (Luke 24:25–27, 44). Therefore, we can take today's reading and ask how Jesus fulfilled it and how He desires to work its principles in us.

Taking that approach, we first begin by seeking the Lord and confessing our sin (1 John 1:9). After confession Israel celebrated the Feast of Unleavened Bread, and so, too, we should celebrate the feast's fulfillment in Christ, as we take and celebrate communion (1 Cor. 11:24). The result of Israel's sanctification then reveals the result of our sanctification now: real joy (Ps. 16:11; 119:14; 1 Cor. 6:11; Gal. 5:22–23).

Confession and celebration are key ingredients in the process of sanctification. And sanctification—being set apart from this world for the glory of Jesus Christ—leads to real joy, the joy of the Lord!

September 11

A Stone, a King, and a Shepherd

TODAY'S READING: **Psalms 118; 129; 148–150; Zechariah 9**

This is the LORD's doing; it is marvellous. *Psalm 118:23*

Picking up where we left off the other day in Psalms and Zechariah, let's look and see more pictures, prophecies, and promises of Jesus in what we read today.

The stone the builders reject will become the chief cornerstone.

> The stone which the builders refused is become the head stone of the corner. This is the LORD's doing; it is marvellous in our eyes. (Ps. 118:22–23)

> Jesus Christ himself [is] the chief corner stone. (Eph. 2:20)

The prophet promised that a humble king will come.

> Rejoice greatly . . . ! Behold, your King is coming to you; He is just and having salvation, lowly and riding on a donkey, a colt, the foal of a donkey. (Zech. 9:9, NKJV)

> Fear not, daughter of Zion; behold, your King is coming, sitting on a donkey's colt. (John 12:15, NKJV)

> Being found in appearance as a man, He humbled Himself and became obedient to the point of death, even the death of the cross. (Phil. 2:8, NKJV)

The prophet promised a shepherd for the flock of God.

> God shall save them in that day as the flock of his people. (Zech. 9:16)

> My sheep hear my voice, and I know them, and they follow me. (John 10:27)

These verses only scratch the surface of the treasures contained in today's reading. Truly, Jesus is spoken of, written about, and prophesied cover to cover. This is the Lord's doing, and it is truly marvelous!

The Crucifixion Foretold

September 12

TODAY'S READING: Zechariah 10–14

They shall look upon me whom they have pierced. *Zechariah 12:10*

The prophet Zechariah wrote a detailed description of Jesus's betrayal and crucifixion, hundreds of years before He was born as the babe of Bethlehem. Note how clearly the Old Testament prophet foretells of our Redeemer.

> If ye think good, give me my price; and if not, forbear. So they weighed for my price thirty pieces of silver. (11:12)

Fulfilled in Matthew 26:15: "What will ye give me, and I will deliver him unto you? And they covenanted with him for thirty pieces of silver."

> I took the thirty pieces of silver, and cast them to the potter in the house of the LORD. (Zech. 11:13)

Fulfilled in Matthew 27:3, 5, 7, 9: "Then Judas . . . threw down the pieces of silver in the temple. . . . And they consulted together and bought with them the potter's field. . . . Then was fulfilled what was spoken" (NKJV).

> They shall look upon me whom they have pierced. (Zech. 12:10)

Fulfilled in John 19:18, 34: "There they crucified him. . . . One of the soldiers pierced his side with a spear" (ESV).

> One shall say unto him, What are these wounds in thine hands? Then he shall answer, Those with which I was wounded in the house of my friends. (Zech. 13:6)

Fulfilled in John 20:20: "He showed them his hands and his side. Then the disciples were glad when they saw the Lord" (ESV).

Keep reading your Bible, dear Christian, and keep seeing Jesus day by day!

September 13

His Watchful Care

TODAY'S READING: Esther 1–3

The king loved Esther above all the women, and she obtained grace and favour in his sight. *Esther 2:17*

Coincidence or providence? Sometimes it's hard to tell the difference. In fact, is it possible that God uses coincidence to work His providence? These are the questions that surround the action-packed book of Esther. Even though God's name is never mentioned, this historic account powerfully demonstrates His providence and testifies to His watchful care over His people.

During Esther's time a handful of Jews had returned to Jerusalem after the Babylonian captivity and were hard at work rebuilding the city of Jerusalem under Nehemiah's direction. However, many of the Jews, including Esther and her cousin Mordecai, chose not to leave Babylon and continued to live in the outlying Persian area. But God did not forsake His people still in Persia.

God is ever gracious and faithful to care for His people. History is "His story," and it is for His glory and His great love that He directs situations and circumstances. That is how we find God using Esther—as a powerful tool to protect His remnant in Persia and a picture of Jesus's work in us, His people. Esther and her people were in Babylon waiting to return to Jerusalem, and all the while God had a plan. We are in this world, eagerly awaiting Jesus's return. We look forward to heaven and know that Jesus has a plan and is working His will in each of us.

Even when circumstances seem to be coincidences, as they did for Esther, we can be certain that Jesus is working in and through us, orchestrating each circumstance. How comforting this is! The ultimate creator, Jesus (John 1:3), the master builder, the supreme designer, and the most faithful watchman, is overseeing the blueprint and details of our lives.

It is God which worketh in you both to will and to do of his good pleasure. (Phil. 2:13)

Approach Your King in Confidence

TODAY'S READING: Esther 4–8

When the king saw Esther the queen standing in the court . . . she obtained favour in his sight. *Esther 5:2*

Have you ever faced fear square in the face? Have you stood toe to toe with a terrifying situation? In such moments we have to decide whether to rely on our own strength or the strength of the Lord. Esther faced fear when she risked her life to save her people. In that culture, in those days, a person could be killed simply for approaching the king without first being called by him. But Esther needed an audience with the king in order to plead for the lives of her people.

We were once in need of favor from the King of kings. Wholly unrighteous, we were unable to approach our holy God (Isa. 59:2). But Jesus, who suffered for our sins, has robed us in His righteousness and ushers us into His throne room, where we have gained everlasting favor with the King (Rom. 5:1–2).

> Christ also suffered once for sins, the righteous for the unrighteous, that he might bring us to God, being put to death in the flesh but made alive in the spirit. (1 Pet. 3:18, ESV)

Well aware of the danger, Esther trusted in God to be the savior of her and all the Jewish people. Through Esther's willingness to approach the king and her trust in the King of kings, a nation was saved. And through that nation came a Messiah, who has made a way for us to approach our King in full confidence.

> Brothers, since we have confidence to enter the holy places by the blood of Jesus . . . let us draw near with a true heart in full assurance of faith, with our hearts sprinkled clean from an evil conscience and our bodies washed with pure water. (Heb. 10:19, 22, ESV)

There's no telling what the Lord wants to do through you as you approach His throne, from which He reigns in amazing grace (4:16)!

Stand Fast in the Victory

TODAY'S READING: Esther 9–10; Ezra 4:6–23; Psalm 105

The Jews smote all their enemies. *Esther 9:5*

After Esther saw God move mightily on her behalf, it was still necessary for the Jewish people to stand firm and fight. Even though Haman's plot was exposed, the declaration against the Jewish people remained in force. The only recourse was to give the Jewish people permission to defend themselves.

> The Jews gathered themselves together in their cities . . . to lay hand on such as sought their hurt: and no man could withstand them; for the fear of them fell upon all people. (Esther 9:2)

Here's a key principle of our life in Christ: victory is already ours, but we still have to stand fast and engage in the fight (Eph. 6:14).

Our Lord has provided what we need for the battle. Jesus has outfitted us with His Holy Spirit (John 16:13). He has given us "the helmet of salvation, and the sword of the Spirit, which is the word of God" (Eph. 6:17). He has promised to equip us with all we need to live in Him (2 Pet. 1:3), and His strength is made perfect in our weakness (2 Cor. 12:9).

Just as God gave Israel victory over Haman, Jesus calls us to stand firm in the victory He has given us.

> It is God who makes both us and you stand firm in Christ. He anointed us, set his seal of ownership on us, and put his Spirit in our hearts as a deposit, guaranteeing what is to come. (2 Cor. 1:21–22, NIV)

The Helper

TODAY'S READING: Psalm 106; Ezra 7:1–8:14

This Ezra went up from Babylon; and he was a ready scribe in the law of Moses. *Ezra 7:6*

Approximately sixty years elapsed between Ezra 6 and 7.[67] During this time the story of Esther took place, the temple in Jerusalem was rebuilt, and those who had returned to life in the Holy City experienced peace for a season.

Ezra, whose name means "help" or "helper,"[68] was a teacher and a priest. During his time of captivity in Babylon, he wasn't able to fulfill his priestly duties. But now the temple has been rebuilt, the people have returned to Jerusalem, and Ezra is finally able to serve in his God-given capacity.

So we find Ezra teaching the people and the people responding and experiencing spiritual revival. Ezra is a wonderful picture of our Christian life. The Bible describes each of us as a temple of the Holy Spirit (1 Cor. 6:19). Before our "temple" was rebuilt or reborn, we were not able to function as God created us to. But now, in Christ, we have ears to hear and hearts to respond exactly the way God intended.

God graciously gave His people in Jerusalem Ezra to be a helper, and He has given you and me His Holy Spirit, the ultimate helper (John 16:7). Just as Ezra taught the people what was acceptable in God's temple, the Holy Spirit does the same for me and you.

When He, the Spirit of truth, comes, He will guide you into all the truth. (v. 13, NASB)

The Holy Spirit testifies of Jesus, always pointing us to Him (15:26). So keep reading His Word, be transformed by the renewing of your mind, and allow God's helper, the Holy Spirit, to teach, instruct, and revive your life—His temple—today!

September 17

Freedom in Jerusalem

TODAY'S READING: Ezra 8:15–10:44

He has granted us new life to rebuild the house of our God.
Ezra 9:9, NIV

Only about fifteen hundred Jews followed Ezra out of captivity in Babylon back to Jerusalem (Ezra 8:1–15). Many of those who had been carried away to Babylon, or who were born during the captivity, had become quite comfortable there. It's easy for you and me to think, *Why would anyone not choose to return to their homeland and live in freedom?* The problem was they knew hard work awaited: the labor of rebuilding their destroyed city.

Ezra beckoned the Jews in Babylon to follow him to Jerusalem, but he did not force anyone to leave. That's how it can often be with you and me. Although we've been set free from sin, we sometimes find it more comfortable to stay where we are and, as a result, end up stuck in captivity (Eph. 2:1–5). We hear our Helper calling us to take up our cross and follow Christ (Matt. 16:24). The question is whether we'll willingly leave the comfort of captivity in order to embark on a long journey to freedom—and embrace the hard work of restoration.

For the Jews, leaving Babylon was just the first step in their journey. Once they reached Jerusalem, Ezra taught them God's law and how to worship in the newly rebuilt temple. Once we decide to follow Christ, He calls us to embark on a journey of obedience, and if we hearken to His call, He instructs us in how we should live and worship (1 Cor. 6:19–20).

How is the Holy Spirit leading you today? Will you follow? The road to Jerusalem isn't easy, but it is where you and I are truly set free.

Keep reading: 1 Chronicles 3:17–24

Rebuild and Rejoice

TODAY'S READING: Nehemiah 1–4

The God of heaven, he will prosper us; therefore we his servants will arise and build. *Nehemiah 2:20*

Ezra and Nehemiah were contemporaries, prophets who lived at the same time. Ezra returned to Jerusalem to rebuild the temple. Nehemiah returned to rebuild the city's walls.

The name Nehemiah means "Comforter from God."[69] He comforted his people and empowered them for the service of rebuilding Jerusalem's walls. Through the power of God's might and because "the good hand of . . . God" (Neh. 2:18, NET) was upon him, Nehemiah strengthened the people and was able to adequately provide for and lead them. Comfort. Empower. Strengthen. Equip. Lead. Are you starting to see how Nehemiah pictures the ministry of the Holy Spirit to you and me?

Jesus sent His Spirit, our comforter, who rebuilds walls and restores the cracked foundations of our lives. Jesus, by His Spirit, rebuilds what sin had left in ruins. Jesus, through His Spirit, comforts (John 15:26), empowers (Acts 1:8), strengthens (2 Cor. 12:9), equips (1 John 2:27), and leads us (Rom. 8:14). We who were once dead in trespasses and sins are now holy, rebuilt with a strong foundation in Jesus Christ.

Much as Nehemiah led Israel, our Leader today has brought us out of bondage and is restoring the "land" of our lives. Walls that were once battered and broken are being rebuilt by Jesus and the power of His Spirit.

As you read through the book of Nehemiah, see Jesus's work in your life. Consider the refortified places, the restored foundations, and the rebuilt walls. And as you do, rejoice that He'll never stop working on you!

Three Steps to Strength

TODAY'S READING: Nehemiah 5:1–7:3

I prayed, "Now strengthen my hands." *Nehemiah 6:9,* NIV

Adversity and opposition follow closely on the heels of opportunity and vision. That's precisely what we find in today's passage. Remember, 1 Corinthians 10:11 tells us that all the things that happened to the Old Testament people are written to teach you and me. So as we see Nehemiah and his men encountering adversity in rebuilding the walls of the Holy City, we know there's a lesson for us.

Nehemiah 6 sets the stage by describing some good old-fashioned bullies simply trying to scare those committed to answering God's call.

> All of them were trying to frighten us, thinking, "They will become discouraged with the work and it will not be done." But now, O God, strengthen my hands. (v. 9, NASB)

Nehemiah, however, did not cower. In his response we see what the Lord wants to teach us. Nehemiah did three things that changed the course of history: he took his cares to the Lord in prayer, he took up a sword in one hand, and he took to the work with the other. That, my friend, is a recipe for success! Nehemiah's three-step strategy enabled him to carry on in the face of adversity. More important, he inspired God's people to fulfill their ministry despite the stress and the threats.

In Jesus, God has made us builders like Nehemiah, for we are His "living stones," building up "a spiritual house" (1 Pet. 2:5, NKJV). Our Adversary constantly tries to bully us into failing at the work Christ has called us to do (Rev. 12:10). But Jesus invites us to do exactly what we see Nehemiah do: take our cares to Him in prayer (1 Thess. 5:17), take "the sword of the Spirit, which is the word of God" (Eph. 6:17), and take up the tools He provides to do what He's called us to do (2 Tim. 3:17).

At the Center of It All

September 20

TODAY'S READING: Psalms 1; 107; 111–112; 117

He sent redemption unto his people. *Psalm 111:9*

Scholars believe that the psalms in today's reading were most likely written while much of Israel remained in exile. As we've seen, only a few Jews had volunteered to leave Babylon under the direction of Ezra and Nehemiah in order to take on the hard work of rebuilding Jerusalem. So whether these psalms were written at the beginning or toward the end of the Babylonian invasion and captivity, they were written from the perspective of a people in bondage, subject to a foreign king, and living in a land where they don't belong. During such times of oppression, little can compare to the hope and comfort of the promises of redemption and restoration. They provide joy to hurting hearts.

Assurances of the coming redeemer are scattered throughout these chapters. Consider:

> He sent his word, and healed them, and delivered them from their destructions. (107:20)

As New Testament believers, we know God did send His Word. Jesus is the Word made flesh (John 1:14). And Jesus healed many while He walked in this world. More important, He offered real healing to all the world as He died for its sins and rose again.

> He calms the storm, so that its waves are still. Then they are glad because they are quiet. (Ps. 107:29–30, NKJV)

The gospel of Mark tells us that Jesus calmed the sea.

> He arose, and rebuked the wind, and said unto the sea, Peace, be still. And the wind ceased, and there was a great calm. (4:39)

Truly, Jesus is the demonstration of God's glory sung about in Psalms and in which we rejoice today.

Life Hidden in the Word

TODAY'S READING: Psalm 119

The entrance of thy words giveth light; it giveth understanding unto the simple. *Psalm 119:130*

As we've seen, the Bible is all about Jesus. He is the Word made flesh (John 1:14). So if we want to be Jesus people, we have to be Bible people. Consider with me what Psalm 119 says, in extensive and exacting detail, about the benefits, importance, and purpose of God's Word, all the while keeping in mind that Jesus is the embodiment of all that is contained in the Word.

God's Word through Jesus

- keeps us from sin and keeps our way pure (vv. 3, 9, 11, 133)
- provides liberty and freedom from affliction and oppression (v. 45)
- gives strength, fulfills our longing, and sets our heart free (vv. 20, 28, 32, 92, 131)
- is our help, gives hope and peace, and renews our trust (vv. 114, 147, 165, 175)
- is our comfort in suffering and is our delight (vv. 16, 24, 35, 50, 52, 76–77, 143)
- gives us a sound heart, an anchor, and a compass for life (vv. 50, 59, 80)
- gives us reason to praise and lift our hands, causing our heart to rejoice (vv. 48, 54, 164, 171)
- is where we find mercies and see His salvation (vv. 41, 58)
- is our teacher, instructor, and a lamp to our feet, giving wisdom (vv. 98–100, 102, 105, 130, 133)
- is an answer for our accuser and frees us from reproach (vv. 6, 42)
- is true, righteous, good, wonderful, trustworthy, faithful, and pure (vv. 30, 39, 42, 75, 86, 128–129, 137, 140, 172)

Next time you're tempted to let your Bible sit on the shelf, think of Psalm 119 and how Jesus is all that the Word says He is and does.

Forgiven, Redeemed, Blessed

September 22

TODAY'S READING: Psalms 121–123; 128; 130; 134–136

There is forgiveness with thee. . . . And he shall redeem Israel from all his iniquities. *Psalm 130:4, 8*

Stop and consider for a minute just what today's verses proclaim: forgiveness and redemption. This is good news! This is the gospel! God does forgive, and Jesus did redeem us from our iniquities.

> And you, being dead in your trespasses . . . , He has made alive together with Him, having forgiven you all trespasses. (Col. 2:13, NKJV)

> . . . in whom we have redemption through his blood, the forgiveness of sins, according to the riches of his grace. (Eph. 1:7)

What God promised in Psalms, He has accomplished through His Son, Jesus.

- We've been shown great mercy and been purchased by the blood of Jesus Christ (Ps. 123:3; 1 Pet. 1:18–19).
- He has forgiven all our sins (Ps. 130:3–4; 1 John 1:9).
- The record that detailed our sin has been taken away, and we are declared innocent (Ps. 130:7–8; Rom. 3:24)!
- Jesus keeps us and preserves our souls (Ps. 121:7; Jude 24).
- God has washed us in the blood of Jesus, sanctified us, and made us into His people (Ps. 135:4; 1 Pet. 2:9; 1 Cor. 6:11).
- He has blessed us and fills us with all good things (Ps. 128:2; James 1:17).

Truly, you have all you need in Him (2 Pet. 1:3; Col. 2:9). So rejoice today, dear Christian! You've been shown the greatest love of all, for in Jesus you're forgiven, redeemed, and blessed.

September 23

Revival That Refreshes

TODAY'S READING: Psalms 146–147; Nehemiah 8–9

> They read from the book, from the Law of God, clearly, and they gave the sense, so that the people understood the reading.
> *Nehemiah 8:8,* ESV

Today we're back in the book of Nehemiah. At this point the walls of Jerusalem have been rebuilt, and the people have settled into life in Jerusalem. Have you noticed that the Lord has a way of stirring our hearts when we get too comfortable? Nehemiah, being a picture of the Holy Spirit, began to stir the people's hearts toward repentance and revival.

The prophet had God's Word read aloud as the whole congregation assembled outside the Water Gate (8:1).

> He read from it . . . from morning until midday . . . and the ears of all the people were attentive to the Book of the Law. (v. 3, NKJV)

Notice that the water of the Word washed over the people, and hearing the Word moved their hearts from complacency to conviction. They wept over their sin and repented. Jesus does that same work in us.

> Christ loved the church and gave himself up for her, that he might sanctify her, having cleansed her by the washing of water with the word, so that he might present the church to himself in splendor. (Eph. 5:25–27, ESV)

Nehemiah comforted the people and encouraged them to rejoice and be glad. The people reveled in real joy (9:5–37). Jesus works this same joy in us as we respond to His Word.

> If you abide in me, and my words abide in you, ask whatever you wish, and it will be done for you. . . . These things I have spoken to you, that my joy may be in you. (John 15:7, 11, ESV)

God's Word stirs hearts and brings conviction, and if we respond with repentance, we'll revel in real joy as we experience revival that refreshes the soul!

Fruit of the Spirit

September 24

TODAY'S READING: Nehemiah 10–11

We will not forsake the house of our God. *Nehemiah 10:39*

The prophet Nehemiah, as we've noted previously, points to the Holy Spirit in Bible typology. His story also illustrates how God's Word can produce big changes in the lives of the people who take in its truths.

Jesus told us to abide in Him and allow His Word to abide in us so that we would "bear much fruit" (John 15:7–8). Consider the fruit Jesus desires to work in and through us with the results of revival, prompted by God's Word. It's the same as what is revealed in Nehemiah 10:

- brotherly love

  They joined with their brothers. (Neh. 10:29, WEB)

  Beloved, let us love one another: for love is of God. (1 John 4:7)

- a renewed dedication to God's Word

  The rest of the people . . . are taking on themselves . . . an oath to walk in God's law. (Neh. 10:28–29, NASB)

  Let the word of Christ dwell in you richly in all wisdom. (Col. 3:16)

- separation from the world

  We will not give our daughters to the peoples of the land or take their daughters for our sons. (Neh. 10:30, ESV)

  Love not the world, neither the things that are in the world. (1 John 2:15)

May you abide in Christ today and allow His Word to abide in you, that you would bear much fruit!

September 25 Encircled with Praise

TODAY'S READING: 1 Chronicles 9:1–34; Nehemiah 12

> . . . to keep the dedication with gladness, both with thanksgivings, and with singing. *Nehemiah 12:27*

When Nehemiah set out to dedicate the newly restored and rebuilt wall, he gathered the Levites from where they lived and brought them to Jerusalem "to celebrate joyfully" (Neh. 12:27, NIV). As part of the celebration, he organized the Levites into two choirs.

> I also assigned two large choirs to give thanks. One was to proceed on top of the wall to the right, toward the Dung Gate. . . . The second choir proceeded in the opposite direction. (vv. 31, 38, NIV)

As the singers proceeded in opposite directions around the city, on top of the wall, they encircled the city with praise!

My friend, you and I can take part in a similar celebration today. We can encircle our lives with praise. The solid rock of Jesus Christ is our strong tower protecting us, just as Nehemiah's towering wall protected Jerusalem. And, like Israel, we have the privilege of dedicating ourselves to praising Him.

> Speaking to yourselves in psalms and hymns and spiritual songs, singing and making melody in your heart to the Lord. (Eph. 5:19)

So no matter your situation, I urge you to encircle your life with praise to Jesus, the rock of your salvation.

Sin Is a Bully

TODAY'S READING: Nehemiah 13; Joel 1–2

I threw all the household goods of Tobiah out of the room. Then I commanded them to cleanse the rooms. *Nehemiah 13:8–9,* NKJV

Anyone who believes it's better to appease rather than to confront or even ignore a bully doesn't understand human nature. They certainly haven't studied world history. Appeasement always leads to trouble, as we see in today's Bible reading.

The temple in Jerusalem had been rebuilt, the city walls had been restored, and the people were rededicated to the Lord. As life in the city became more comfortable, Eliashib, the priest, eased up on the troublemaker Tobiah. The Scriptures make it clear that Eliashib gave Tobiah shelter in the temple (Neh. 13:4–6). That sounds crazy. Didn't he remember all the trouble Tobiah had caused for Nehemiah?

Before we give Eliashib too hard a time, we'd be wise to consider how we deal with trouble in our own lives. You see, Tobiah is a picture of sin. If we don't deal firmly with sin but instead give it sanctuary, we will find it taking up residence in our lives. We are the temples of the living God (1 Cor. 6:19), and there shouldn't be any rooms reserved for the old troublemaker and bully of sin! In fact, no room should be left empty, but every room filled with things that glorify the Lord.

Jesus affirmed this truth when He delivered a demon-possessed man. Jesus warned the people that a life cleansed must be filled with God's Spirit. Otherwise, wickedness floods back in with vengeance (Luke 11:24–26).

Nehemiah 13 reminds us to pray that the Lord would search our hearts. When He reveals a room that's been reserved for something other than Jesus, we need to deal with it directly, lest the bully of sin creep in. Praise be to our Lord, for His blood washes us and sets us free.

Last Shadow Before the Sun

TODAY'S READING: Joel 3; Malachi 1–4

The Lord, whom ye seek, shall suddenly come. *Malachi 3:1*

The Old Testament contains 39 books, 929 chapters, and 23,145 verses (in the King James Version).[70] And as we've seen, it's one big glorious picture book with all the pictures, prophecies, foreshadows, and typologies pointing to the person of Jesus Christ. Remember, Jesus is the very essence of the Scriptures. Soon we'll see Him not in shadows but as the Word made flesh (John 1:14).

First, let's take one last look for our prophesied Messiah in Malachi.

> Behold, I will send my messenger, and he shall prepare the way before me: and the Lord, whom ye seek, shall suddenly come to his temple, even the messenger of the covenant, whom ye delight in: behold, he shall come, saith the Lord of hosts. (3:1)

Indeed, God sent His messenger. John the Baptist prepared the way and declared the glorious entrance of the Messiah.

> Behold the Lamb of God, which taketh away the sin of the world. (John 1:29)

In Malachi God promised a resolution of righteousness.

> Unto you that fear my name shall the Sun of righteousness arise with healing in his wings. (4:2)

Jesus, the sun of righteousness, is our light and brought healing in His hands.

> Because of the tender mercy of our God, whereby the sunrise shall visit us from on high to give light to those who sit in darkness and in the shadow of death, to guide our feet into the way of peace. (Luke 1:78–79, ESV)

The real power is found not in simply recognizing Jesus in the Old Testament but in trusting wholly in the one pictured!

He Is Here

September 28

TODAY'S READING: Luke 1:1–2:20

. . . that you may know the certainty of those things in which you were instructed. *Luke 1:4,* NKJV

As we begin the New Testament, keep in mind that from the time of Malachi until the angel appeared to Zacharias, Israel endured four hundred silent years. That reality helps explain Mary's heart poured out in gratitude when the angel appeared. Mary's song is referred to as the Magnificat, and it is truly magnificent (Luke 1:46–56)! If you feel like you're in the midst of your own set of silent years, I hope you'll see in today's story that God has spoken definitively through His Son, Jesus Christ. There are no more silent years, my friend. We have Jesus, God's final Word, made flesh.

As we've done through the Old Testament, we'll be reading through the Gospels in chronological order. We'll compare the same stories as they were recorded by different writers, each of whom addresses a distinct audience while supernaturally meeting the needs of every devoted truth seeker:

- Matthew, writing to the Jews, shows Jesus as the promised king.
- Mark, writing to the Romans, shows Jesus as a servant.
- Luke, a doctor and a scholar, addressed the Greeks' fascination with Plato's ideal man by describing Jesus as the perfect son of man.
- John, writing to a universal audience, focused on Jesus as God's love shown to the world.

Such glory! Jesus, the one who appeared to Abraham as King of Salem (Gen. 14:18; Heb. 7:1–2), the one pictured by the priests and sacrifice (Lev. 14:13; Rev. 13:8), the one prophesied as the "Son of man" in Daniel (7:13; Luke 9:22; 22:69), and the one God promised to Ezekiel who would love and shepherd His people (34:11–16; John 10:11–18)—He is here!

September 29

Jesus's Genealogy

TODAY'S READING: Matthew 1; Luke 2:21–40; 3:23–38

This is how the birth of Jesus Christ came about. *Matthew 1:18,* NIV

Remember how our study in Genesis 5 pointed to the gospel through the names in Adam's family? Here in the genealogies in Matthew and Luke, we gain more divine insight into our Savior.

The genealogy in Matthew traces Jesus's lineage through His adoptive father, Joseph. This was not Jesus's bloodline, due to His virgin birth, but it was His legal line through adoption. Matthew presents Jesus as the Son of David and, thus, the rightful heir to David's kingly throne (2 Sam. 7:12–16). Matthew continues back past David, all the way to Abraham—for Jesus "is the Seed of Abraham in whom all nations would be blessed" (Gen. 12:3).[71]

Luke, by contrast, traced Mary's line, an appropriate choice considering Jesus's virgin birth. While Matthew went back as far as Abraham, Luke continued all the way back to Adam. For you see, Jesus is the "last Adam" (1 Cor. 15:45), bringing life not only to the Jewish people but to all mankind.

Matthew's genealogy shocks the ancient Jewish mind by including and highlighting four women: Tamar, who resorted to deception and seduction rather than trusting God's provision, demonstrates God's mercy; Rahab, the harlot who hid the spies, demonstrates God's forgiveness and redemption; Ruth, the Moabitess who put her faith in God, demonstrates God's willingness to adopt non-Jewish peoples into His family; and Bathsheba, who had been the wife of Uriah, demonstrates God's restoration.

Jesus, the son of Mary and Joseph, is truly the Son of God, the Son of David, the promised messiah, our redeemer, the king of the whole earth.

His Plan Revealed

TODAY'S READING: Matthew 2:1–3:12; Luke 2:41–3:20; Mark 1:1–8; John 1:1–18

Jesus was born in Bethlehem of Judaea. *Matthew 2:1*

Jesus came as the babe of Bethlehem, born in a stable. But His humble beginnings don't detract from the fact that He was the King of kings. As we saw yesterday, Jesus's genealogies prove He had the legal and spiritual right to the throne of Israel. In today's reading we find a few wise men who discerned His majesty and followed a star in order to pay homage to the newborn King, fulfilling several Old Testament prophecies.

The prophet Micah foretold where the Messiah would be born.

> Bethlehem . . . you are small among the clans of Judah; one will come from you to be ruler over Israel for me. His origin is from antiquity, from ancient times. (5:2, CSB)

Jesus, born in Bethlehem, from the tribe of Judah, is indeed our everlasting ruler!

The prophet Hosea spoke of the Messiah as coming out of Egypt (11:1). Matthew's gospel records how Joseph and Mary took the baby Jesus to Egypt (2:13) in order to escape Herod's decree, which was itself prophesied in Jeremiah 31:15. And the prophets Isaiah and Malachi, both with miraculous and majestic eloquence, describe the ministry of John the Baptist proclaiming the entrance of the long-awaited Messiah.

> The voice of him that crieth in the wilderness, Prepare ye the way of the LORD, make straight in the desert a highway for our God. (Isa. 40:3)

> Behold, I will send my messenger, and he shall prepare the way before me. (Mal. 3:1)

No wonder the apostle Luke wrote, "Of Him all the prophets bear witness" (Acts 10:43, NASB). Jesus is God's promised messiah, His plan from the beginning, His purpose throughout the Scriptures.

October 1

Temptation

TODAY'S READING: Mark 1:9–20; Matthew 3:13–4:11; 4:18–22; Luke 3:21–22; 4:1–13; 5:1–11; John 1:29–51

> Jesus answered him, saying, It is written, That man shall not live by bread alone, but by every word of God. *Luke 4:4*

It's been said, "Life is not a playground but a battleground." As Christians, we are engaged in serious combat on a spiritual battleground where temptation abounds. Even Jesus experienced this, as of course He had to.

> We have not an high priest which cannot be touched with the feeling of our infirmities; but was in all points tempted like as we are, yet without sin. (Heb. 4:15)

Jesus showed us how to face temptation and win. Satan tempted Jesus by misusing, misquoting, and then questioning God's Word. That was his tactic in the Garden of Eden when he tempted Eve, and it remains his tactic today. So how did Jesus defeat Satan? He intimately knew God's Word, responded with God's Word, and submitted to God's Word. Can you see, in today's reading, the power and beauty of faithfully reading and knowing God's Word? Let's take note of a few more things.

First, Jesus didn't defeat Satan simply by quoting Scripture. It was His submission to God's Word that led to victory.

Second, Jesus was intimately familiar with His Father's Word and appropriately applied it line upon line, precept upon precept. Our Lord read the Scriptures, knew the Scriptures, and applied the Scriptures to His daily life. How much more should you and I?

Finally, notice that Jesus called Satan out for his Bible manipulation. Every verse Satan used was only part of the truth. Without reading and studying God's Word, we'll find ourselves confused by demonic manipulations and twisting of the truth (2 Tim. 2:15). So keep reading and submitting to the Word, and then watch as Satan and temptations flee (James 4:7).

You Must Be Born Again!

TODAY'S READING: John 2:1–4:26

Verily, verily, I say unto thee, Except a man be born again, he cannot see the kingdom of God. *John 3:3*

In today's reading Jesus turned water into wine, foretold His death and resurrection, shared the gospel with a Pharisee named Nicodemus, promised living water to a Samaritan woman, and fulfilled Psalm 69:9, "Zeal for your house has consumed me" (ESV), as He overturned tables in the temple.

While Jesus walked on earth, He was a living, breathing demonstration of God's love for humanity. In fact, the Bible tells us that Jesus is "the brightness of [God's] glory, and the express image of his person" (Heb. 1:3).

No matter our situation, Jesus offers all we need. If your life is empty like those jars at the wedding, He can fill it with the fruit of the Spirit. If you're a skeptic who doubts Jesus is the Son of God, just take a look at how He fulfilled all the law and prophecies. If you're a religious person like Nicodemus but still dead in your spirit, He wants to give you new life through a relationship with Him. If you're making choices that will leave you lonely and unsatisfied like the woman at the well, He offers you *living* water so you'll never thirst again. If your life is filled with sin like the temple, He can cleanse it.

But what must I do to have these things done in my life? you wonder. You must be born again!

> That which is born of the flesh is flesh; and that which is born of the Spirit is spirit. Marvel not that I said unto thee, Ye must be born again. (John 3:6–7)

Through Jesus Christ, God proved His love for us (John 3:16), washed and cleansed us from sin (1 John 1:7), gave us peace and forgiveness (Eph. 1:7; 2:14–15), and gave us new life (2 Cor. 5:17). Jesus stands ready, willing, and able to meet your every need today, but you must be born again!

Living Promise

TODAY'S READING: John 4:27–46; Mark 1:14–15, 21–45; Matthew 4:12–17; 8:1–17; Luke 4:14–44; 5:12–16

> The people living in darkness have seen a great light. *Matthew 4:16,* NIV

What a Savior we serve! The Gospels detail how Jesus healed the brokenhearted, proclaimed freedom for those enslaved in sin, and comforted those who mourned. Over seven hundred years before the birth of Christ, Isaiah prophesied that the Messiah would do every single one of those things!

> The Spirit of the Lord God is upon me . . . to preach good tidings unto the meek . . . to bind up the brokenhearted, to proclaim liberty to the captives, and the opening of the prison to them that are bound . . . to comfort all that mourn . . . to give unto them beauty for ashes, the oil of joy for mourning, the garment of praise for the spirit of heaviness; that they might be called trees of righteousness . . . that he might be glorified. (61:1–3)

The Old Testament pointed to Jesus through prophecies, pictures, shadows, and types. Now it's as though a curtain has been lifted and the light of God's glory reveals Jesus Christ as the living, breathing promise of God Almighty, fulfilling everything the prophets had foretold, including

- living water flowing from Jerusalem (Zech. 14:8; John 4:14; 7:38)
- life proclaimed to Galilee (Isa 9:1–2; Matt. 4:12–17)
- good news preached to the poor and freedom preached to the oppressed (Isa. 61:1–3; Luke 4:16–21)
- the sick healed and our sorrow carried by Him (Isa. 53:4; Matt. 8:14–17)

What a Savior indeed!

Sins Forgiven

TODAY'S READING: Mark 2:1–28; Matthew 9:1–17; 12:1–8; Luke 5:17–32; 6:1–5

Friend, your sins are forgiven. *Luke 5:20,* NIV

Several months back we saw God prompt the prophet Isaiah to pen these promises:

> Say to those who are fearful-hearted, "Be strong, do not fear! Behold, your God will come . . . He will come and save you." Then the eyes of the blind shall be opened, and the ears of the deaf shall be unstopped. (35:4–6, NKJV)

Jesus fulfilled those prophecies perfectly. But the greatest miracle of all is that Jesus forgives our sins.

> "Which is easier, to say, 'Your sins are forgiven you,' or to say, 'Rise up and walk'? But that you may know that the Son of Man has power on earth to forgive sins"—He said to the man who was paralyzed, "I say to you, arise, take up your bed, and go to your house." Immediately he rose up before them, took up what he had been lying on, and departed to his own house, glorifying God. (Luke 5:23–25, NKJV)

Like that man, we were paralyzed by sin. We broke the law and owed a penalty we could not pay (Rom. 3:20–23; 6:23; James 2:10). Because Jesus paid our insurmountable debt (Rom. 4:25; 5:9; Gal. 2:16; 3:13), God forgives us and declares us not guilty of sin (Acts 13:39; Rom. 3:24–26). The record that detailed our sin has been destroyed (Col. 2:14).

If you are bound today by sin's shame or condemnation, there is good news! Like the blind man, look and see Jesus offering you forgiveness. Like the deaf man, allow the Holy Spirit to open your ears to hear His words of life. And like that paralyzed man, rise, walk, and leap for joy, for you are forgiven (Luke 5:25)!

October 5

He Left Nothing Undone

TODAY'S READING: Mark 3:1–19; Matthew 12:9–21; Luke 6:6–16; Matthew 4:23–5:12

> . . . that it might be fulfilled which was spoken by Isaiah the prophet. *Matthew 12:17,* NKJV

The Scriptures declare that Jesus Christ is the express image of God's glory (Heb. 1:3). He created the universe and holds it together by the power of His Word (Col. 1:17). Yet He became a man and walked among us (Phil. 2:7–8). As He walked out the letter of the law—full of grace and truth—the world witnessed perfection and peace personified.

> We beheld his glory, the glory as of the only begotten of the Father . . . full of grace and truth. (John 1:14)

Jesus kept the law, satisfying all its requirements and fulfilling God's promises as declared by the prophets. Isaiah prophesied that the Messiah would heal the sick (35:4–6; Mark 3:1–5) and in gentleness would lead His people like a shepherd (Isa. 40:11; John 10:11). Today's reading repeatedly reveals the healing touch, guiding hand, and saving grace of Jesus Christ, the good shepherd.

Isaiah described Him as giving strength to the weak (40:29; Matt. 8:14–15) and opening the eyes of the blind (Isa. 42:7, 18; Mark 8:22–25). As the light of the world, Jesus shone brightly into the darkness (Isa. 42:16; John 1:4–5). But as we've seen, His greatest act as the promised messiah was the redemption and salvation of sinners (Isa. 41:14; Eph. 1:7)! Truly, Jesus fulfilled every promise God made concerning healing, leading, and saving lost sheep like you and me.

As Christ followers, we rejoice and stand in the confidence the Good Shepherd has given us through His healing touch, His guiding hand, and His saving grace. Jesus left nothing undone.

Perfection for the Imperfect

October 6

TODAY'S READING: **Matthew 5:13–7:29**

By their fruits ye shall know them. *Matthew 7:20*

When we claim the name of Christ through an identifying statement, like "I'm a Christian," are we referring to the fact that we once said a prayer of salvation or responded to an altar call? Or, in the context of our lives, does the name *Christian* represent a lifestyle? Ultimately, do we as Christians live differently than we did before coming to Christ? If so, why?

Jesus addressed these challenging questions in the Sermon on the Mount. Let's read this familiar passage with these questions in mind and consider the Sermon on the Mount as practical instructions, our road map for daily life. Ultimately, that road map leads to an impossible standard.

> Be ye therefore perfect, even as your Father which is in heaven is perfect. (Matt. 5:48)

Uh-oh. I'm certainly not perfect! And I'm guessing you'd say the same for yourself. So where does that leave us? Jesus knows we're not perfect. That's why He came, to make us perfect in Him—to substitute His perfect life for our imperfect ones (2 Cor. 5:21). Does that mean we will never sin again? No. The point is that we are undergoing a process of sanctification, being transformed day by day into Jesus's likeness.

The beauty of the call to perfection is that it reflects God's amazing grace. Jesus calls us to impossible perfection and then makes it possible through His death and resurrection.

> With God nothing shall be impossible. (Luke 1:37)

Because of Jesus we have the ability to be genuine Christians—Jesus imitators and followers—not because we're so great but because He's so gracious.

October 7

See Him, Hear Him, Touch Him

TODAY'S READING: Luke 6:17–7:17; Matthew 8:5–13; John 4:46–54

The whole multitude sought to touch him. *Luke 6:19*

The narrative in Luke 6–7 echoes the message found in Matthew's record of the Sermon on the Mount—a message that proved irresistible to the crowds around Jesus. The people living in Israel at the time of Christ desperately wanted to hear His message. They wanted to listen to His words of truth and joyous hope spoken with authority from on high (Matt. 7:29; Mark 1:22). They couldn't comprehend what drew them to Him, but they knew they wanted to be near this teacher.

The Bible tells us that multitudes sought Jesus and traveled great distances to see Him and hear His words of truth. They knew that virtue flowed from Him and if they could just touch Him, they would be healed.

Virtue still flows from Him, and truth is still contained in His Word. How far are you and I willing to travel to see Him, to hear Him, and to touch Him? No doubt the distance we're called to traverse is not measured in miles but rather in the sacrifices to our schedules, deliberately setting aside time to quiet our hearts, hear His voice, and take in His Word.

Let's keep going the extra mile, my friend, and continue to make time to see Him, hear Him, and touch Him through time spent in His presence.

Reassurance

TODAY'S READING: Luke 7:18–8:3; Matthew 11:1–19; 12:22–45; Mark 3:20–30; Luke 11:14–26

Go your way, and tell John what things ye have seen and heard. *Luke 7:22*

It's easy to believe in God's faithfulness when things are going smoothly, isn't it? When times get tough, however, we often find ourselves beginning to doubt and praying for reassurance. Even the great John the Baptist wrestled with such sentiments.

God had promised to send a messenger ahead of the Messiah to proclaim His coming (Mal. 3:1; Isa. 40:3). Jesus confirmed that John the Baptist was that messenger (Luke 7:27). John was the voice crying in the wilderness. And when Jesus came to him to be baptized, John had the unsurpassed privilege of unveiling the Messiah to the world!

> Behold, the Lamb of God, who takes away the sin of the world! (John 1:29, ESV)

But then John found himself in prison, facing death and seeking confirmation of what he had previously preached and boldly proclaimed—that Jesus Christ was the messiah.

> John, calling two of his disciples . . . , sent them to Jesus, saying, "Are You the Coming One, or do we look for another?" (Luke 7:19, NKJV)

Jesus responded to John's questioning not by delivering him from captivity but by turning his focus toward eternity.

> Go and tell John the things you have seen and heard: that the blind see, the lame walk, the lepers are cleansed, the deaf hear, the dead are raised, the poor have the gospel preached to them. (v. 22, NKJV)

Jesus met John's doubting heart with words of comfort and reassurance. If you have questions today, remember that Jesus has sent you a message of comfort through His Word. Continue to read it and see Jesus.

October 9

The Soil of the Soul

TODAY'S READING: Mark 3:31–4:29; Matthew 12:46–13:23; Luke 8:4–21

> He said unto them, He that hath ears to hear, let him hear.
> *Mark 4:9*

The complexity of God's Word is extraordinary. Consider what the Old Testament prophets wrote about Jesus's teachings.

> I will open my mouth in a parable: I will utter dark sayings of old. (Ps. 78:2)

Indeed, Jesus spoke in parables full of wisdom and instruction. Take today's reading, for example. In the parable of the sower, Jesus used four different types of soil to describe the willingness of people to receive the Word. The examples He gave also describe our own hearts in different seasons of life, various circumstances, or even throughout any given day. In this parable we find an exhortation to keep our hearts prepared to receive God's Word at all times and in every situation.

What does the soil of your heart look like today? Is His Word falling along the path where Satan comes and takes it away or on rocky ground, where it's joyfully received but quickly wilts for lack of roots? Have you allowed thorny areas crowded with the cares of the world to choke His Word? Or are you tending your heart to prepare good soil where God's Word can be heard, applied, take root, and bear much fruit?

> These are they which are sown on good ground; such as hear the word, and receive it, and bring forth fruit, some thirtyfold, some sixty, and some an hundred. (Mark 4:20)

God, in His mercy, gave us the water of His Word, which breaks up the fallow ground and brings refreshment to the parched areas of our souls (Eph. 5:26). It can change a bad mood into a soft, yielded attitude.

Ask the Lord to soften the soil of your heart. Take in the water of His Word, and cultivate the areas that need tilling so that you may bear much fruit for His kingdom.

Even in the Storm

TODAY'S READING: Mark 4:30–5:20; Matthew 13:24–52; 8:23–34; Luke 8:22–39

Even the wind and the waves obey him! *Mark 4:41,* NIV

Surely all of us have encountered a storm here and there. Or maybe you feel as if your life is one big storm. Regardless of which camp you find yourself in, you can be certain that everyone experiences storms.

As we navigate the raging storms of life, we can find comfort in remembering God's repeated promises to take care of us and to take us from glory to greater glory.

The disciples found themselves terrified by a ferocious storm. But Jesus's previous instruction to them was still in play. You see, before Jesus and His disciples set sail on the Sea of Galilee, Jesus had made clear His intention: "Let us go over to the other side" (Mark 4:35, NASB). Yet in the midst of that squall, His disciples had completely forgotten His command. They were totally freaked out at the possibility of sinking.

Jesus practically met His disciples in their moment of distress, but He also gloriously fulfilled the prophetic words of Psalm 107.

> He caused the storm to be still, so that the waves of the sea
> were hushed. Then they were glad because they were quiet,
> so He guided them to their desired haven. (vv. 29–30, NASB)

When it comes to our own storms, God has made His intention clear: Jesus has gone to prepare a place for us so that where He is, we may be too (John 14:2). God's Word is true, and we can rest on His promises. Of course, He can simply speak an end to the storms in our lives, should He so choose. But even if He doesn't, we know we're crossing the sea and will indeed arrive safely on the other side.

He Is Able

TODAY'S READING: Mark 5:21–6:6; Matthew 9:18–34; 13:53–58; Luke 8:40–56; John 5:1–15

Jesus said . . . , "Don't be afraid; just believe." *Luke 8:50,* NIV

Jesus Christ stands ready, willing, and able to meet every single need you could ever have. There is simply no need under the sun that cannot be met by the Son. In today's reading we see Jesus heal the sick (Mark 5:25), show compassion to the hopeless (v. 34), answer a father's prayer for his dying daughter (v. 22), silence the mockers and doubters (v. 40), give life to the dead (v. 41), give sight to the blind (Matt. 9:30), heal the lame (John 5:8), and free the possessed and afflicted (Matt. 9:32).

In these demonstrations of His divine power and authority, Jesus showed us that He hears our cries for help and responds with compassion to those who cry out to Him. Like the sick woman with the issue of blood, we had a sin issue that Jesus cured by shedding His own blood (1 John 1:7). Like Jairus's daughter, we were dead in our sins, but Jesus made it possible for us to be born again (Eph. 2). Like the blind man who could suddenly see, Jesus touched each of us, and now we, too, can say, "One thing I do know. I was blind but now I see!" (John 9:25, NIV). Like the lame man, we can leap for joy because Jesus has forgiven all our sins (5:14). Like the possessed man who was released from chains of bondage, Jesus has released us from the chains of sin and death (Heb. 2:14).

> [Jesus] asked them, "Do you believe that I am able to do this?"
> "Yes, Lord," they replied. (Matt. 9:28, NIV)

Whatever your need is today, look to Jesus! Respond to His Word with a resounding "Yes, Lord," and believe that He is able to do all that He says He will do for you.

All Scripture Points to Him

TODAY'S READING: John 5:16–47; Mark 6:6–11; Matthew 9:35–10:42; Luke 9:1–5

You search the Scriptures . . . ; it is these that testify about Me.
John 5:39, NASB

The concept of looking for Jesus throughout the Scriptures is not new. It wasn't developed through the scholarly work of a theologian or suggested by leaders of a reformation of biblical engagement. Its first mention goes back further than the earliest epistles—all the way back to the foundation of the world. For you see, Christ came according to the plan of God, established from the beginning (1 Pet. 1:20; Rev. 13:8).

After God revealed His plan of redemption to Adam and Eve (Gen. 3:15), He continued to provide signs, prophecies, and pictures that pointed to His Son, Jesus Christ, the promised messiah.

> Philip found Nathanael and said to him, "We have found him of whom Moses in the Law and also the prophets wrote, Jesus of Nazareth, the son of Joseph." (John 1:45, ESV)

Indeed, Jesus is the one to whom all the law pointed, of whom all the prophets spoke, and to whom all Scripture gave witness.

> You search the Scriptures . . . ; it is these that testify about Me. (5:39, NASB)

Here the scribes and Pharisees were searching the Scriptures for eternal life, but they failed to recognize the one to whom all the Scriptures pointed: Jesus.

> Truly, truly, I say to you, he who hears My word, and believes Him who sent Me, has eternal life. (v. 24, NASB)

Jesus said that it wasn't good enough to simply search the Scriptures; we must believe in Him. Today, may you read the Scriptures with a longing to see Jesus and with a firm belief in Him (12:21).

October 13

Little Becomes Much

TODAY'S READING: Mark 6:12–44; Matthew 14:1–21; Luke 9:6–17; John 6:1–15

He said, "Bring them here to Me." *Matthew 14:18,* NKJV

Have you found it to be true that whatever you give to God, He will gladly receive and multiply it in a way that brings Him glory and at the same time ministers to people practically? That's exactly what Jesus did in today's famous reading about a little boy who brought Jesus his five small barley loaves and two small fishes. Jesus took that little lunch and miraculously fed a multitude.

Consider, too, the twelve men who left all they had in order to follow Jesus. Jesus took those twelve ordinary men and, minus Judas, transformed them into apostles that He would use to forever shape the course of history.

Jesus chose a despised tax collector, several uneducated fishermen, and a bunch of Galileans who were not normally counted among Israel's elite, and He used these meager, sometimes-mocked men to share the greatest message in all of history!

> They went out, and preached that men should repent. And they cast out many devils, and anointed with oil many that were sick, and healed them. (Mark 6:12–13)

God uses the small and weak things of this world to confound the wise.

> God hath chosen the foolish things of the world to confound the wise; and God hath chosen the weak things of the world to confound the things which are mighty. (1 Cor. 1:27)

Whether it's our resources, like the little boy's loaves and fishes, or our very lives, like those of the disciples, Jesus sure can do a lot with a little. He uses the ordinary to accomplish the extraordinary.

Whatever you have to give Jesus, regardless of how small it may be, give it to Him gladly today. Then watch and see what He does with it!

The Bread of Life

TODAY'S READING: Mark 6:45–56; Matthew 14:22–36; John 6:16–59

Our fathers did eat manna in the desert; as it is written, He gave them bread from heaven to eat. *John 6:31*

As the Israelites journeyed through the wilderness, God provided them manna, bread from heaven (Exod. 16). God was not only miraculously providing for a practical need but was also giving His people a picture of Jesus, the one who would come from heaven as the bread of life. What manna was to Israel, Jesus is to us.[72]

- The manna was essential (Exod. 16:3–4). Without it, the people of Israel would have died. Jesus is essential, and without Him no man has eternal life (John 3:15).
- The manna came from heaven and was a gift from God (Exod. 16:4). Jesus was sent from heaven as God's "unspeakable gift" (John 3:13; 2 Cor. 9:15).
- The manna was available to all and easily accessible as it fell outside their tents (Exod. 16:14–16). God sent His only Son, that whoever believes in Him finds eternal life (John 3:16). Jesus is accessible to all and never turns us away (6:37).
- The manna was sufficient for the day (Exod. 16:18–20). Jesus is our sufficiency. He supplies all our needs (Matt. 6:31–34; Phil. 4:19).

The people following Jesus asked Him to perform a miracle equivalent to manna (John 6:30–31). What they failed to recognize was that the Bread of Life Himself, the miracle that manna foreshadowed, stood before their very eyes.

Jesus said unto them, I am the bread of life: he that cometh to me shall never hunger; and he that believeth on me shall never thirst. (v. 35)

October 15
Wisdom Versus Legalism

TODAY'S READING: **Mark 7:1–8:10; Matthew 15**

> This people draweth nigh unto me with their mouth . . . but their heart is far from me. *Matthew 15:8*

Our Savior warned the hyper-legalistic Pharisees not to mistake their own rules and regulations for the heart behind God's law. You see, the Pharisees had all sorts of interpretations of the Old Testament law that they thought would keep them pure in God's eyes. But then Jesus Christ came on the scene, and His teachings rocked the Pharisees' legalistic concern with outward cleanliness.

> Woe to you, scribes and Pharisees, hypocrites! For you are like whitewashed tombs which indeed appear beautiful outwardly, but inside are full of dead men's bones and all uncleanness. (Matt. 23:27, NKJV)

Jesus was and is always focused on the heart.

> Not that which goeth into the mouth defileth a man; but that which cometh out of the mouth, this defileth a man. (15:11)

No doubt most Pharisees started out with good intentions and used their rules as "guardrails" to keep them from sin. In and of itself, that's not a bad idea. Many problems we see today would be avoided if more Christians had guardrails in place to help them steer clear of sin. This is wisdom, not legalism. But God Himself, not human-designed rules, is meant to be our ultimate guide.

> In vain they worship Me, teaching as doctrines the commandments of men. (v. 9, NKJV)

What we really need is Jesus, "the author and finisher of our faith" (Heb. 12:2). As we spend time with the Savior, learning of Him through His Word, our love for Him deepens while our desire for sin lessens. Let the Light of the World be your guide for daily life!

Unexpected Paths

October 16

TODAY'S READING: Mark 8:11–9:1; Matthew 16:1–28; Luke 9:18–27; John 6:60–71

We believe and are sure that thou art that Christ, the Son of the living God. *John 6:69*

Jesus is the Christ, the Son of the living God. He has revealed Himself to us, been at work within us, and spoken words of life to us. With that in mind, we can eagerly join with our beloved brother Peter in echoing his great confession:

> Lord, to whom shall we go? thou hast the words of eternal life. (John 6:68)

Indeed, Jesus Christ alone speaks words of eternal life, but sometimes those words work themselves out in ways we don't expect. For example, the disciples did not expect that Christ's promise of life would cost Him His own.

> The Son of man must suffer many things, and be rejected . . . and be slain, and be raised the third day. (Luke 9:22)

Suffering was not what the disciples had anticipated as they followed their Messiah. Their expectation was deliverance from the Romans, their earthly oppressors. But God's plans are eternal, and He intended to deliver His people from spiritual oppression and usher them into eternal victory. The prophet Isaiah spoke of this when he said,

> Of the increase of his government and peace there shall be no end, upon the throne of David, and upon his kingdom, to order it, and to establish it with judgment and with justice from henceforth even for ever. (9:7)

God was perfectly fulfilling His Word and His plan, even though this eternal victory came through a tremendous heartbreak.

Regardless of your circumstances today, rest assured that what God has promised, He will perform. He will never let you go (49:16).

October 17

Keeping Company with Jesus

TODAY'S READING: Mark 9:2–37; Matthew 17:1–23; 18:1–5; Luke 9:28–48

> After six days Jesus took Peter, James and John with him and led them up a high mountain, where they were all alone. *Mark 9:2,* NIV

Jesus knew His disciples needed time alone with Him, away from the crowds and the demands of life and ministry. Indeed, all of us need time with Jesus apart from the hectic pace of this world. The Holy Spirit beckons us to spend time with the Lord in His Word, in prayer, and in worship. Accepting the invitation can be life changing. That's why we're committing to spend time with Jesus, through His Word, every single day!

What if Peter, James, and John had declined Jesus's invitation to accompany Him to the Mount of Transfiguration? Turns out that was the day when Jesus quite literally glowed in His glory before their very eyes. Needless to say, those three disciples would have missed out on a life-altering revelation had they said "Sorry, we're busy fishing" or "We're scheduling your next meeting" or even "We're ministering to the masses."

But Peter, James, and John chose to keep company with Jesus and, as a result, got to see His glory that day, a revelation that was instrumental in preparing them for the events to come—Jesus's crucifixion and their own persecution.

God Almighty desires fellowship with you. If He calls you to a quiet place to talk with Him today, don't decline. Remember that time in the Lord's presence reveals His glory, and fellowship with Him prepares us for what lies ahead.

Go Fish

TODAY'S READING: Matthew 17:24–27; 18:6–19:2; 8:18–22; 11:20–24; Mark 9:38–10:1; Luke 9:49–10:20

Take up the fish that first cometh up; and when thou hast opened his mouth, thou shalt find a piece of money.
Matthew 17:27

Jesus is glorious not only in His divinity but also in His practicality and, as we see in today's story, even in His irony. I find it comforting that He not only cares for His followers spiritually but also cares for us practically, even when it comes to something like taxes (Matt. 17:24–27)!

The collectors of the temple tax approached Peter to ask if Jesus had paid His fair share. The tribute in question was not a civil fee demanded by the Romans but a temple tax required to support worship in the temple.[73] The temple tax was referred to in Exodus as a *ransom* or *atonement for the soul* (30:12, 15).

Jesus answered in humility and willingly submitted to these earthly authorities. But at the same time, He demonstrated His divinity and authority over all creation by telling His disciples they would find the funds furnished in a fish's mouth!

Jesus was God, yet He put Himself under the law that He might completely fulfill all its requirements (Gal. 4:4). Having become a servant of all (Phil. 2:7–8), He paid the *atonement price* for Himself. Oh, the irony in this scene—for He is the atonement!

May we follow our Lord's example today and walk humbly, giving Him tribute. And if the Lord tells us to "go fish," as He did Peter, may we obey quickly. In so doing, we just might see a miracle. With certainty we will be blessed and refreshed and will see our practical needs provided for.

Rest for Your Soul

TODAY'S READING: **Luke 10:21–24; 10:38–11:13; 11:27–12:21; Matthew 11:25–30**

I will give you rest. *Matthew 11:28*

Throughout the Gospels we repeatedly see Jesus offer rest and reprieve to those who followed Him.

> Come unto me, all ye that labour and are heavy laden, and I will give you rest. Take my yoke upon you, and learn of me; for I am meek and lowly in heart: and ye shall find rest unto your souls. For my yoke is easy, and my burden is light. (Matt. 11:28–30)

This was not a new concept for God's people. Throughout the Old Testament God continually offered His people rest. God gave them the Sabbath, a day of rest (Exod. 34:21). God gave them a year of rest (Lev. 25:4), and God gave them a land of rest (Deut. 12:10). Most of all, God extended to them a life of rest.

> He said, My presence shall go with thee, and I will give thee rest. (Exod. 33:14)

What the Old Testament shadowed, Jesus demonstrated (Heb. 4:8–11). Jesus gave a practical lesson in resting. Consider how He admonished Martha to rest from her toil. No doubt, Martha considered her work a labor of love, for her messiah, Jesus, was in *her* house. As Martha hurried about, her sister, Mary, sat at Jesus's feet and listened. When Martha chastised Mary for not helping, Jesus said,

> Martha, Martha, you are worried and troubled about many things. But one thing is needed. (Luke 10:41–42, NKJV)

Mary chose the one thing needed: to rest in the presence of Jesus. Although Martha was doing necessary work, it didn't need to be done at that time, when Jesus was speaking. So today, if He calls you to sit for a bit, choose to kneel at your Lord's feet and listen. There you will find rest for your soul.

Be Sure You're Sure

TODAY'S READING: Luke 12:22–13:17; 13:22–14:24

Strive to enter in at the strait gate: for many, I say unto you, will seek to enter in, and shall not be able. *Luke 13:24*

Have you ever missed a train or a plane? If so, you know that sinking feeling you get as the train pulls away or the doors close while you're running toward the gate. That temporary frustration reminds me of a parable Jesus told—though His lesson has eternal consequences.

Some of the religious people asked Jesus whether many or few would be saved. Jesus answered,

> When once the Master of the house has risen up and shut the door, and you begin to stand outside and knock at the door, saying, "Lord, Lord, open for us," and He will answer and say to you, "I do not know you, where you are from," then you will begin to say, "We ate and drank in Your presence, and You taught in our streets." But He will say, "I tell you I do not know you, where you are from. Depart from Me, all you workers of iniquity." (Luke 13:25–27, NKJV)

Jesus said there would be those who seemingly fellowshipped with Him here on earth, and yet on that day He'll say He never knew them. This is sobering, to say the least! Many people, even churchgoers, have lived as if serving God, yet their hearts are far from the saving knowledge of Jesus Christ. That's why Paul admonished us to examine ourselves to be sure Jesus Christ is in us (2 Cor. 13:5).

So today, please make sure He's not just *the savior* but that He's *your savior* and that on that day you'll hear Him say, "Well done, good and faithful servant" (Matt. 25:21, NKJV).

October 21

The Shepherd's Care

TODAY'S READING: Luke 14:25–16:17

> I say to you that likewise there will be more joy in heaven over one sinner who repents than over ninety-nine just persons who need no repentance. *Luke 15:7,* NKJV

Nearly six hundred years before Jesus's birth, the prophet Ezekiel spoke of the coming redeemer and described Him as a shepherd who would seek His lost sheep.

> As a shepherd seeks out his flock on the day he is among his scattered sheep, so will I seek out My sheep and deliver them from all the places where they were scattered on a cloudy and dark day. (Ezek. 34:12, NKJV)

God's relentless care and faithfulness to Israel give us a precious and precise picture of the love Jesus has for us. As Jesus spoke to His disciples, He poetically fulfilled Ezekiel's prophecy, declaring,

> I am the good shepherd: the good shepherd giveth his life for the sheep. (John 10:11)

Our Good Shepherd did give His life for us. We were lost, but He found each of us who are His.

> What man of you, having an hundred sheep, if he lose one of them, doth not leave the ninety and nine in the wilderness, and go after that which is lost, until he find it? And when he hath found it, he layeth it on his shoulders, rejoicing. (Luke 15:4–5)

Truly, He is the tender caretaker who has given His life for His sheep. May you follow where He leads, listen to His instruction, and find rest in His pasture today. Let Him be your shepherd.

Rivers of Living Water

October 22

TODAY'S READING: Luke 17:20–18:14; John 7

If any man thirst, let him come unto me, and drink. *John 7:37*

Thirst can be a mighty force. Ancient civilizations rose and fell based on access to a reliable source of water. The Sumerians, through their water management system, established what is generally considered the first known civilization. The Nabataeans seemingly conquered the desert and built a water paradise in the arid region of Petra. The Khmer empire engineered a marvel of a man-made reservoir that stretched over 460 square miles and is visible from space. Humanity, driven by its need for water, has accomplished great architectural feats as a matter of life and death.

But it's not just our bodies that thirst; our spirits do as well. Jesus spoke of this spiritual thirst and gave an eternal solution to this ever-present need. On the final day of the Feast of Tabernacles—the eighth day, signifying completion (Lev. 23:36)—Jesus stood at the temple and proclaimed to the people,

> If anyone thirsts, let him come to me and drink. Whoever believes in me, as the Scripture has said, "Out of his heart will flow rivers of living water." (John 7:37–38, ESV)

The prophet Zechariah had prophesied about living water in relation to a time when the Lord would be king over all the earth.

> It shall be in that day, that living waters shall go out from Jerusalem. (14:8)

Through Jesus it did—and it will! Jesus is the living water who came once and is coming again.

Just as thirst is impartial, so is Christ. He compels *anyone* who thirsts to come and be filled, to have his or her spiritual thirst supernaturally, eternally satisfied. So keep reading and drinking in the water of the Word, my friend. May you find your thirst continually satisfied in Him!

October 23

What Do You Need Today?

TODAY'S READING: **John 7:53–9:34**

If the Son therefore shall make you free, ye shall be free indeed.
John 8:36

In the Gospels we see Jesus repeatedly meet people in their time of need. Right when there seemed to be no hope, Jesus came to provide it. So, too, He meets you and me today. Just look at our Savior in John 8–9 and see the practical ways Jesus ministered to those who came to Him.

- He defended those who needed a defender. "He said unto her, Woman, where are those thine accusers? hath no man condemned thee? She said, No man, Lord" (8:10–11).
- He offered forgiveness to those who needed a new start. " 'Neither do I condemn you,' Jesus declared. 'Go now and leave your life of sin' " (v. 11, NIV).
- He offered light to those who stumbled in the darkness. "I am the light of the world: he that followeth me shall not walk in darkness, but shall have the light of life" (v. 12).
- He offered freedom to those who were in bondage. "If the Son therefore shall make you free, ye shall be free indeed" (v. 36).
- He offered sight to those who were blind. "One thing I know, that, whereas I was blind, now I see" (9:25).

And that, my friend, is your story. It's my story too. He found us in sin and came to defend us, forgive us, offer us a fresh start, liberate us from the past and the power of sin, be our light in the darkness, and open our eyes. Amazing grace!

Count the Cost

TODAY'S READING: John 9:35–10:21; Mark 10:2–22; Matthew 19:3–22; Luke 16:18; 18:15–23

Come, take up the cross, and follow me. *Mark 10:21*

We should live with eternity always in view. Having an eternal perspective makes all the difference in how we approach our daily choices. Jesus admonished a rich young man to sell all he had and follow Him. Despite Jesus's evident love, that young man was unwilling to obey and follow Christ.

> Jesus beholding him loved him, and said unto him, One thing thou lackest: go thy way, sell whatsoever thou hast, and give to the poor, and thou shalt have treasure in heaven: and come, take up the cross, and follow me. And he was sad at that saying, and went away grieved: for he had great possessions. (Mark 10:21–22)

The message of this story is not that selling everything would have gained this young man salvation but that in following Jesus, he would find all his heart desired and more. This young man, following after the things of the world, was unwilling to abandon his affections for his earthly possessions in order to follow Jesus.

Just as Jesus loved that rich young man, He loves you too. Is He asking you to lay something down and take up a cross? Don't hesitate! Don't delay in this wonderful opportunity to obey. What may seem a tremendous sacrifice is a tiny price to exchange for eternal rewards. Will you follow your Lord today?

October 25

The Impossible Made Possible

TODAY'S READING: Mark 10:23–31; Matthew 19:23–20:16; Luke 18:24–30; John 10:22–11:16

With men it is impossible, but not with God: for with God all things are possible. *Mark 10:27*

With God all things are possible. For example, we know it was impossible for us to live up to God's perfect standard, as revealed in the Old Testament. We all sinned and fell short of God's glory (Rom. 3:10, 23). It was impossible for us to make up for our shortcomings and redeem ourselves (James 2:10). That is why God promised a redeemer. It was impossible for us to earn eternal life by our own efforts (Rom. 6:23). That was what God revealed through the law (Gal. 3:24).

But Jesus, fulfilling all the law and the prophets, accomplished the impossible for us on the cross. Just consider all the "impossibilities" He has made reality for you:

- You've been purchased with the blood of Jesus Christ (1 Pet. 1:18–19), forgiven of all your sins (Col. 2:13), justified and the record that detailed your sins removed, and declared innocent (Rom. 3:24).
- God has washed you and sanctified you (1 Cor. 6:11); He has given you new life (2 Cor. 5:17), eternal life through Jesus Christ (Titus 3:7).

It doesn't stop there!

- He fills you with His Spirit and dwells within you (1 John 4:13).
- He has given you joy in exchange for sadness and fills a heavy heart with praise (Isa. 61:3).
- Once you're saved, He offers all you need to live life in Him (2 Pet. 1:3).

Rejoice! God Himself made a way for you to have fellowship with Him. What was impossible for you is completely possible with Him.

Jump to Your Feet

TODAY'S READING: **John 11:17–57; Mark 10:32–52; Matthew 20:17–34; Luke 18:31–43**

Immediately he received his sight, and followed Jesus in the way. *Mark 10:52*

I love the story of blind Bartimaeus! A couple of things particularly interest me. First, notice how Bartimaeus tenaciously and repeatedly cries out to Jesus before the Savior stops. That fits perfectly with the instructions Jesus gave us to ask, seek, knock—or keep asking, keep seeking, and keep knocking—when we need something (Matt. 7:7; Luke 11:9). Second, notice how when Jesus commanded that Bartimaeus be brought to Him, Bartimaeus obeyed immediately and enthusiastically.

> Throwing aside his cloak, he jumped up and came to Jesus. . . . Jesus said, "What do you want Me to do for you?" And the blind man said to Him, "Rabboni, I want to regain my sight!" And Jesus said to him, "Go; your faith has made you well." (Mark 10:50–52, NASB)

Prophetically, Jesus was fulfilling the Old Testament prophecies that the messiah would give sight to the blind (Isa. 29:18; 35:4–6; 42:6–7; Ps. 146:8). But spiritually speaking, Jesus was giving a wonderful hope to you and me. We were just like blind Bartimaeus. But unlike so many other needs where Jesus tells us to ask, seek, and knock to show our sincerity, when it comes to healing the spiritually blind, the Bible tells us He's the one who's knocking (Rev. 3:20).

The question is, Have we thrown off the old cloak (who we were before we came to Christ) and jumped to our feet in response to Jesus's call?

Like those crowds around Bartimaeus, let's encourage one another on as we seek Him. Cheer up, dear friend. On your feet! He's calling you because He wants you to see Him!

October 27

To See Jesus

TODAY'S READING: Luke 19:1–10, 28–48; Mark 11:1–25; Matthew 21:1–11; John 12:12–19

Jesus entered and passed through Jericho. *Luke 19:1*

Today's story marvelously mirrors a famous Old Testament one. The setting: Jericho, the famous walled city that Joshua conquered as he led the Israelites into the Promised Land. The characters: Jesus and Zacchaeus (and a sycamore tree) in the New Testament; Rahab and the spies in the Old.

Think back with me to our reading many months ago when we saw Joshua march around Jericho in faith that its fortress walls would come tumbling down. In the gospel of Luke, we see King Jesus not marching into Jericho but simply walking into Jerusalem on his way to the Cross—not as a political or military conqueror but to seek and save the lost (19:9–10).

Joshua was sent to conquer Jericho, a wicked city that represents our old self, the flesh, in Bible typology. Jesus came to conquer our hearts so that we could live victorious over our old self, the flesh.

Now let's consider Rahab, the harlot whose life was spared in Jericho because, in faith, she hid the Israelite spies and then let them down the wall to freedom by a scarlet cord. That scarlet cord is, of course, a powerful picture of Jesus's precious blood. Now fast-forward to another sinner, Zacchaeus. He was the chief among the publicans, a despised group of tax collectors who regularly cheated people (Luke 19:2, 8). But Zacchaeus wanted to know Jesus and, in faith, let himself down from the sycamore tree so he, too, could be set free, not by a scarlet cord but by the scarlet blood of Jesus.

Jesus called Zacchaeus to come down from the tree, knowing He would soon be lifted up on the tree at Calvary. There He would pay for the sins of Zacchaeus, of you, and of me.

Today, if you, like Zacchaeus, want to see Jesus, remember you'll find Him on every page of His Word, which tells the story of His wonderful redemption plan.

The Cornerstone

TODAY'S READING: Mark 11:27–12:17; Matthew 21:23–22:22; Luke 20:1–26

The stone which the builders rejected is become the head of the corner. *Mark 12:10*

Jesus is our sure foundation (1 Cor. 3:11), the cornerstone (Ps. 118:22–23; Matt. 21:42; Acts 4:11; Eph. 2:20), the solid rock (1 Sam. 2:2), a stronghold and refuge for those who trust in Him (2 Sam. 22:3). The Old Testament repeatedly points to Jesus as this foundation stone.

> Behold, I lay in Zion a stone for a foundation, a tried stone, a precious cornerstone, a sure foundation; whoever believes will not act hastily. (Isa. 28:16, NKJV)

Not only does Christ give us a solid foundation, but from Him flow rivers of living water. He Himself is the rock that followed Israel in the wilderness.

> They drank from the supernatural Rock which followed them, and the Rock was Christ. (1 Cor. 10:4, RSV)

Jesus unveiled Himself to the religious rulers as the fulfillment of the Old Testament type, but they could not see it. Just as prophesied, they rejected their cornerstone (Matt. 21:42).

Today, you and I have the opportunity to build our lives on the rock of Jesus Christ, if we choose to believe He is who and what He says.

> Whosoever heareth these sayings of mine, and doeth them, I will liken him unto a wise man, which built his house upon a rock. (7:24)

He remains the chief cornerstone, the firm foundation, the rock of ages. May we build our lives, our homes, our very existence on Him.

Know and Speak Truth

TODAY'S READING: Mark 12:18–40; Luke 20:27–47; 10:25–37; Matthew 22:41–23:36

> Jesus answering said unto them, Do ye not therefore err, because ye know not the scriptures . . . ? *Mark 12:24*

The Sadducees were religious leaders who did not believe in the resurrection of the dead. They believed that once this life was over, that was it. Since Jesus spoke often of life after death, the Sadducees frequently tried to trick Him with questions about the resurrection. Jesus's response to one such attempt teaches you and me how we should answer questions.

> Jesus answered them, "You are wrong, because you know neither the Scriptures nor the power of God. . . . And as for the resurrection of the dead, have you not read what was said to you by God . . . ?" (Matt. 22:29, 31–32, ESV)

Jesus first pointed out the Sadducees' lack of Bible knowledge and then proceeded to answer their question with the Word. There's the key for you and me: we must train ourselves to think biblically!

Jesus was full of wisdom (1 Cor. 1:24), and in His mouth there was no deceit (1 Pet. 2:22). As He spoke, He revealed God to us (Col. 1:15), thus wonderfully fulfilling the psalm.

> Good and upright is the LORD: therefore will he teach sinners in the way. (25:8)

God promised to send a redeemer and put His words in His mouth (Deut. 18:18; Isa. 50:4). Indeed, Jesus came and spoke God's Word and taught us in the way. For He is "the way, the truth, and the life" (John 14:6). May we take His example and apply it to our thinking today. How often do our responses to those around us reflect only our ideas or personal experiences? But God's Word holds absolute truth. It keeps our minds right and gives us a firm foundation for our opinions, our doctrine, and our daily conduct (2 Tim. 3:16).

Let Not Your Heart Be Troubled

October 30

TODAY'S READING: Matthew 23:37–24:28; Mark 12:41–13:23; Luke 21:1–24

See that you are not troubled. *Matthew 24:6,* NKJV

We're living in the last days. We can choose to live with our hearts full of fear as we watch the world unravel around us, or we can follow the lead of the psalmist who sang, "I will lift up mine eyes unto the hills, from whence cometh my help" (121:1). If we choose to trust the Lord, then we'll truly be able to proclaim that we have the privilege of watching prophecy unfold right before our very eyes.

The darkness of the day shouldn't be a surprise because the Bible tells us the last days will indeed be shadowed with evil (2 Tim. 3:1–5). But Jesus encourages us with His words:

> You will hear of wars and rumors of wars. See that you are not troubled; for all these things must come to pass. (Matt. 24:6, NKJV)

Jesus brought us hope and good news, just as Isaiah prophesied He would (52:7–9).

> I, even I, am He who comforts you. Who are you that you are afraid of man who dies and of the son of man who is made like grass? (51:12, NASB)

Jesus warned us of the dark days to come, but He encouraged us to remember that He has overcome the world. Jesus is our hope, and His Word gives us wisdom to navigate the world around us, reminders to anticipate the place being prepared for us, and encouragement from the words Jesus speaks to us.

> These things I have spoken unto you, that in me ye might have peace. In the world ye shall have tribulation: but be of good cheer; I have overcome the world. (John 16:33)

So keep turning your eyes upward, looking to Jesus, and let not your heart be troubled, my friend!

A Life Changer

TODAY'S READING: Mark 13:24–37; Matthew 24:29–25:30; Luke 21:25–38; 19:11–27

> Heaven and earth shall pass away: but my words shall not pass away. *Mark 13:31*

Knowing, studying, meditating on, and loving God's Word matters. Jesus said that all heaven and earth will pass away, but His Word will never pass away. What else does God say about His Word? He tells us that He's esteemed it above His very name (Ps. 138:2). Incredible! Just ponder that for a minute. God also tells us that all Scripture is given by His inspiration (2 Tim. 3:16). God tells us that His Word is itself creative power, for He spoke all creation into existence (Gen. 1). God tells us that His Word is cleansing (Eph. 5:26). It's also sanctifying (Ps. 119:9; John 17:17). His Word is guiding and enlightening (Ps. 119:105). God tells us that His Word is sustaining (Matt. 4:4) and that it's dividing.

> The word of God is living and powerful, and sharper than any two-edged sword, piercing even to the division of soul and spirit, and of joints and marrow, and is a discerner of the thoughts and intents of the heart. (Heb. 4:12, NKJV)

Ultimately, God's Word is totally fulfilling and lifesaving. The beginning of the gospel of John tells us,

> In the beginning was the Word, and the Word was with God, and the Word was God. . . . And the Word was made flesh, and dwelt among us. (1:1, 14)

God's Word is complete, not lacking anything, because in it we see, hear, and feel the heart of Jesus Christ, the Word of God made flesh.

Keep taking in God's Word, my friend. Don't grow weary in reading it, for the Bible will feed your soul, change your world, set your perspective straight, give you truth to believe, and show you righteous standards to obey. It really is a life changer.

Death That Brings Life

November 1

TODAY'S READING: Matthew 25:31–26:16; John 12:1–11, 20–50; Mark 14:1–11; Luke 22:1–6

> Unless a grain of wheat falls into the earth and dies, it remains alone; but if it dies, it bears much fruit. *John 12:24,* NASB

God gives meaning to the seemingly meaningless, even to death.

> Precious in the sight of the LORD is the death of his saints. (Ps. 116:15)

In today's reading Jesus begins to prepare His disciples for His death. What would feel to them like the end of the world was the perfect fulfillment of all God's promises, types, pictures, and prophecies!

> I, if I be lifted up from the earth, will draw all men unto me. This he said, signifying what death he should die. (John 12:32–33)

Jesus makes it clear that He had to be lifted up on the cross so that everyone—including you and me—might be drawn to Him. This was God's plan from the beginning (Gen. 3:15; Isa. 53:1–12). Through Jesus's death God brought us life. Jesus died once for all (Rom. 6:10) so that we might live victorious.

We enter into that victory by daily crucifying our own flesh. The apostle Paul grasped this important spiritual principle when he wrote in 1 Corinthians 15:31, "I die daily." Paul understood what Jesus meant when He said, "If any man will come after me, let him deny himself, and take up his cross daily, and follow me" (Luke 9:23).

Herein lies a paradox of the gospel: death is our victory. On the cross Jesus Christ conquered sin and death. And every day that we take up our cross, die to sin, and live for Christ, we experience the victorious Christian life.

November 2

Our Passover Lamb

TODAY'S READING: Mark 14:12–21; Matthew 26:17–25; Luke 22:7–18; John 13:1–30

> I have earnestly desired to eat this Passover with you before I suffer. For I tell you I will not eat it until it is fulfilled in the kingdom of God. *Luke 22:15–16,* ESV

The disciples were experiencing the actual fulfillment of the Passover feast they had so faithfully celebrated all their lives, though they didn't realize it at the time. With every symbolic act of that Passover meal, Jesus understood that He was the sacrificial lamb who fulfilled its promise (1 Cor. 5:7; John 1:29–36).

Think back to that first Passover night in Egypt, when God instructed the Israelites to apply the blood of a lamb to the doorposts of their homes so the angel of death would pass over (Exod. 12). God instructed His people to prepare a feast that night consisting of a sacrificed lamb, unleavened matzah bread, and bitter herbs (v. 8). The lamb was the core requisite for Passover (34:25; Deut. 16:1–7). Without a lamb there was no blood to apply and, therefore, no deliverance.[74]

God commanded His people to observe Passover as a memorial forever (Exod. 12:14, 26–27). Over a thousand years later, Jesus, the perfect lamb of God, sat at this meal with His disciples and said to them, "I have earnestly desired to eat this Passover with you." For Jesus knew it would soon be fulfilled through His suffering (Luke 22:15–16, ESV).

Just as the people of Israel escaped death by marking their doorposts with the blood of the lamb, so we are spared eternal death because our hearts are covered with the blood of Jesus.

> Ye know that ye were not redeemed with corruptible things . . . but with the precious blood of Christ, as of a lamb without blemish and without spot. (1 Pet. 1:18–19)

Jesus was the perfect lamb of God (John 1:29), sacrificed for the sins of the world. He was the perfect fulfillment of the Passover feast, and His blood covers our sins and completely sets us free.

Oh, the Blood of Jesus

November 3

TODAY'S READING: Mark 14:22–25; Matthew 26:21–29; Luke 22:19–30; John 13:31–38

This is my blood of the new testament, which is shed for many for the remission of sins. *Matthew 26:28*

That old hymn that so sweetly sings over and over "Oh, the blood of Jesus" is perhaps my favorite of all. For without the shedding of His blood, there would be no remission for our sin (Lev. 17:11; Heb. 9:22). At that meal in the upper room, Jesus comprehended both the suffering He would face on the cross and the everlasting joy it would usher in. The cup He extended to the disciples holds what the Old Testament looked forward to: the redeeming blood of Jesus Christ, shed for our sin.

Soon the disciples would look back and recognize that Jesus was fulfilling all that the Old Testament sacrifices shadowed:

- The Passover lamb protected Israel from physical death, but Jesus's blood brought everlasting life (John 3:16; 5:24).
- The Old Testament sacrifices atoned for a season, but Jesus's sacrifice satisfied the price for sin once and for all (Exod. 30:10; Rom. 5:11; Heb. 10:10).
- The blood of bulls and goats could not cleanse a person's conscience, but the blood of Jesus frees us from the power of guilt (Col. 2:14; John 3:17; 1 John 3:21; Rom. 8:1).

The precious, innocent blood of Jesus (1 Pet. 1:19; Matt. 27:3–4) brought us redemption (Eph. 1:7) and reconciliation (Col. 1:20). The cleansing power of Jesus's blood has sanctified us (Heb. 13:12) and washed us clean (1 John 1:7).

What life-altering power, what joy and utmost significance was represented by the cup Jesus extended to His unknowing disciples!

Jesus extends to you that same cup. Consider its precious contents today, and may your heart sing, "Oh, the blood of Jesus! It washes white as snow."

On the Doorstep of Despair

TODAY'S READING: John 15–17; Mark 14:26–31; Matthew 26:30–35; Luke 22:31–38

> In the world ye shall have tribulation: but be of good cheer; I have overcome the world. *John 16:33*

As Jesus and His disciples left the upper room after the Last Supper, they headed toward the Garden of Gethsemane, where Jesus had retreated on other occasions to pray. By this point it was dark, and Judas had already left to betray Christ.

On the way Jesus spoke to His beloved disciples regarding their coming hardships. He advised them to plan for the future (Luke 22:35–38). He prayed for them (John 17), and He sang with them (Matt. 26:30; Mark 14:26). Jesus was preparing His friends for what would take place over the next few hours. But as is His nature, Jesus gave them hope to hang on to.

He told His disciples that they would all forsake Him (Matt. 26:31) but that He would again see them in Galilee after His resurrection (v. 32; Mark 14:28). He predicted Peter's three-part denial (Matt 26:33–35; Mark 14:29–31) but told the impulsive disciple that He had prayed for him and that Peter was to strengthen his fellow believers once he turned back to his faith (Luke 22:32). He told the disciples that He had to depart and go to the Father but that He would send the Holy Spirit to comfort them and lead them in all truth (John 15:26; 16:7–15).

Jesus also gave His disciples four powerful promises: that their present sorrows would turn to joy, that they could ask the Father for all their needs in Jesus's name, that they would have peace in the midst of tribulation, and that He would overcome the world (vv. 22–23, 33).

These promises from Jesus are promises you and I also possess because of His resurrection! So today, ask Him for joy, petition the Father in Jesus's name, let the Holy Spirit bring peace in tribulation, and remember you have overcome the world because greater is He who is in you than he who is in the world.

A Man of Sorrows

TODAY'S READING: Mark 14:32–52; Matthew 26:36–56; Luke 22:39–65; John 18:1–12

My soul is exceeding sorrowful unto death. *Mark 14:34*

Isaiah prophesied that the redeemer would be "a man of sorrows, and acquainted with grief" (53:3). We read of many sorrowful moments in Jesus's life: the death of His friend Lazarus (John 11), the sorrow He felt as the rich young ruler walked away (Mark 10:21–23), and the grief He showed as He wept over Jerusalem (Luke 19:41). But none of these compare to the grief He experienced as He prayed in the Garden of Gethsemane.

> Being in an agony he prayed more earnestly: and his sweat was as it were great drops of blood falling down to the ground. (22:44)

Jesus's grief so encompassed Him that "it threatened his very life" (Mark 14:34).[75] Yet this suffering was not a waste or an unnecessary trial. It was all part of God's gracious redemptive plan.

In Jesus's prayer it was "the cup" that He so agonized over and petitioned to have removed. I haven't found a better explanation of this cup than that given by Dr. Harold Willmington:

> The Scriptures plainly inform us that the Gethsemane cup was filled with the sins of all humanity! Our Lord looked deeply into the cesspool of human sin that dark night and groaned as he smelled its foul odor and viewed the rising poisonous fumes.[76]

Indeed, Jesus knew sorrow and grief well, but it was on account of our actions. He willingly drank the cup of our sin and offered us the cup of His blood, which atoned, covered, and paid the price. Oh, the grace of Jesus!

Seven Trials of Jesus

TODAY'S READING: Matthew 26:57–27:26; Luke 22:66–23:12; Mark 14:53–15:5; John 18:13–38

When they had bound him, they . . . delivered him to Pontius Pilate. *Matthew 27:2*

In the Bible the number seven represents completion. God created the world and rested on the seventh day (Gen. 2:2). Naaman the leper was told to bathe in the Jordan River seven times in order to be healed (2 Kings 5:10). Joshua marched around Jericho for seven days before the walls came down (Joshua 6:3–4). And in the book of Revelation, we find Jesus's seven letters to the seven churches (2–3). So when we see Jesus put on trial seven times before His crucifixion, we can be sure it's significant! With each trial we find humanity's utter failure contrasted with Christ's perfect fulfillment of God's divine plan.

- In the first trial, at Annas's house (John 18:12–14), Jesus, the lamb, was examined by the high priest, just as the law required (Exod. 12:3–6).
- In the second and third trials, Jesus was taken to Caiaphas (Matt. 26:57–27:1; Luke 22:66–23:1). Here He was rejected, spat on, struck, and mocked (Isa. 50:6).
- In the fourth, fifth, and sixth trials, Jesus was ushered between Pilate and Herod (John 18:28–38; Luke 23:7–12; Matt. 27:15–26). And so it had to be! For Psalm 22:16 prophesied that the Messiah would be delivered to the wicked and His death had to come by way of the Roman cross (Deut. 21:23).
- In the seventh trial, Jesus was taken to the court of scourging (Mark 15:16–20) where His back was striped, He was given a crown of thorns, and He was mocked (Isa. 53:5; 50:6).

In these seven trials of Jesus, we find God's perfect work perfectly completed.

Wounded for Us

TODAY'S READING: Mark 15:6–21; Luke 23:13–32; John 18:39–19:17; Matthew 27:27–32

They smote him on the head with a reed, and did spit upon him. *Mark 15:19*

How could God possibly be at work in the midst of this darkness, devastation, and death? And yet we know He was. When we look closely at the events surrounding Jesus's crucifixion, we see God at work in the smallest of details.

In today's reading we see Jesus taken to the court of scourging, called the Praetorium (Matt. 27:27–31; Mark 15:16–20). After the soldiers gathered together, they stripped Jesus, clothed Him in a purple robe, put a crown of thorns on His head, placed a reed in His hand, bowed to Him in mock homage, spat in his face, and ridiculed Him, saying, "Hail, King of the Jews!" (Mark 15:18, ESV).

> I gave my back to the smiters, and my cheeks to them that plucked off the hair: I hid not my face from shame and spitting. (Isa. 50:6)

All the scourging, all the mockery, and all this wretched abuse were part of God's plan, foretold by the prophets and ordained before the foundations of the earth (Eph. 1:4; Heb. 10:4–7; 1 Pet. 1:18–20; Rev. 13:8).

> Surely he hath borne our griefs, and carried our sorrows: yet we did esteem him stricken, smitten of God, and afflicted. But he was wounded for our transgressions, he was bruised for our iniquities: the chastisement of our peace was upon him; and with his stripes we are healed. (Isa. 53:4–5)

Jesus endured all this for the joy of what it would accomplish: the salvation of you and me (Heb. 12:2)!

Lifted High

TODAY'S READING: Mark 15:22–41; Matthew 27:33–56; Luke 23:33–49; John 19:17–37

When they were come to . . . Calvary, there they crucified him.
Luke 23:33

As Jesus hung on Calvary's cross, the prophecies describing the Messiah's death were fulfilled in explicit detail.

Isaiah prophesied that Jesus would be counted as a transgressor (53:12; Matt. 27:38) and buried with the rich (Isa. 53:9; Matt. 27:57–60).

The psalms prophesied of the vinegar Jesus would be given to drink (69:21; Matt. 27:34).

Zechariah declared that His hands and feet would be pierced and the people would gaze at Him (12:10; Ps. 22:16; Mark 15:25; Matt. 27:36).

David spoke of His garments being torn and gambled for (Ps. 22:18; Luke 23:34) and His great thirst on the cross (Ps. 22:15; John 19:28). He stated that none of His bones would be broken (Ps. 34:20; John 19:33–36).

Jesus is God's perfect promise fulfilled.

- Jesus is the ram Abraham had anticipated, the Son offered as a willing sacrifice (Gen. 22:1–2, 10, 13; Heb. 11:17–19).
- Jesus is the branch cast into the water—His cross making our bitter waters sweet (Exod. 15:22–25; 1 Cor. 10:1–2).
- Jesus is the smitten rock (Exod. 17:5–6; 1 Cor. 10:4) from which comes the living water.
- Jesus is what the brass serpent pictured: lifted high, He brings healing (Num. 21:5–9; Isa. 53:5; John 3:14–16).
- Jesus is the perfect Passover lamb (Exod. 12; 1 Cor. 5:7).

Truly, Jesus Christ, our lord and savior, is the promised messiah.

He Is Risen

TODAY'S READING: Mark 15:42–16:8; Matthew 27:57–28:10; Luke 23:50–24:12; John 19:38–20:18

He said to them, "Do not be alarmed. You seek Jesus of Nazareth, who was crucified. He is risen! He is not here."
Mark 16:6, NKJV

Just as He promised, Jesus rose from the dead and is alive! Had Jesus not risen to new life, all that preceded His death would have been for naught. Without His resurrection we would still be lost and with no hope of heaven. Jesus's victory over death is the final piece that completes the picture of our salvation. As Dr. Harold Willmington noted regarding the Resurrection,

> It is the final side making up the divine triangle of salvation. Thus:
> 1. Jesus' birth made it possible.
> 2. Jesus' death made it actual.
> 3. Jesus' resurrection made it certain.[77]

You and I are redeemed, forgiven, and justified—because Jesus is risen!

> Jesus said unto her: I am the resurrection, and the life: he that believeth in me, though he were dead, yet shall he live. (John 11:25)

We no longer have to live in fear, condemnation, or uncertainty!

> Do not be afraid, for I know that you are looking for Jesus, who was crucified. He is not here; he has risen, just as he said. Come and see the place where he lay. Then go quickly and tell his disciples: "He has risen from the dead." (Matt. 28:5–7, NIV)

The angel said to Mary at the garden tomb, "Come and see." Our Savior extends the same invitation to you and me: "Come and see"—because He is risen. He is risen indeed.

The Greatest Bible Study Ever

TODAY'S READING: Matthew 28:11–20; Luke 24:13–53; John 20:24–21:25

> Beginning at Moses and all the prophets, he expounded unto them in all the scriptures the things concerning himself. *Luke 24:27*

Have you ever pictured yourself on the road to Emmaus, listening in as the risen Jesus, unrecognized by His bewildered and grieving disciples, explains to them the meaning of His crucifixion?

> He said to them, "What kind of conversation is this that you have with one another as you walk and are sad? . . . Ought not the Christ to have suffered these things and to enter into His glory?" And beginning at Moses and all the Prophets, He expounded to them in all the Scriptures the things concerning Himself. (Luke 24:17, 26–27, NKJV)

Those blessed students in that most amazing of Bible studies were awed as they reflected on their conversation: "Were not our hearts burning within us while he talked with us on the road and opened the Scriptures to us?"(v. 32, NIV). Had they never read Isaiah 53 or Psalm 22 or Daniel 9? Certainly they had, but it wasn't until Jesus Himself removed the veil from their eyes and gave them understanding that these portions of Scripture began to make sense. As Bible commentator Matthew Henry wrote,

> Jesus Christ is himself the best expositor of scripture, particularly the scriptures concerning himself; . . . it was in this way that he led people into the knowledge of the mystery concerning himself; not by advancing new notions independent upon the scripture, but by showing how the scripture was fulfilled.[78]

May we open God's Word and see Jesus! He is there from beginning to end.

Witness to the World

TODAY'S READING: Mark 16:9–20; Acts 1–2

He said unto them, Go ye into all the world, and preach the gospel. *Mark 16:15*

Every single person has the same need: to be forgiven of his or her sins. What a moment it is when Jesus comes in and cleans the house of our hearts. The Scriptures declare that the angels rejoice when even one sinner repents and is saved (Luke 15:10).

Jesus gave a final command to His followers as He ascended into heaven, directing us to share the gospel message with the whole world:

- *We have all sinned.* We have broken God's law, we are all sinners, and the wages of sin is death (Rom. 3:10, 23; 6:23).
- *But while we were sinners, God sent Jesus to die for us.* While we were sinners, our merciful God loved us and sent His only Son, Jesus, to pay the penalty for us (5:8–10).
- *Jesus took our place on the cross.* Jesus bore our sin on Calvary, rose again, and conquered sin and death (1 Pet. 2:24; 1 Cor. 15:3–4).
- *Believe in your heart and confess out loud* that Jesus Christ is Lord (Rom. 10:9). "If we confess our sins, he is faithful and just to forgive us our sins, and to cleanse us from all unrighteousness" (1 John 1:9).
- *Rejoice! He makes all things new.* "If any man be in Christ, he is a new creature: old things are passed away; behold, all things are become new" (2 Cor. 5:17).

Remember, Jesus called His disciples to be witnesses. What do witnesses do? They speak of those things they have seen.

What have you seen Jesus do for you, dear Christian? Can you tell somebody about the goodness, the love, the forgiveness, and the life-changing work you've seen Him bring in your heart or home? That's all it takes to be a witness. What a privilege we have to tell the world of such wonderful news!

November 12

The Acts of the Living God

TODAY'S READING: Acts 3:1–5:16

The God of our fathers, hath glorified his Son Jesus. *Acts 3:13*

As New Testament believers, we witness Jesus through the foreshadowing and prophecies of the Old Testament, in the gospel accounts of His life on earth, and through His church, for the church is His body (1 Cor. 12:27; Eph. 4:12).

The church begins to take shape after the ascension of Jesus, and its early days are detailed in the book of Acts, sometimes titled the Acts of the Apostles. I once heard someone suggest that it be retitled the Acts of the Living God Through the Lives of His Apostles. I like that because Jesus tells us that without Him we can do nothing (John 15:5), and His Word also tells us that we can do all things through Christ who strengthens us (Phil. 4:13). Those truths are demonstrated in what He accomplished through the apostles in the book of Acts, and He desires to demonstrate them in you and me too. He works His glory in and through our lives as we yield to His will.

As we dive into the history of the early church, we will see Jesus, alive and well and working in and through His people via His Spirit. The Holy Spirit continues to convict, comfort, and point to the Son. God used the apostles to declare Jesus Christ to the world, and He continues to use His church to reach the world with Jesus's message that "you must be born again" (John 3:7, ESV). He desires to use us, to work in us, and to shine through us. Quite simply, He appoints us to be living demonstrations of the acts of the living God.

The Stephen Style

TODAY'S READING: Acts 5:17–7:60

Go, stand in the temple courts . . . and tell the people the full message of this new life. *Acts 5:20,* NIV

Despite persecution, ridicule, and even execution, the disciples continued to share the good news of Jesus Christ. One such example was Stephen, whom the Bible tells us was full of faith and power in the Holy Spirit (Acts 6:5, 8). Being falsely accused, Stephen was seized and brought before the Jewish council. There he delivered the longest recorded sermon in the book of Acts. This glorious message would be Stephen's last words as he became the first martyr of the early church.

One thing that should stand out to us is how much Scripture Stephen quoted. Virtually his entire sermon was made up of Old Testament references, and when he was not quoting Scripture, he was giving a summation of it. Oh, that more pastors would consider adopting the Stephen style! Nothing can replace the power of speaking directly from God's Word.

Stephen began with Abraham, their father, and walked these Jewish rulers through their history, a history they knew well. They were proud of their heritage but failed to recognize the fulfillment of its purpose in the righteous one, Jesus Christ. This was the culmination of Stephen's message.

> Which of the prophets did your fathers not persecute? And they killed those who announced beforehand the coming of the Righteous One, whom you have now betrayed and murdered. (7:52, ESV)

As you read through Stephen's sermon, be encouraged! You're adopting the Stephen style and learning to see Jesus, the purpose of all the Scriptures. Consider the cost Stephen was willing to pay to follow Christ and speak the truth: it cost him his very life. But in the end he looked up and saw the glory of God and Jesus standing in heaven (v. 55–57). What a prize!

November 14

Great Joy

TODAY'S READING: Acts 8:1–9:31

There was great joy in that city. *Acts 8:8*

It is an undisputable biblical truth that the absence of sin brings joy. That theme is seen throughout the history of humanity as revealed in the Scriptures, and we hear it echoed in the stories of the early church.

> Unclean spirits, crying with loud voice, came out of many that were possessed with them: and many taken with palsies, and that were lame, were healed. And there was great joy in that city. (Acts 8:7–8)

Don't you just love that last phrase: "And there was great joy in that city"? Being cleansed from sin brings joy! Why? Because sin is a brutal master, but forgiveness equals freedom (Rom. 6). Once we're free from sin, we are free to be sanctified, the process of being made more and more into the image of our creator, Jesus Christ. Someday that sanctification will turn into glorification, where not only will we see Him, but "we will be like Him" (1 John 3:2, NASB). I know of nothing that can bring greater joy than those truths!

The message of the Messiah brings forgiveness, sanctification, and someday, not too long from now, glorification—all of which translates into great joy for you and me here and now. As the Scriptures say,

> May the God of hope fill you with all joy and peace in believing [through the experience of your faith] that by the power of the Holy Spirit you will abound in hope and overflow with confidence in His promises. (Rom. 15:13, AMP)

The Gospel Within Our Walls

November 15

TODAY'S READING: Acts 9:32–11:18

It was known throughout all Joppa; and many believed in the Lord. *Acts 9:42*

The gospel of Jesus Christ is quite literally a Godsend—a message the world needs to hear. How wonderful that the same message that impacts nations and revitalizes civilizations is a message we can share on a daily basis within our own four walls, with the family and friends we hold nearest and dearest. The gift Jesus has given us of a clean conscience, through the forgiveness of sin, is a reality we can live out and lovingly remind one another of day by day. Living for Jesus in our hearts and homes will inevitably spill out into our communities.

Tabitha, a woman in the early church, demonstrated this truth as she walked out the gospel in her home and loved those around her. Tabitha was loved by all who knew her. When she died, her friends called Peter to come quickly (Acts 9:38).

Peter went with them, and when he arrived he was taken upstairs to the room. All the widows stood around him, crying and showing him the robes and other clothing that [Tabitha] had made while she was still with them. (v. 39, NIV)

Tabitha had left her mark of service: the work of her hands and her acts of love. Peter got on his knees and prayed. God heard, and Tabitha was given life again.

It was known throughout all Joppa; and many believed in the Lord. (v. 42)

May we, too, love those around us well and leave a trail of good works that reflect Jesus. Like Tabitha, may we live so that our neighbors know that Jesus has breathed new life into us and many may believe in the Lord!

Perfectly Mature

TODAY'S READING: James 1–3

> Even so faith, if it hath not works, is dead, being alone.
> *James 2:17*

Today we jump to the book of James, perhaps the earliest letter we have to the church in Jerusalem, written around AD 45. James had been the first pastor of those local believers (Acts 12:17; 15:13), and at the time he wrote this book, the severe persecution that eventually caused the dispersion of that church had just begun.

There are at least four men named James in the New Testament (Matt. 10:2–3; Luke 6:16; Acts 12:2). This James is the half brother of Jesus (Matt. 13:55), who didn't come to faith in the Messiah until after the Resurrection (John 7:3–10; 1 Cor. 15:7), when Jesus appeared to him personally.[79]

At the time James wrote this letter, the church in Jerusalem was in its infancy and these believers were still very much Jewish in thought and practice. Knowing his audience, James referenced the Old Testament at least fifty-three times.[80] He pointed the believers' attention to Old Testament illustrations and applied them to their current obligation: maturity in Christ.

> Let patience have her perfect work, that ye may be perfect and entire, wanting nothing. (James 1:4)

James emphasized faith demonstrated by outward action. Just think of James's experience, having watched Jesus throughout his life. If anyone knew the answer to "What would Jesus do?" I'd expect His younger brother James would. As you read through this concise letter, consider it from James's perspective. All that James admonishes us to do, he saw demonstrated by Jesus. As Christians, we are to be Jesus imitators, and the book of James gives us insight as to what that looks like.

Humility

TODAY'S READING: James 4–5; Acts 11:19–12:25

God resisteth the proud, but giveth grace unto the humble.
James 4:6

History tells us that James was called "James the Just" and was known to be "an unusually good man."[81] He was present on that powerful day of Pentecost when flames of fire rested over the disciples' heads as they were filled with the Holy Spirit (Acts 2:1–4). Oh, the experiences James could have boasted of or the names he could have dropped, being the son of Mary and Joseph, the half brother of Jesus. Yet he simply referred to himself as "a servant of God and of the Lord Jesus Christ" (James 1:1). This, dear Christian, is a sign of a mature believer, one who has experienced the presence of God and has been left with the fruit of humility.

Humble yourselves in the sight of the Lord, and he shall lift you up. (4:10)

James reminds the believer to grow in Christ through humble submission to God (vv. 1–17). He admonishes us to be humble as we live selflessly, not living for this world but for Christ (5:1–6). Jesus did not accumulate earthly possessions, and He came to serve others (Luke 9:58; Matt. 20:28). James exhorts us to continue to humbly serve and love one another (5:9–11), just as Jesus loved us (John 13:34).

Today, may we humble ourselves under the mighty hand of God, keeping our eyes fixed on Jesus, "the author and perfecter of our faith" (Heb. 12:2, NIV). May we, like James, be more consumed with who He is than who we are. Let's spend our days praising His works rather than worrying about what great works we might accomplish. Today, let us fall at His feet in humble adoration and lift Him high.

History Lesson

TODAY'S READING: Acts 13–14

> What God promised . . . he has fulfilled to us. *Acts 13:32–33,* ESV

Before Paul was the apostle Paul, he was Saul—a devout Pharisee (Acts 23:6), a lover of the rabbinic law who venomously persecuted the church (26:5, 9–11; Gal. 1:14). In a miraculous conversion Jesus opened Paul's spiritually blind eyes as He appeared to him on the road to Damascus (Acts 9:1–8). Now this once religious ruler stood before his fellow Jews and gave them a history lesson that pointed straight to Jesus.

Paul began with what they knew—the law and the prophets. He reminded them of the Exodus, the Promised Land, the judges, the prophets, and the covenant God made with David (13:15–23). All this spoke of what would take place when the Messiah came. Then Paul declared that the Messiah had come and that all that was written had been fulfilled.

> When they had carried out all that was written concerning Him, they took Him down from the cross and laid Him in a tomb. But God raised Him from the dead; and for many days He appeared to those who came up with Him from Galilee to Jerusalem, the very ones who are now His witnesses to the people. And we preach to you the good news . . . that God has fulfilled this promise to our children in that He raised up Jesus, as it is also written in the second Psalm, "YOU ARE MY SON; TODAY I HAVE BEGOTTEN YOU." (vv. 29–33, NASB)

Paul understood the power of seeing Jesus throughout the Scriptures and used the pictures and prophecies of the Old Testament to proclaim the gospel of Jesus Christ, the risen Lord. When we see Jesus throughout His Scriptures, it adds depth to our comprehension of God's faithfulness throughout the ages. Let's pray for the wisdom to put the pieces together in order to more effectively share Him with others.

Legalism Versus Obedience

TODAY'S READING: Galatians 1:1–4:7

> God sent forth his Son . . . made under the law, to redeem them that were under the law. *Galatians 4:4–5*

Paul's ministry to the new believers in Galatia had been fruitful, and many Gentiles were converted to Christ. But after Paul left, these new converts started listening to some other voices who were spreading the doctrine of legalism, claiming that certain acts, like circumcision, were required for salvation.

In this short but strong letter, Paul wrote through the inspiration of the Holy Spirit about the result of legalism—depending on the law for salvation—compared to the fruit of obedience to God's commands. He explained to the believers in Galatia that the law's purpose was to reveal God's holy nature and our need for a savior.

> The law was our schoolmaster to bring us unto Christ, that we might be justified by faith. (3:24)

Paul reminded them that they were utterly incapable of earning salvation by keeping the law. Everyone has fallen short in every aspect of God's righteousness. But where we failed, Jesus triumphed. Jesus kept the law completely by fulfilling it in the tiniest of details (Matt. 5:18; Gal. 4:4–5). Salvation comes not through our adherence to the law but through our obedience to the Father by believing in His Son. As Paul proclaimed,

> By grace are ye saved through faith; and that not of yourselves: it is the gift of God: not of works, lest any man should boast. (Eph. 2:8–9)

If you've placed your faith in Jesus's finished work on the cross, you are a child of the King (Gal. 3:26), adopted into His family (4:6). No longer in bondage to the law, you are free to walk obediently in the Spirit. All praise to Jesus, who fulfilled all the law and the prophets perfectly!

November 20

Fruit of the Spirit

TODAY'S READING: Galatians 4:8–6:18

> This I say then, Walk in the Spirit, and ye shall not fulfil the lust of the flesh. *Galatians 5:16*

Paul's letter to the church in Galatia contains an emphatic reminder of grace that shifts the believers' focus to Jesus and away from the legalism found in the Old Testament law. But this doesn't mean the law is bad; after all, Paul tells us in Romans 7:12 that "the law is holy . . . and just, and good." Its purpose was not to make us perfect but to be a schoolmaster that teaches us about and leads us to our Savior (Gal. 3:24). The law leads us to Jesus because we simply can't keep it, so we eventually cry out, "Lord, save me!"

At that moment we're justified by Jesus. As we've talked about previously, being justified means "just-if-I'd" never sinned. After we're justified, we begin the process of being sanctified—and the whole point of sanctification is to produce the fruit of the Spirit, to make us like Jesus.

> The fruit of the Spirit is love, joy, peace, longsuffering, gentleness, goodness, faith, meekness, temperance: against such there is no law. (5:22–23)

If our appetite is for sin, then we're not feasting on Jesus, the bread of life. If we find ourselves thirsty for worldly entertainment, then we need to drink in the Living Water and let it cleanse our minds. If we are filled with the Spirit, we will hunger and thirst for what Jesus has to offer.

> They that are Christ's have crucified the flesh with the affections and lusts. If we live in the Spirit, let us also walk in the Spirit. (vv. 24–25)

As a Christian, your life belongs to Jesus. He has justified you and is sanctifying you. Hunger after the things of Christ, and let the Spirit produce His fruit in your life.

Let Freedom Ring

TODAY'S READING: Acts 15–16

Why do you test God by putting a yoke on the neck of the disciples which neither our fathers nor we were able to bear?
Acts 15:10, NKJV

As we read in Paul's letter to the Galatians, the traditions and legalism of Judaism were a constant issue in the early church. Many Jews were coming to faith in Christ and bringing along their strong convictions regarding ceremonial laws. As the number of Gentile believers grew, so did the conflict between law and grace.

Here in Acts we find Paul, Barnabas, and Peter standing before a council in Jerusalem and laying forth in detail the foundational understanding of what we now refer to as the Church Age—the time in God's history when He is building His church from every tribe and nation (Matt. 16:18; Rev. 7:9). The church is rooted in the New Covenant that God promised through His prophet Jeremiah and ushered in through the death and resurrection of Jesus (Jer. 31:33–34).

> This is the covenant that I will make with the house of Israel . . . I will put my laws into their mind, and write them in their hearts: and I will be to them a God, and they shall be to me a people: and they shall not teach every man his neighbour, and every man his brother, saying, Know the Lord: for all shall know me, from the least to the greatest. For I will be merciful to their unrighteousness, and their sins and their iniquities will I remember no more. (Heb. 8:10–12)

We are no longer burdened by the weight of sin that was made evident by the law. Through God's mercy we've been saved by the blood of Jesus. His Spirit lives and abides in us, and God has written His Word in our hearts. This is the glorious New Covenant: we are free to know the Lord!

November 22

Be a Berean

TODAY'S READING: Acts 17:1–18:17; 1 Thessalonians 1–2

The brothers sent Paul and Silas away to Berea. *Acts 17:10,* NIV

Here's an interesting and challenging question we should ask ourselves from time to time: *Am I a Berean or a Thessalonian? Do I study the Scriptures to search out truth like the Bereans, or do I treat God's Word with indifference like many of the Thessalonians?*

Paul and Silas encountered both types of Christians as they traveled throughout the Middle East ministering to the church.

> The brethren immediately sent Paul and Silas away by night to Berea. When they arrived, they went into the synagogue of the Jews. These were more fair-minded than those in Thessalonica, in that they received the word with all readiness, and searched the Scriptures daily to find out whether these things were so. (Acts 17:10–11, NKJV)

Knowing, studying, meditating on, and loving God's Word matters! We live in a time when truth is rarely celebrated. Wrong is represented as right, and evil is seen as good. It's crucial that we search the Scriptures as the Bereans did in order to find and know truth. But as we do, we must keep Jesus at the forefront, daily abiding in Him and allowing His words to abide in us.

> I am the vine; you are the branches. Whoever abides in me and I in him, he it is that bears much fruit, for apart from me you can do nothing. . . . If you abide in me, and my words abide in you, ask whatever you wish, and it will be done for you. (John 15:5, 7, ESV)

So keep reading, keep studying, keep being a Berean, daily abiding in Jesus and allowing His Word to abide in you.

Faithful He Was, Faithful He Will Be

November 23

TODAY'S READING: 1 Thessalonians 3–5; 2 Thessalonians 1

Comfort one another with these words. *1 Thessalonians 4:18*

God is faithful. He always keeps His promises! He promised to send His Son, and He did. He promised to save us from our sin, and He did. He promised to rise from the grave, and He did. He promised to come again, and He will!

> The Lord Himself will descend from heaven with a shout, with the voice of an archangel, and with the trumpet of God. And the dead in Christ will rise first. Then we who are alive and remain shall be caught up together with them in the clouds to meet the Lord in the air. And thus we shall always be with the Lord. Therefore comfort one another with these words. (1 Thess. 4:16–18, NKJV)

No matter your circumstances, you have reason to rejoice today: our Redeemer lives. Soon and very soon we will stand in His presence and see Him face to face. What a glorious day that will be. He "will wipe away every tear" (Rev. 21:4, NKJV), and all will be made right. Although Paul emphasized to his beloved brothers and sisters at Thessalonica the necessity of holy living and sanctification, he reminded the church that such discipline and endurance is propelled by the hope of our Savior's return and the glorification of the saints.

> We beseech you, brethren, and exhort you by the Lord Jesus, that as ye have received of us how ye ought to walk and to please God, so ye would abound more and more. (1 Thess. 4:1)

Dear Christian, remember that the Lord Jesus is coming again! Let this be your living hope, your joy and rejoicing, and your encouragement to endure. He was faithful to come as our redeemer. He will be faithful to come as our king.

Stand Fast

TODAY'S READING: 2 Thessalonians 2–3; Acts 18:18–19:41

Therefore, brethren, stand fast. *2 Thessalonians 2:15*

Have you ever heard the command "Stand fast"? It's a military phrase often heard in war movies. Picture a climactic scene with the enemy fast approaching the last line of defense. The commanding officer yells at his men to "stand fast" in order to hold the line and preserve victory.

To "stand fast" means to have a firm, fixed, or settled position. The apostle Paul commands you and me—soldiers of Christ—to "stand fast" no fewer than six times throughout his epistles (1 Cor. 16:13; Gal. 5:1; Phil. 1:27; 4:1; 1 Thess. 3:8; and here in 2 Thess. 2:15). Why would Paul so often use this military term? It's because he knows that you and I, as believers in Christ, are in a battle and that the Lord has called us to be soldiers in His army.

But it's what follows Paul's admonition to stand firm that gives us the strength to endure.

> Now may our Lord Jesus Christ himself, and God our Father, who loved us and gave us eternal comfort and good hope through grace, comfort your hearts and establish them in every good work and word. (vv. 16–17, ESV)

It is Jesus Christ Himself and the love of God that establishes us. It is the grace of God that outfits us, equips us, and prepares us for the battles we face. In 2 Corinthians 10:4 Paul notes that "the weapons of our warfare are not carnal, but mighty through God." Our defense is to clothe ourselves in the armor of God (Eph. 6:13–17) and to be consumed only by the Lord Jesus Christ (Rom. 13:14).

So, dear fellow soldier of Christ, stand fast in God's love and be established in the eternal comfort and good hope of His grace. Put on the Lord Jesus—His ways and His attributes—and stand firm in Him.

A Mess of a Church

November 25

TODAY'S READING: 1 Corinthians 1:1–3:11

Unto the church of God which is at Corinth . . .
1 Corinthians 1:2

Arguably the greatest missionary of all time and the author of no fewer than thirteen of our twenty-seven New Testament books was an ex-Pharisee and a former persecutor of Christians. After the apostle Paul was radically saved (Acts 9), he went on to establish dozens of churches, mending, defending, and tending to that which he once tried to destroy.

The church at Corinth particularly needed lots of mending and tending. The members of this church were teaching false doctrine on baptism (1 Cor. 1:10–17), were arrogant regarding their ignorance (vv. 18–31), were as worldly as could be (3:1), were willfully deceived (v. 18), had embraced immorality (v. 17), were full of pride (4:18), were suing one another in court (6:1), were misguided regarding marriage (7:1), were confused about liberty and grace (8:9), were immodest (11:6), failed to esteem the Lord's table (vv. 28–30), were misusing the gifts of the Holy Spirit (14:1–40), were confused when it came to the Resurrection (15:1–58), and had become selfish and neglectful of their tithing (16:1–24).

In short, it was a mess of a church! But a closer look at the first verses of Paul's letter reveals the longsuffering of our Lord.

> Unto the church of God which is at Corinth, to them that are sanctified in Christ Jesus, called to be saints . . . (1:2)

Jesus has clothed His church in His righteousness. He loves His people—they are His bride (2 Cor. 11:2; Eph. 5:27; Rev. 19:7). He is in the midst of His church (Matt. 18:20; Rev. 1:13), and regardless of the Corinthians' situation, they were still being sanctified through Christ and called to be saints.

Regardless of past or current failings, Jesus saves and sanctifies His people. We're still clothed in His righteousness and called to be saints. Amen and praise the Lord for that!

November 26

All for His Glory

TODAY'S READING: 1 Corinthians 3:12–6:20

> The wisdom of this world is foolishness with God.
> *1 Corinthians 3:19*

What a mystery that God chooses to use humans to bring Him glory. God fashioned us in His image, giving each of us abilities, talents, wisdom, skills, and knowledge—all to be used for His glory. Yet in our own human tendencies and propensities, we so easily forget that these abilities came from the Lord. We often start to think we're pretty . . . well . . . great. Nothing could be further from the truth!

> The wisdom of this world is foolishness with God. . . . The Lord knoweth the thoughts of the wise, that they are vain. Therefore let no man glory in men. (1 Cor. 3:19–21)

God does not need us. By His mercy and grace alone He chooses to work through us. Jesus reminded us of this very thing when He said,

> I am the vine; you are the branches. Whoever abides in me and I in him, he it is that bears much fruit, for apart from me you can do nothing. (John 15:5, ESV)

We are Jesus's workmanship, being used by Him to bring Him glory (Eph. 2:10). And Jesus uses "the foolish things of the world to confound the wise" (1 Cor. 1:27).

God used a little lamb to picture Jesus's atoning blood (Exod. 12). He used a rock struck by Moses to picture Jesus, the living water (Exod. 17). He used David, a small shepherd boy, to picture Jesus, our good shepherd (1 Sam. 17). And He used Paul, who persecuted His church (Acts 8:3), to shepherd His flock.

Whether you are foolish, weak, simple, or polluted—as we all are in one way or another—Jesus desires to use you to point others to Him, all for His glory!

One Big Picture Book

TODAY'S READING: 1 Corinthians 7–10

All these things happened unto them for examples.
1 Corinthians 10:11

As we've seen, Jesus is the very essence of the Scriptures. The Old Testament points to Him, and the New Testament reveals Him. Today's reading contains possibly the single best verse for understanding how to read the entire Old Testament. In fact, it inspired the idea for this book.

> All these things happened unto them for examples: and they are written for our admonition, upon whom the ends of the world are come. (1 Cor. 10:11)

This is our key to understanding the Old Testament. It was given for our encouragement, as an example of God's attributes and love for His people. Many other verses make it unmistakably clear that the Old Testament is one big picture book centered singularly on Jesus Christ as revealed in the New Testament.

> We have found him, of whom Moses in the law, and the prophets, did write, Jesus of Nazareth. (John 1:45)

> You search the Scriptures because you think that in them you have eternal life; it is these that testify about Me. (5:39, NASB)

> Beginning at Moses and all the prophets, he expounded unto them in all the scriptures the things concerning himself. (Luke 24:27)

> Then said I, Lo, I come (in the volume of the book it is written of me). (Heb. 10:7)

Beyond debate and dispute, all Scripture points to and speaks of Jesus the Christ, our savior and redeemer. To Him be all the praise and honor and glory!

November 28 — Unity for His Glory

TODAY'S READING: 1 Corinthians 11–13

> Now are they many members, yet but one body. *1 Corinthians 12:20*

Throughout the book of 1 Corinthians, Paul teaches that believers are the body of Christ and, as such, we need to function as a healthy body, in unity (12:12–13). In fact, in John 17 Jesus prayed for unity among believers.

> I do not pray for these alone, but also for those who will believe in Me through their word; that they all may be one, as You, Father, are in Me, and I in You; that they also may be one in Us, that the world may believe that You sent Me. (vv. 20–21, NKJV)

As a good Father, God cares about His family; therefore, He cares about unity (1 Cor. 12:25). But unity is not intended to be simply for the sake of community. Rather, unity in the body of Christ is to be for Christ's glory!

Please don't get me wrong. I'm not suggesting that living in community is in any way a bad thing. After all, that's what the body of Christ did at its very beginning in the book of Acts (2:42–47). What I am saying is that the unity Christ desires is so much more than our having fellowship and fun and friends to laugh with and lean on. All those things are good. But if unity stops with living in community with the body, we're missing what Jesus really prayed for: unity for Christ's sake as His people stand together on His Word, in His truth, showing forth His love, so the "world may believe" that God sent His Son (John 17:21). That's what unity is all about: that the world may believe and be saved as we bear one another's burdens, not for our ease but for His glory!

> . . . that ye may with one mind and one mouth glorify God, even the Father of our Lord Jesus Christ. (Rom. 15:6)

A Timely Reminder

TODAY'S READING: 1 Corinthians 14:1–15:34

I want to remind you . . . *1 Corinthians 15:1,* NIV

Can you think of a time when you received the kind of good news that made you giddy? What joy! What excitement! But like most things in this world, even the giddiness of good news is fleeting. As those fantastic feelings dull, we require something new to keep us engaged. The apostle Paul knew that, so he reminded us about the greatness of Jesus's message—the gospel we've received!

> I want to remind you of the gospel I preached to you, which you received and on which you have taken your stand. By this gospel you are saved. (1 Cor. 15:1–2, NIV)

Do you remember that great day when you received the gospel and Jesus Christ saved you and brought you to new life? As Christians, we need to be reminded of the good news of Jesus. Otherwise, there's a distinct possibility we will forget just how amazing our salvation is and that the wonder of first receiving new life will fade. The real threat is that as time goes by and that fading takes place, compromise can take root.

Just as the apostle Paul reminded the Corinthian church of their foundation—Jesus—so, too, should we be reminded of Christ and all He has done for us.

You Can Do It!

TODAY'S READING: 1 Corinthians 15:35–16:24; Acts 20:1–6; 2 Corinthians 1:1–2:4

> My dear brothers, stand firm. Let nothing move you.
> *1 Corinthians 15:58,* NIV

When my kids ran cross-country, my husband and I would run across the route, zigzagging back and forth to position ourselves at the most challenging sections of the race so we could cheer our little runners on as they huffed and puffed up those exhausting hills. That, my friend, is precisely what the apostle Paul aimed to do for us in today's reading. He's cheering us on as we run the race of faith!

More specifically, Paul encourages us to stand firm, reminding us of our future hope and admonishing us to abound in the work of the Lord.

And just like in those cross-country races my kids ran, Paul reminds us that we will one day cross the finish line.

> But thanks be to God, which giveth us the victory through our Lord Jesus Christ. (1 Cor. 15:57)

So permit me to cheer you on today, dear friend. You have all the hope in the world because Jesus has overcome the world (John 16:33)! You are more than a conqueror through Him who loved you and gave Himself for you (Rom. 8:37). These are the truths that we need to hear—the cheers, if you will—that fill our hearts and minds and encourage us to keep running each and every day for His glory.

> My beloved brethren, be ye steadfast, unmovable, always abounding in the work of the Lord, forasmuch as ye know that your labour is not in vain in the Lord. (1 Cor. 15:58)

Run your race with renewed faith today, my friend. God is for you and working all things out for your good (Rom. 8:28). His strength is made perfect in your weakness. So give all things to Him, and race for the prize He has for you (1 Cor. 9:24).

Don't Lose Heart

TODAY'S READING: 2 Corinthians 2:5–6:18

We do not lose heart. *2 Corinthians 4:16,* NKJV

We may not be able to see today how God intends to fulfill His promises and prophecies, but we can be certain He will. As we've so clearly seen through almost an entire year of reading the Bible, He is faithful to every word He has spoken. He promised to come and redeem us from our sin, and He did. He promises to return and take us to heaven, and He will. Soon and very soon we'll be going to see our King!

> Therefore we do not lose heart. Even though our outward man is perishing, yet the inward man is being renewed day by day. (2 Cor. 4:16, NKJV)

No matter the situation you're in or the temptation you're facing, our redeemer, Jesus, lives. Soon we will stand before Him and see Him face to face. The message of 2 Corinthians 4 is a challenge to persevere and continue living for Jesus. We can do so, despite whatever challenges we face, because "our light affliction, which is but for a moment, worketh for us a far more exceeding and eternal weight of glory" (v. 17).

One day Jesus "will wipe away every tear from [our] eyes" (Rev. 21:4, NKJV) and all will be made right. Until then, remember that the Bible says our afflictions are temporary. So let's continue to stay in His Word, which helps us maintain an eternal perspective.

> The things which are seen are temporal; but the things which are not seen are eternal. (2 Cor. 4:18)

A New Heart

TODAY'S READING: 2 Corinthians 7:1–11:15

> Having these promises, beloved, let us cleanse ourselves from all filthiness of the flesh and spirit, perfecting holiness in the fear of God. *2 Corinthians 7:1,* NKJV

Simply trying to be good is not enough to bring us near to God (Jer. 2:22). Jesus focused on this as He rebuked the Pharisees for washing their hands yet leaving their hearts filthy.

> Even so ye also outwardly appear righteous unto men, but within ye are full of hypocrisy and iniquity. (Matt. 23:28)

Paul echoed this truth, explaining to the Corinthian church the difference between obedience to external rules and the behavior that flows from a transformed heart.

> Now I rejoice, not that you were made sorry, but that your sorrow led to repentance. . . . For godly sorrow produces repentance leading to salvation. (2 Cor. 7:9–10, NKJV)

Our hearts need Jesus and the transformation that only He can bring. Only after we've been born again (John 3:6–7) can we experience a change of heart that brings about holy living. This is accomplished as our reborn hearts are cleansed by washing in the water of the Word of God and as the indwelling Holy Spirit gives us power over sin.

> If anyone is in Christ, he is a new creation; old things have passed away; behold, all things have become new. (2 Cor. 5:17, NKJV)

If you've declared Jesus as your lord and savior, if you've been born again and made new, then you have been cleansed from all unrighteousness and are being transformed into His image. Praise the Lord for a new heart that brings a new way of life!

The Glorious Book of Romans

TODAY'S READING: 2 Corinthians 11:16–13:14; Romans 1

I am not ashamed of the gospel of Christ: for it is the power of God unto salvation to every one that believeth. *Romans 1:16*

Romans is the perfect book to read during the Christmas season. It underscores the truth that the little babe born in a manger came to bring us joy and justification. This book changed the perspective of Martin Luther and brought about the Protestant Reformation. In his preface to Romans, he wrote,

> This letter . . . is purest Gospel. It is well worth a Christian's while not only to memorize it word for word but also to occupy himself with it daily, as though it were the daily bread of the soul. It is impossible to read or to meditate on this letter too much or too well. The more one deals with it, the more precious it becomes and the better it tastes.[82]

Romans can be divided into seven parts:

1. The entire world is guilty of sin.
2. The remedy is justification through faith in Christ.
3. The Christian life means dying to sin and experiencing new life.
4. The gospel brings the blessings.
5. God's covenant promises to Israel remain because God keeps His promises.
6. The Christian is called to a life of service to the Lord.
7. The world will know we are Christians by our love.

Ready your heart to be reminded of the remarkable, incomprehensible gift of salvation as we consider what that babe in a manger came to do.

December 4

Paid in Full

TODAY'S READING: Romans 2–4

> . . . being justified freely by his grace through the redemption that is in Christ Jesus. *Romans 3:24*

Can you imagine your excitement if you found out that someone had paid off all your debt, no matter the size? Anything you owed, of any sort to anyone, was covered. What a gigantic, grand gift that would be, wouldn't it?

Friend, that is exactly what Jesus did for us! We owed an insurmountable debt as a result of our sin, and He took care of it all.

> All have sinned, and come short of the glory of God. (Rom. 3:23)

We serve an awesome God who not only paid our debt and cleared our account of unrighteousness but actually added to our account and gave us a surplus of benefits.

> He that spared not his own Son, but delivered him up for us all, how shall he not with him also freely give us all things? (8:32)

The gift of our salvation cost Him everything. Yet to receive it, all we have to do is accept His free gift of love.

> . . . being justified freely by his grace through the redemption that is in Christ Jesus. (3:24)

Through Christ we are forgiven of our sins—our debt has been paid (Col. 1:14). The demands of justice were met, the debt satisfied, and our guilt removed (Ps. 103:12; Col. 2:14; Heb. 10:14).

We have so very much to thank God for, and it starts with salvation. Because of Jesus, God's riches are poured out on us.

You're Free!

TODAY'S READING: Romans 5:1–8:17

> Having been set free from sin, and having become slaves of God, you have your fruit to holiness, and the end, everlasting life. *Romans 6:22,* NKJV

The Bible tells us that without Jesus we are slaves to sin (Rom. 6:20). But with Jesus the bondage of sin is broken, and by His grace we are freed from the chains of guilt (8:1).

> There is therefore now no condemnation to those who are in Christ Jesus, who do not walk according to the flesh, but according to the Spirit. For the law of the Spirit of life in Christ Jesus has made me free from the law of sin and death. (vv. 1–2, NKJV)

How wonderful to know that not only are we forgiven, freed, and refreshed but that the same grace is offered to the people all around us. Whether or not the rest of our family has been set free from slavery to sin, the realization that the grace of God is freely offered to them will most assuredly affect how we pray for and interact with them.

> If children, then heirs; heirs of God, and joint-heirs with Christ; if so be that we suffer with him, that we may be also glorified together. (v. 17)

You are a child of the King who shares an inheritance with Christ. Walk today in graciousness, in forgiveness, in kindness, recognizing that those who don't know Jesus are slaves to sin and He wants to set them free, just as He did you and me. Jesus is a gift worth sharing. This is a truth to hold close, especially during the Christmas season.

December 6

All Means All

TODAY'S READING: Romans 8:18–11:10

> The sufferings of this present time are not worthy to be compared with the glory which shall be revealed in us.
> *Romans 8:18*

Today's reading is full of promises, encouragement, good news, and exhortation—the sort of stuff that sets our perspective straight and leads us to sound biblical reasoning. Let's look at just a few of Paul's important reminders:

- *All* things are working together for our good. "All things work together for good to them that love God, to them who are the called according to his purpose" (Rom. 8:28).
- We have forgiveness of *all* sin. "With the heart man believeth unto righteousness; and with the mouth confession is made unto salvation" (10:10).
- He has given us *all* we need. "He that spared not his own Son, but delivered him up for us all, how shall he not with him also freely give us all things?" (8:32).
- In *all* things we are more than conquerors. "Who shall separate us from the love of Christ? . . . Yet in all these things we are more than conquerors through Him who loved us" (vv. 35, 37, NKJV).

Jesus gave all of Himself for you and me. Nothing can separate us from all His love (v. 39). May this be our perspective today and all our days: your life, my life, our lives should be all about Jesus since all our blessings, all our forgiveness, all our provision, and all our hope are all because of Him.

You Are What You Eat

TODAY'S READING: Romans 11:11–14:23

> Put ye on the Lord Jesus Christ, and make not provision for the flesh, to fulfil the lusts thereof. *Romans 13:14*

Don't be fooled by the folly of this fallen world. God has a better and higher plan for us. Paul tells us to "put . . . on the Lord Jesus Christ" (Rom. 13:14). This phrase means to "put on," like you would clothing.[83] Jesus used a similar phrase when He told us to "abide," or to live, in Him and to allow His Word to live in us (John 15:7).

We accomplish this by feasting on the Bread of Life and drinking from the Living Water. Jesus satisfies our souls and anchors our perspectives as He shows us a better way!

> Be not conformed to this world: but be ye transformed by the renewing of your mind, that ye may prove what is that good, and acceptable, and perfect, will of God. (Rom. 12:2)

In Jesus Christ you and I have the perfect model for how we should act, think, and speak. The question is often asked, "What would Jesus do?" Perhaps we should be asking, "What did Jesus do?" Because God inspired men to write an account of what He did while here on earth, we can look at His life, we can hear His heart, we can study His sermons, and we can marvel at His miracles. We don't have to wonder what He would do; we can see what He actually did do.

> The night is far spent, the day is at hand: let us therefore cast off the works of darkness, and let us put on the armour of light. (13:12)

Let's determine that we, as Jesus followers, would be clothed in Him today and shine forth His glorious praise.

December 8 Planned from the Beginning

TODAY'S READING: Romans 15–16; Acts 20:7–38

Rejoice, O Gentiles, with his people. *Romans 15:10,* ESV

In today's reading Paul points out how God promised from the very beginning to extend His grace to not only the Jews but also the Gentiles. This wasn't an afterthought. It was His purpose and plan from the foundation of the world (Deut. 32:43; 2 Sam. 22:50; Ps. 18:49; 117:1; Isa. 11:10; 52:15; Rom. 15:8–12). This gives me great hope! Seeing God's plans unfolded and revealed through the Scriptures should remind us that His plans are not haphazard but carefully orchestrated.

Throughout the Old Testament we find hundreds of promises regarding a coming redeemer who would restore our fellowship with God. From generation to generation Israel looked forward to the promised messiah. In today's reading the apostle Paul points out yet another level of prophecy and promise fulfilled: God's faithfulness to all humankind.

> Jesus Christ has become a servant to the circumcision for the truth of God, to confirm the promises made . . . that the Gentiles might glorify God for His mercy, as it is written: "For this reason I will confess to You among the Gentiles, and sing to Your name." (Rom. 15:8–9, NKJV)

God's gift of salvation was meant for everyone, not just Israel. He's "not willing that any should perish, but that all should come to repentance" (2 Pet. 3:9). Through Jesus, God made a way for every single one of us to have fellowship with Him. He's extended forgiveness to everyone who will accept it. Receiving that forgiveness opens the floodgates to fellowship with our Lord. Let's enjoy the fellowship He has brought and dig into His Word today!

He Prepares Us

TODAY'S READING: Acts 21–22

The will of the Lord be done. *Acts 21:14*

Today we find Paul bidding farewell to dear friends and submitting to the guidance of the Spirit despite the danger ahead as he sets sail for Jerusalem. Along the way Paul stopped in several cities where, through the gifts of the Holy Spirit, the believers repeatedly prophesied that dire things would befall him in Jerusalem (Acts 20:23). Paul's friends, out of a deep love and concern for him, attempted to convince the apostle not to continue on. But Paul, convinced that God wanted him to go, was ready to face whatever the future held.

> Paul answered, "What do you mean by weeping and breaking my heart? For I am ready not only to be bound, but also to die at Jerusalem for the name of the Lord Jesus." (21:13, NKJV)

Knowing how loved Paul was and what impact his death would have on the church, the Lord, in His mercy, had prepared His people for the loss. What a gracious God we serve! Because of this gift of foresight, both Paul and his friends would later be able to look back and know that God was in control. Instead of struggling with confusion and questions, they would be built up by the assurance that God knew this would happen all along and had a purpose in it.

This reminds me of Jesus's words to His disciples. Knowing His death was approaching, He prepared His disciples for what was to come (John 13:21–38). And that continues to be the ministry of His Spirit: preparing our hearts for what lies ahead (16:13).

As God writes His Word on your heart and guides your steps, remember you are not following a whim into the great unknown! You are trusting the Good Shepherd, who is preparing a place for you, and you can walk steadily forward in faith, ready to face whatever God's sovereign plan may hold.

December 10

Be of Good Cheer

TODAY'S READING: Acts 23:1–25:22

The Lord stood by him, and said, Be of good cheer. *Acts 23:11*

Paul had been arrested, chained up, falsely accused, and interrogated. This would be cause for discouragement for me, for sure! But Paul seized the opportunity and continued to preach the gospel. Despite the injustices he faced, Paul knew that God was using the situation for good and for His glory and that He had a purpose in it all.

> The following night the Lord stood by him and said, "Be of good cheer, Paul; for as you have testified for Me in Jerusalem, so you must also bear witness at Rome." (Acts 23:11, NKJV)

Jesus appeared to Paul in his time of difficulty and encouraged him by saying, in essence, "Don't lose heart, Paul. I have a plan." In tomorrow's reading we'll see that Paul listened to Jesus's encouragement to "be of good cheer," remembered it, and soon shared it with others around him.

Just as Paul was the Lord's servant, so are you and I. As we walk with our Lord, He will meet us in times of adversity. And He has given us words to share with those around us; we just have to read and heed them.

No matter the situation, no matter the injustice, God's plans are steadfast. He is good and is faithful to accomplish His perfect will and to speak words of encouragement that we can share with others. So be of good cheer, my friend, and spread some cheer to those who need a reminder of Jesus's love and care.

Redeeming the Situation

December 11

TODAY'S READING: Acts 25:23–28:10

Having therefore obtained help of God, I continue unto this day, witnessing both to small and great. *Acts 26:22*

Paul knew a thing or two about hard circumstances. His legal fiasco began in Jerusalem but eventually ended in Rome. Along the way he endured conspiracies, accusations and interrogations, shipwreck, and imprisonment. A tremendous benefit of reading the Bible in chronological order is that we gain insight into Paul's thoughts on all this as we read the letters he wrote while in prison: Ephesians, Philippians, Colossians, and Philemon.

Paul tells us why he was willing to undergo such difficulties.

> I count all things to be loss in view of the surpassing value of knowing Christ Jesus my Lord, for whom I have suffered the loss of all things, and count them but rubbish so that I may gain Christ. (Phil. 3:8, NASB)

Paul's entire aim was to live for Christ, regardless of the cost (2 Tim. 2:4; 2 Cor. 5:9). Through his ups and downs, Paul sought to lead others to Jesus. He preached the gospel, shared his testimony (Acts 26), saved lives in the midst of a storm (27:42–44), took the gospel to the island of Malta (28:1–31), was an example of Christ's power (vv. 5–6), prayed for the sick (vv. 8–9), and shared the good news with the soldiers he was chained to (Phil. 4:22).

God used Paul's circumstances to ensure that lives changed, people were healed, and the gospel was spread.

Whatever situation you find yourself in today, remember this encouragement:

> My brethren, count it all joy when you fall into various trials. (James 1:2, NKJV)

Like Paul, you can redeem each situation for the glory of Christ. Your life can be a testimony to His great power.

December 12

Ransomed

TODAY'S READING: Acts 28:11–31; Ephesians 1–3

> . . . in whom we have redemption through his blood, the forgiveness of sins, according to the riches of his grace.
> *Ephesians 1:7*

The word *redeemed* means "to be released . . . by payment of a ransom."[84] As believers in Jesus Christ, we have been redeemed from the penalty of sin, bought with "the precious blood of Christ" (1 Pet. 1:19; Col. 1:14).

This redemption was promised throughout the Old Testament.

> I will ransom them from the power of the grave; I will redeem them from death: O death, I will be thy plagues; O grave, I will be thy destruction. (Hosea 13:14)

The Christmas season brings constant reminders of that precious babe in the manger. But let's be mindful of what that baby came to do: He came to die for you and me! Jesus Christ was the long-promised redeemer. He perfectly fulfilled God's promise through His death and resurrection. He paid the ultimate price, and, as a result, we were released upon the payment of His blood, were forgiven by His grace, were justified by His righteousness, and are being sanctified through His Spirit and Word.

> Blessed be the Lord God of Israel; for he hath visited and redeemed his people. (Luke 1:68)

Let's not neglect His Word during this busy holiday season. Let's dig in, feast on the Bread of Life, drink from the Living Water, and be transformed by the renewing of our minds. Thanks be to Jesus, who paid our ransom!

Imitators of Christ

December 13

TODAY'S READING: Ephesians 4–6

> Be ye therefore followers of God, as dear children; and walk in love, as Christ also hath loved us, and hath given himself for us. *Ephesians 5:1–2*

Today's Bible reading encourages us to leave the world far behind and look forward to the great things God has in store for us as we walk with Him and in His ways. When we allow God to have His way in our lives and we obey the things the Spirit calls us to do, we find ourselves withdrawing from the world and the things that once gave us pleasure. Our appetites change, and we find ourselves desiring the things of God and fellowship with Him. The Bible tells us that if we draw close to Him, He will draw close to us (James 4:8). This is all part of that vital process of sanctification.

To be sanctified is to be set apart for God's purposes. God Almighty has plans for us, but sin keeps us from those plans and pollutes the joy we can experience in Him. God's Word tells us to keep our eyes fixed on Jesus and imitate the way He walked in love (Heb. 12:2; Eph. 5:1–2).

> Christ also loved the church, and gave himself for it; that he might sanctify and cleanse it with the washing of water by the word. (vv. 25–26)

This is how Jesus loved us: He gave Himself for us. Our aim should be to give our lives in sharing His love with others.

As you read about the Christ you celebrate at Christmas, as you fellowship with Him, as you read His Word looking for Jesus, may you be transformed into His image, showing His love to the world around you.

December 14

The Greatest Christmas Gift

TODAY'S READING: Colossians 1–4

. . . having forgiven you all trespasses. *Colossians 2:13*

In the midst of the hectic holiday season, I challenge you to stop and consider afresh the miracle of forgiveness, the greatest Christmas gift ever given. All our sins, faults, and imperfections have been forgiven and separated from us as far as the east is from the west, thrown to the deepest depths of the sea. That reality should cause the most distracted of hearts to hush in adoration.

> If You, LORD, should mark iniquities, O Lord, who could stand? But there is forgiveness with You, that You may be feared. . . . And He shall redeem Israel from all his iniquities. (Ps. 130:3–4, 8, NKJV)

> You, being dead in your sins and the uncircumcision of your flesh, hath he quickened together with him, having forgiven you all trespasses; blotting out the handwriting of ordinances that was against us, which was contrary to us, and took it out of the way, nailing it to his cross. (Col. 2:13–14)

We have been miraculously and completely redeemed! The blood of Jesus Christ has purchased our freedom, releasing us from slavery to sin (1 Pet. 1:18–19). We have been forgiven (Col. 2:13), justified, and declared innocent (Rom. 3:24). God has washed us white as snow (1 Cor. 6:11). He has given us new life (2 Cor. 5:17). He has given us eternal life (Titus 3:7). He has given us His Spirit, and He dwells within us (1 John 4:13). He has replaced our sadness with joy and filled our heavy hearts with praise (Isa. 61:3). He has given us all we need to live life in Him (2 Pet. 1:3).

May the song of our hearts be "O come, let us adore Him" as we hear Jesus say to you and me, "Friend, your sins are forgiven" (Luke 5:20, NIV).

His Good Work in You

December 15

TODAY'S READING: Philemon 1:1–25; Philippians 1:1–2:30

> He which hath begun a good work in you will perform it until the day of Jesus Christ. *Philippians 1:6*

This might be one of the most encouraging verses in the entire Bible! It promises you and me that Jesus Christ, personally, will never give up on us. You might be thinking, *But don't we see that same promise in several places throughout the Bible?* Yes, we sure do! Genesis 28:15, Deuteronomy 31:6, Joshua 1:5, and Hebrews 13:5 are just a few. But here in Philippians 1:6 we hear our brother the apostle Paul beautifully and succinctly summarize our Christian walk. I find this verse incredibly encouraging in view of what "good work" means, according to John 6:29:

> This is the work of God, that ye believe on him whom he hath sent.

The "good work" is our *salvation* through faith in Jesus Christ. That precious prayer of salvation was just the beginning! The Bible speaks of our salvation as a process taking us from justification through sanctification and culminating someday in glorification. Justification is being set free from the penalty of sin, which happened the moment we believed in Him. Sanctification is His Spirit giving us power over sin, which continues to happen until we're with Him. And glorification is being delivered from the presence of sin, which will happen the moment we see Him.

> When he shall appear, we shall be like him. (1 John 3:2)

Justification, sanctification, and glorification are all part of God's good work of salvation. And this is precisely what the apostle Paul so beautifully described through the powerful promise that "He which hath begun a good work in you will perform it until the day of Jesus Christ" (Phil. 1:6).

December 16

Take All of Me

TODAY'S READING: Philippians 3–4; 1 Timothy 1–2

The peace of God, which passeth all understanding, shall keep your hearts and minds through Christ Jesus. *Philippians 4:7*

As Paul sat in a Roman prison, falsely accused and wrongly imprisoned, he wrote this little letter to the Philippians, encouraging them to let their lives be consumed by Jesus and to not be overcome by their present problems. Jesus wants all of us, our entire being—heart, soul, and mind. Paul not only knew this but had also lived it.

What things were gain to me, those I counted loss for Christ. (3:7)

As you read Paul's letter, may you, too, be pressed to invite Jesus to take over every aspect of your life.

- Let Jesus rule your emotions. "Rejoice in the Lord always: and again I say, Rejoice" (4:4).
- Let Jesus consume your thoughts. "Whatsoever things are true, whatsoever things are honest, whatsoever things are just, whatsoever things are pure, whatsoever things are lovely, whatsoever things are of good report; if there be any virtue, and if there be any praise, think on these things" (4:8).
- Let Jesus set your goals and ambitions. "I press toward the mark for the prize of the high calling of God in Christ Jesus" (3:14).
- Let Jesus be your conversation. "Our conversation is in heaven; from whence also we look for the Saviour, the Lord Jesus Christ" (3:20).

Let Jesus take all of you!

Good Advice

TODAY'S READING: 1 Timothy 3–6

> Watch your life and doctrine closely . . . because if you do, you will save both yourself and your hearers. *1 Timothy 4:16,* NIV

Timothy, a convert of the apostle Paul, was pastoring the local church in Ephesus. As a young pastor shepherding a new church, he likely faced a lot of questions. But God, through the apostle Paul, equipped Timothy with the answers and practical advice he needed.

In contrast to Paul's letter to the church in Corinth, which dealt with what should not be in the church (adultery, fornication, immodesty, gossip), Paul's first letter to Timothy affirmed those things that should abound in the church.

> Be an example to the believers in word, in conduct, in love, in spirit, in faith, in purity. (4:12, NKJV)

Think back with me to our readings in Exodus and Leviticus, and remember how God gave Israel specific instructions on how to build His sanctuary. Every detail was described precisely, measured out, and orchestrated by the Lord. Every detail was important because every detail pointed to Jesus, foreshadowing Him as a picture of redemption. That same God of specificity gave His people instructions on how His church was to be built and organized in and through its pastors, teachers, and overseers.

Had the Israelites taken liberties with the design, God's intended picture of Jesus would have been distorted. As New Testament believers, God is using us to point others to His Son. We are to follow His example and reflect Him to the world (Eph. 5:1–2).

Our call is to heed God's detailed, specific instructions on the qualifications of a pastor (1 Tim. 4:12) and other overseers (3:1–13), realizing they are not standards implemented by mere mortals but our Lord's divine design for how He desires His church to be built—all pointing to Jesus.

O Come, Let Us Adore Him

TODAY'S READING: Titus 1–3; 1 Peter 1

> Ye know that ye were not redeemed with corruptible things, as silver and gold. *1 Peter 1:18*

As we enjoy our Christmas celebrations, let's take time to again consider our redemption and how it began with Christ's birth. Almighty God, the maker of heaven and earth, humbled Himself by becoming a man. He was born in a lowly manger. He lived a simple life, serving those He came to die for. Had He not been willing to take our infirmities and bear our iniquities, we would not have been redeemed and couldn't be saved from our sins. Christmas is certainly a time to say "Thank You, Jesus" and, with humbled hearts, "Happy Birthday, Savior."

Before we were saved, we were in a spiritual state of debt. Our salvation started with God buying us back—redeeming us—with the proper payment for our sin (1 Pet. 1:18–19).

This redemptive reality was foreshadowed years and years ago in the book of beginnings. In Genesis 22:8, where Father Abraham is about to sacrifice his son Isaac, we read,

> Abraham said, My son, God will provide himself a lamb.

Amazing! God did provide a lamb. Jesus Himself was the lamb, perfect and without spot or blemish as He lived a sinless life but willingly offered Himself for our sins—the perfect sacrifice. It's because He paid the price to buy us back from sin that you and I have been born again.

> Being born again, not of corruptible seed, but of incorruptible, by the word of God, which liveth and abideth for ever . . . (1 Pet. 1:23)

As the old hymn so rightly proclaims,

> Jesus paid it all,
> All to Him I owe;
> Sin had left a crimson stain,
> He washed it white as snow.[85]

The Perfect Time to Rejoice

December 19

TODAY'S READING: 1 Peter 2–5; Jude 1

Rejoice, . . . be glad also with exceeding joy. *1 Peter 4:13*

The holidays can be a tough time for many, but if you are hurting this holiday season, I encourage you to focus on eternity—and what Christ did to secure it for us. We have abundant reason to rejoice, to literally "joy again" or "re-joy." No matter your circumstances, you can celebrate because Jesus came to die that you and I might live.

> . . . who his own self bare our sins in his own body on the tree, that we, being dead to sins, should live unto righteousness: by whose stripes ye were healed. For ye were as sheep going astray; but are now returned unto the Shepherd and Bishop of your souls. (1 Pet. 2:24–25)

Consider all these truths this Christmas season:

- Jesus Christ willingly became a man and took our filthy rags upon Himself (1 Pet. 2:24).
- He robed us in His righteousness (Isa. 61:10).
- He gave us a crown of "beauty for ashes, the oil of joy for mourning"; He replaced our despair with praise (v. 3).
- He brought our dead spirits to life (Rom. 8:10).
- He's given us heaven; without Him we were headed for hell (John 14:2–3).

These are truly reasons to "joy again" in Jesus Christ! So rejoice, dear Christian, and be full of hope. You are returned to the shepherd of your soul, Jesus.

> You are a chosen generation, a royal priesthood, a holy nation, His own special people, that you may proclaim the praises of Him who called you out of darkness into His marvelous light. (1 Pet. 2:9, NKJV)

December 20

Patient Promise

TODAY'S READING: 2 Peter 1–3; 2 Timothy 1

> The Lord is not slack concerning His promise . . . but is longsuffering toward us, not willing that any should perish but that all should come to repentance. *2 Peter 3:9,* NKJV

God's patience is one of His most encouraging and amazing attributes. For a clear example, we need look no further than Peter himself. Remember, Peter denied Jesus three times, just as the Savior had predicted. But then our Lord beautifully restored Peter as He commissioned him to shepherd His sheep (John 21:15–17).

How interesting and appropriate that a man who personally experienced the Lord's longsuffering would be inspired by His Spirit to pen these encouraging words about God patiently waiting for that long-lost sinner to come home, "not willing that any should perish, but that all should come to repentance" (2 Pet. 3:9). Peter reminded the believers of God's longsuffering love and admonished them not to listen to the scoffers who mocked their belief in the Lord's second coming. Peter reminded them, and in so doing reminded us, that the Lord is indeed coming again.

> Wherefore, beloved, seeing that ye look for such things, be diligent that ye may be found of him in peace, without spot, and blameless. (v. 14)

God promised to send a redeemer, and in His time He did (John 3:16). Jesus promised that the world would grow dark in the last days, and it has. But He also promised to come again, and in His time He will.

> We, according to his promise, look for new heavens and a new earth, wherein dwelleth righteousness. (2 Pet. 3:13)

This Christmas season, like those wise men of old, look for His promise! God is longsuffering, but in His perfect time He will come again.

Last Words for the Last Days

December 21

TODAY'S READING: 2 Timothy 2–4

> . . . that the man of God may be perfect, thoroughly furnished unto all good works. *2 Timothy 3:17*

As Paul wrote this second letter to Timothy, his son in the faith, the apostle was in prison, awaiting his death sentence. In his final words Paul told Timothy to watch and be ready for the last days (3:1–13) when men will be self-lovers, money lovers, boastful, proud, blasphemers, disobedient to parents, unthankful, profane, unloving, promise breakers, false accusers, without self-control, savage, despisers of good, betrayers, reckless, high minded, lovers of pleasure, religious without knowing Christ, knowledgeable without wisdom, sorcerers, deceivers, and deceived.

What a dismal situation! Yet I think you'll agree that Paul's description of the last days aptly captures the world in which you and I are living. I am thankful that Paul did not simply itemize the problems but specifically gave Timothy the remedy: Jesus!

> Continue in the things that you have learned . . . the sacred writings (Hebrew Scriptures) which are able to give you the wisdom that leads to salvation through faith which is in Christ Jesus [surrendering your entire self to Him and having absolute confidence in His wisdom, power and goodness]. All Scripture is God-breathed [given by divine inspiration] and is profitable for instruction, for conviction [of sin], for correction [of error and restoration to obedience], for training in righteousness [learning to live in conformity to God's will, both publicly and privately—behaving honorably with personal integrity and moral courage]; so that the man of God may be complete and proficient, outfitted and thoroughly equipped for every good work. (vv. 14–17, AMP)

Jesus is the cure the world so desperately needs. So keep reading His Word, keep obeying what He says, and keep sharing His truth with the world around you.

December 22

A Better Way

TODAY'S READING: Hebrews 1–5

We see Jesus . . . crowned with glory and honour. *Hebrews 2:9*

The focus throughout the treasure trove of the book of Hebrews can be summed up with one word: *better.* Throughout Hebrews we'll see a sharp contrast between the rules and regulations of the Old Testament and the better way through Jesus Christ. Consider these truths:

- Jesus is better than the law because He fulfilled the law (Matt. 5:17).
- Jesus is better than Moses. Moses gave the law, but Jesus freed us from the law (Heb. 10:1).
- Jesus is better than Joshua and Aaron. They led the Israelites into the Promised Land and conquered their Canaanite enemies, but Jesus leads us to an eternal land He has promised to prepare for us. He makes us "more than conquerors" (Rom. 8:37; Heb. 4:8–9).
- Jesus is better than the Old Testament priests and sacrificial offerings. He is our great high priest and the perfect sacrificial lamb of God (vv. 14–16).
- Jesus is better than the Mosaic Covenant. He brought us the New Covenant based on grace and His work alone!

> Being made perfect, he became the author of eternal salvation unto all them that obey him. (5:9)

As we celebrate the birth of our Savior during this holiday season, let's glory in His righteousness and in His free gift of salvation. He came not to do away with the Old Testament rules and regulations but to fulfill every single one of them because we could not. Let's dig into His Word and look for Jesus—the better way—all throughout the book of Hebrews.

Because of the Cross

December 23

TODAY'S READING: Hebrews 6:1–10:18

Which hope we have as an anchor of the soul . . .
Hebrews 6:19

Perhaps you find yourself a bit distracted today by hectic holiday preparations. The book of Hebrews addresses the dangers of another kind of distraction: the works of law. The remedy it offers is to continually point our eyes to Jesus and His work.

Through Christ's work on the cross . . .

- God proved His love (1:3–6).
- He became sin for us (2:9).
- We are reconciled to God (10:14).
- Our sins are blotted out (9:28).
- We will never be separated from God (7:25).

By it we have received . . .

- God's grace (2:9)
- peace and forgiveness (10:17)
- new life (v. 20)
- access to God (4:16)
- an everlasting inheritance (9:15)
- a clean conscience and no condemnation (v. 14)
- a better way and abundant life (8:13; 10:4; 12:24)
- eternal life (2:3; 4:3; 5:9; 13:14)

I hope you'll take time today to sit at the foot of the cross and reflect on all Christ has done for you.

December 24
Faith in the Figures

TODAY'S READING: Hebrews 10:19–12:29

> Faith is the substance of things hoped for, the evidence of things not seen. *Hebrews 11:1*

How fitting that on Christmas Eve, as we celebrate Jesus, the cornerstone of our faith, we consider God's examples of true faith. Hebrews 11 details the faith of Old Testament heroes who were familiar with the promise of a coming savior and redeemer and whose lives pointed to and pictured Him. Just consider:

> By faith Abraham . . . offered up Isaac, and he who had received the promises was in the act of offering up his only son. . . . He considered that God was able even to raise him from the dead, from which, figuratively speaking, he did receive him back. (vv. 17, 19, ESV)

Oh, how I love these verses! Abraham was willing to offer his only son because he *knew* Isaac was a "type" of Christ. Incredible!

Joshua, the captain of the host of Israel, in faith led the children of the Lord into the Promised Land, just as Jesus, the captain of our salvation, leads us into our Promised Land of eternity.

Then there's the prostitute Rahab, who, in faith, hid the spies and let them escape by a scarlet cord draped down her window built right into the wall of Jericho. That scarlet cord pictured the way of escape by the scarlet blood of Jesus covering our sins.

Faith is believing that God's Word is true and acting in accordance with it. Today, let's follow in the footsteps of the faithful, knowing that our lives, too, can reflect Him and His sacrifice.

Merry Christmas

TODAY'S READING: 1 John 1–3; Hebrews 13

Now, little children, abide in him. *1 John 2:28*

Merry Christmas! Today we unwrap the gift of 1 John, which highlights the physical reality that is the person of Jesus Christ.

> That which was from the beginning, which we have heard, which we have seen with our eyes, which we have looked upon, and our hands have handled, concerning the Word of life—the life was manifested, and we have seen, and bear witness, and declare to you that eternal life which was with the Father and was manifested to us. (1:1–2, NKJV)

What a great way to celebrate Christmas Day, being encouraged in the physical manifestation of Jesus Christ, which was revealed that holy night back in Bethlehem.

This little book of 1 John centers on God's love and His forgiveness—the reasons Jesus came. Jesus's willingness to be born as the babe of Bethlehem made a way for you and me to be born again as the children of God.

> Truly our fellowship is with the Father, and with his Son Jesus Christ. And these things write we unto you, that your joy may be full. (vv. 3–4)

Our joy truly is full because of Jesus Christ. He gives eternal life (1:2; 2:25), He brought us into God's family (2:1–6), He gave us fellowship with Himself (1:3), He is our light (1:5), He is our "advocate with the Father" (2:1), and He is our forgiveness (2:12).

I hope and pray that today our Lord fills your heart and mind with His love. He loves you so much that He was born just to die for your sin.

Love, Sweet Love

TODAY'S READING: 1 John 4–5; 2 John 1; 3 John 1

We love him, because he first loved us. *1 John 4:19*

As a song from the mid-1960s declared, "What the world needs now is love, sweet love."[86] Well, here's some great news: "God is love" (1 John 4:8), and love has come. His name is Jesus!

> Herein is love, not that we loved God, but that he loved us, and sent his Son to be the propitiation for our sins. (v. 10)

From the time Adam and Eve sinned, God's plan of salvation was set in motion. Remember that marvelous first mention of the gospel back in Genesis 3:15. God loved humankind so much that as soon as Adam introduced sin into the world, God determined to save us. His one and only Son would bear the burden of sin so that all who believe would live eternally.

> This is the record, that God hath given to us eternal life, and this life is in his Son. He that hath the Son hath life; and he that hath not the Son of God hath not life. These things have I written unto you that believe on the name of the Son of God; that ye may know that ye have eternal life, and that ye may believe on the name of the Son of God. (1 John 5:11–13)

That name, the name of the Son of God, is Jesus. He is the Word that even now gives witness on your behalf in heaven (v. 7). Through the name of Jesus we have overcome because "greater is he that is in [us], than he that is in the world" (4:4). Because of His perfect love, we no longer need to be afraid (v. 18). And with this powerful, perfect love, He first loved you and me and draws us near in order to provide us eternity.

The world does indeed need love—and Jesus meets that need completely.

> Greater love hath no man than . . . that [he] lay down his life for his friends. (John 15:13)

A Revelation of Jesus

December 27

TODAY'S READING: Revelation 1–5

The Revelation of Jesus Christ . . . *Revelation 1:1*

The book of Revelation holds the potential to either captivate or intimidate, depending on your perspective. A glimpse of heaven can captivate, but insight into earth's future can intimidate. The promise of Christ's second coming can captivate, but the sheer volume of the varying Revelation interpretations can intimidate.

However, the point of this powerful prophetic book is not primarily about getting the skinny on future events. Revelation is about the same thing the rest of the Bible is about: Jesus Christ! So let's read Revelation looking not for our Lord but rather right at Him, for in this book we see Him as He is today—glorified! Plus, reading Revelation brings a promised blessing.

> Blessed is he that readeth, and they that hear the words of this prophecy, and keep those things which are written therein: for the time is at hand. (1:3)

The book of Revelation reveals the person of Jesus in chapter 1, His heart for the church in chapters 2–3, His home in heaven in chapters 4–5, His righteous judgment in chapters 6–19, and His eternal life for you and me in chapters 20–22. Fix your eyes on Jesus.

> Behold, he cometh with clouds; and every eye shall see him, and they also which pierced him: and all kindreds of the earth shall wail because of him. Even so, Amen. (1:7)

December 28

The Saints' Song

TODAY'S READING: Revelation 6–10

> Salvation to our God which sitteth upon the throne, and unto the Lamb. *Revelation 7:10*

As we anticipate the start of a new year, it's natural to reflect on the old and consider what's to come. So what could be a more fitting backdrop for the next few days than the book of Revelation?

As we read the chapters pertaining to God's righteous judgment, remember your previous condition apart from Jesus Christ. We were each in a state of rebellion toward God, and had it not been for the saving grace of Jesus, this is the punishment we all deserved. But Revelation also reminds us that the future is all about Jesus—His return, His judgment, His power, His redemption, and the place He has prepared for us in heaven. He has given us a sure future, an expected end, and a living hope.

The Christian life holds a magnificent dichotomy in that our everlasting beginning awaits at our earthly end. As Matthew Henry noted, "Such a glorious appearance will the faithful servants of God make at last, when they have fought the good fight of faith, and finished their course."[87]

> After this I beheld, and, lo, a great multitude, which no man could number, of all nations, and kindreds, and people, and tongues, stood before the throne . . . and cried with a loud voice, saying, Salvation to our God which sitteth upon the throne, and unto the Lamb. (7:9–10)

If Jesus is your Lord, if you are born again and sealed by His Spirit, then this is your glorious future. You will stand before the throne and sing with a loud voice, "Salvation to our God . . . and unto the Lamb."

Fight the good fight, dear saint. Finish your race well. Your glorious prize awaits!

Satan Silenced

TODAY'S READING: Revelation 11–14

They overcame him by the blood of the Lamb, and by the word of their testimony. *Revelation 12:11*

As believers, we are joint heirs with Christ, adopted into and made part of His family. But the Bible tells us that we have an accuser who stands before God day and night (Rev. 12:10). We saw this story played out on an individual level in Job 1 and Zechariah 3. Indeed, Satan is, as Revelation calls him, the "accuser of our brethren" (12:10).

But in verse 11 we are given a surefire means of silencing Satan. How? By the blood of the Lamb and the word of our testimonies! Through Christ's shed blood on the cross, He set us free from the power of sin and death. And Satan can't say a thing to change that truth.

The phrase "the word of their testimony" translated is "word," which is the same as the Greek term *logos.* We find *logos* used in John 1 to describe God becoming man in the form of the babe of Bethlehem.[88] The word *testimony* is from the Greek word *martyria,* which is, in its essence, a declaration of a witness who speaks with the authority of one who knows because he has seen.[89] Put together, we can plainly see that we overcome the "accuser of our brethren" by the blood of the Lamb and our witness to what Jesus, the Word made flesh, has done for you and me.

Dear Christian, it's so important to be aware that Satan is accusing you, just as he did Job and Joshua the high priest. But also know that you can—and do—overcome him by being bathed in the blood of the Lamb and by being a faithful witness to the wonder-working power of the great "I am."

December 30

The Righteous Judge

TODAY'S READING: Revelation 15–18

> They sing . . . the song of the Lamb, saying, Great and marvellous are thy works, Lord God Almighty; just and true are thy ways, thou King of saints. *Revelation 15:3*

What an awesome song! These words remind me of the energetic spiritual "When the Saints Go Marching In," but instead of being about the saints, it's about the King of saints!

> Who shall not fear thee, O Lord, and glorify thy name? for thou only art holy: for all nations shall come and worship before thee; for thy judgments are made manifest. (Rev. 15:4)

Many people have difficulty reconciling Jesus the good shepherd, meek and mild, with Jesus as the righteous judge demonstrating His holiness and justice. The core problem is a fundamental misunderstanding of what justice and righteousness and holiness actually are. Consider this: we don't condemn a judge when he or she sentences a guilty criminal. On the contrary, we're thankful and rejoice at justice being done. It brings peace and safety. From our perspective it's the right thing to do. So, too, as we read of the Lord's judgment on a Christ-rejecting, sinful world, we need to trust that when He judges the guilty and punishes wickedness, He is acting in righteousness and holiness.

> True and righteous are his judgments: for he hath judged the great whore, which did corrupt the earth with her fornication, and hath avenged the blood of his servants at her hand. (19:2)

Our hearts grieve at the wickedness in the world. We ache to witness so much pain and sorrow as a result of sin. But Jesus is the good and righteous judge of all the earth. His enemies will face their day of judgment. We, however, are clothed in His righteousness and adopted into His family. We are His children, loved by our Father and sealed by His Holy Spirit. We will stand in our Lord's presence not in judgment but as joint heirs with Christ, who paid our ransom price.

Come Quickly, Lord Jesus

December 31

TODAY'S READING: Revelation 19–22

Behold, I come quickly. *Revelation 22:12*

With today's reading we complete our journey through the whole of God's Word. Congratulations! I pray that as you took in God's Word, seeing Jesus day by day, a new understanding has taken root in your heart. I hope you now see for yourself that Jesus is the very essence of the Scriptures. The Old Testament points to Him, and the New Testament reveals Him. He was, from the beginning, woven throughout the lives and experiences of His saints, pictured in the sacrifices, and proclaimed through the prophecies that promised He would come to save His people.

And here in the book of Revelation, He promises to come again, to set all things right, and to reign eternally as the king of glory!

> God shall wipe away all tears from their eyes; and there shall be no more death, neither sorrow, nor crying, neither shall there be any more pain: for the former things are passed away. And he that sat upon the throne said, Behold, I make all things new. (21:4–5)

Through every Scripture passage we've witnessed how faithful our Father is to keep His promises. He is coming again, and we will see Him face to face. The Bible says that when we see Him, "we shall be like Him" (1 John 3:2, NKJV). The end we read of here in Revelation is just the beginning because we will live with Him eternally. So finish strong, dear Christian. Keep your eyes fixed squarely on Jesus. May He be your daily delight, the treasure you uncover as you continue to look for Him in His Word. And you can begin again tomorrow looking for our King in the beautiful book of beginnings as you read through the Bible yet again.

> He which testifieth these things saith, Surely I come quickly. Amen. Even so, come, Lord Jesus. The grace of our Lord Jesus Christ be with you all. Amen. (22:20–21)

Notes

1. *Strong's,* s.v. "'adam" (H120), Blue Letter Bible, www.blueletter bible.org/lang/lexicon/lexicon.cfm?t=kjv&strongs=h120.
2. M. G. Easton, *Easton's Bible Dictionary,* s.v. "Seth," www.eastons bibledictionary.org/3291-Seth.php.
3. *Strong's,* s.v. "'enowsh" (H582), Blue Letter Bible, www.blueletter bible.org/lang/Lexicon/lexicon.cfm?strongs=H582&t=KJV.
4. *Strong's,* s.v. "Qeynan" (H7018), Blue Letter Bible, www.blueletter bible.org/lang/Lexicon/Lexicon.cfm?strongs=H7018&t=KJV.
5. *Strong's,* s.v. "Mahalal'el" (H4111), Blue Letter Bible, www.blue letterbible.org/lang/Lexicon/Lexicon.cfm?strongs=H4111&t=KJV.
6. *Strong's,* s.v. "Yered" (H3381, H3382), Blue Letter Bible, www .blueletterbible.org/lang/Lexicon/Lexicon.cfm?strongs=H3382 &t=KJV.
7. *Strong's,* s.v. "chanak" (H2585, H2596), Blue Letter Bible, www .blueletterbible.org/lang/lexicon/lexicon.cfm?strongs=H2596 &t=KJV.
8. *Strong's,* s.v. "Měthuwshelach" (H4968), Blue Letter Bible, www .blueletterbible.org/lang/lexicon/lexicon.cfm?strongs=H4968. Methuselah, or Měthuwshelach, means "man of the dart." This name is derived from two root words. Transliterations of the first include *men, few, small, friends,* and *persons.* Transliterations of the second include *sword, weapon, sprout,* and *shoot.* For purposes of this reading, our emphasis is placed on the transliteration *men* and *friends.* However, here is an example of divine nuances as we see that Christ, who was pierced with a sword, was the offshoot of the stump of Jesse (Isa. 11:1), sprouted from the branch of David (Jer. 33:15), and is the one in whom we find our greatest weapon against sin and death: Jesus has equipped us with the sword of His Spirit, which is the Word of God.

9. *Strong's,* s.v. "Lemek" (H3929), Blue Letter Bible, www.blueletter bible.org/lang/lexicon/lexicon.cfm?strongs=H3929.
10. *Strong's,* s.v. "Noach" (H5146), Blue Letter Bible, www.blueletter bible.org/lang/lexicon/lexicon.cfm?Strongs=H5146&t=KJV.
11. Matthew Henry, "Commentary on Genesis 11," Blue Letter Bible, www.blueletterbible.org/Comm/mhc/Gen/Gen_011.cfm?a =11003.
12. Dr. Harold L. Willmington, *Willmington's Guide to the Bible* (Carol Stream, IL: Tyndale, 2011), 1146.
13. Edward Mote, "The Solid Rock," Indelible Grace Hymn Book, public domain, http://hymnbook.igracemusic.com/hymns/the -solid-rock.
14. C. I. Scofield, ed., *The Scofield Reference Bible,* rev. ed. (New York: Oxford University Press, 1945), 569.
15. Robert Jamieson, A. R. Fausset, and David Brown, "Job: Introduction," *Commentary Critical and Explanatory on the Whole Bible,* 1871, www.biblestudytools.com/commentaries/jamieson-fausset -brown/job/job-introduction.html.
16. Matthew Henry, "Commentary on Job 28," Blue Letter Bible, www.blueletterbible.org/Comm/mhc/Job/Job_028.cfm?a =464012.
17. David Guzik, "Study Guide for Job 42," Blue Letter Bible, www .blueletterbible.org/Comm/guzik_david/StudyGuide2017-Job/Job -42.cfm.
18. Robert Jamieson, A. R. Fausset, and David Brown, "Job 42:14," *A Commentary, Critical, Practical, and Explanatory on the Old and New Testaments,* 1882, Bible Hub, https://biblehub.com /commentaries/job/42-14.htm.
19. "Job 42:14," *Geneva Study Bible,* Bible Hub, https://biblehub.com /commentaries/job/42-14.htm.
20. "Job 42:14," *Geneva Study Bible.*
21. *Strong's,* s.v. "Shalem" (H8004), Blue Letter Bible, www.blueletter bible.org/lang/lexicon/lexicon.cfm?Strongs=H8004&t=KJV.
22. *Willmington's Guide to the Bible,* 1146.

23. *Jon Courson's Application Commentary: Old Testament,* vol. 1, *Genesis–Job* (Nashville: Thomas Nelson, 2005), 150.
24. *Willmington's Guide to the Bible,* 29.
25. *Willmington's Guide to the Bible,* 29.
26. *Strong's,* s.v. "Beyth-'El" (H1008), Blue Letter Bible, www.blue letterbible.org/lang/lexicon/lexicon.cfm?strongs=H1008.
27. *Willmington's Guide to the Bible,* 1144.
28. *Strong's,* s.v. "Shĕkem" (H7927), Blue Letter Bible, www.blue letterbible.org/lang/lexicon/lexicon.cfm?Strongs=H7927&t=KJV.
29. Billy Apostolon, *Homiletic Outlines* (Grand Rapids, MI: Baker, 1959), 47.
30. *Willmington's Guide to the Bible,* 45–46.
31. Abraham Alexandre Weill, "The Wonderful Vitality of the Jewish Race," in *Physical Culture,* ed. Bernarr MacFadden, vol. 10 (New York: Physical Culture Publishing, 1903), 416.
32. *Strong's,* s.v. "mow`ed." (H4150), Blue Letter Bible, www.blue letterbible.org/lang/lexicon/lexicon.cfm?Strongs=H4150&t=KJV.
33. Kevin Howard and Marvin J. Rosenthal, *The Feasts of the Lord* (Nashville: Thomas Nelson, 1997), 12–23.
34. Walter L. Wilson, *A Dictionary of Bible Types* (Peabody, MA: Hendrickson, 1999), 300–301.
35. Wilson, *Dictionary of Bible Types,* 257.
36. Wilson, *Dictionary of Bible Types,* 346–47.
37. *Strong's,* s.v. "Yĕhowshuwa`" (H3091), Blue Letter Bible, www .blueletterbible.org/lang/lexicon/lexicon.cfm?strongs=H3091.
38. Matthew Henry, "Commentary on Deuteronomy 21," Blue Letter Bible, www.blueletterbible.org/Comm/mhc/Deu/Deu_021.cfm ?a=174023.
39. *Scofield Reference Bible,* 259.
40. *Strong's,* s.v. "Yĕhowshuwa`."
41. The events recorded in Judges 17 "took place before the time of Israel's first judge, Othniel. Evidence for placing these events at an earlier time of the judges comes in verse 18:1, which says the tribe of

Dan had not yet received its inheritance—its land. Judges 1:1–3:6 records the Israelites' struggle to take possession of the promised land from the Canaanites. Thus, the story in Judges 17:1–18:31 fits in with this time period." *The One Year Chronological Bible: New International Version* (Carol Stream, IL: Tyndale, 1995), annotation in April 1 reading, 357.

42. A. B. Simpson, *The Christ in the Bible Commentary,* vol. 2 (Camp Hill, PA: Christian Publications, 1992), 161.
43. *Strong's,* s.v. "`Othniy'el" (H6274), Blue Letter Bible, www.blueletterbible.org/lang/lexicon/lexicon.cfm?strongs=H6274.
44. "Samson's adulthood, late in the period of the Judges, may have overlapped with Samuel's youth." *One Year Chronological Bible,* annotation in April 9 reading, 390.
45. *Scofield Reference Bible,* 608n3.
46. Simpson, *Christ in the Bible Commentary,* 281.
47. *Strong's,* s.v. "Yĕhuwdah" (H3063), Blue Letter Bible, www.blueletterbible.org/lang/lexicon/lexicon.cfm?strongs=H3063.
48. *Strong's,* s.v. "Shim`own" (H8095), Blue Letter Bible, www.blueletterbible.org/lang/lexicon/lexicon.cfm?strongs=H8095.
49. *Strong's,* s.v. "Binyamiyn" (H1144), Blue Letter Bible, www.blueletterbible.org/lang/lexicon/lexicon.cfm?strongs=H1144.
50. *Strong's,* s.v. "Mĕnashsheh" (H4519), Blue Letter Bible, www.blueletterbible.org/lang/lexicon/lexicon.cfm?strongs=H4519.
51. *Strong's,* s.v. "charizomai" (G5483), Blue Letter Bible, www.blueletterbible.org/lang/lexicon/lexicon.cfm?Strongs=G5483&t=KJV.
52. *Willmington's Guide to the Bible,* 1206.
53. C. H. Spurgeon, "The Incomparable Bridegroom and His Bride," Blue Letter Bible, www.blueletterbible.org/Comm/spurgeon_charles/sermons/2469.cfm.
54. "Solomon's Temple and Solomon's Mines," Creation Concepts, www.creationconcepts.org/resources/SOLOMON.pdf.
55. Matthew Henry, "Commentary on John 1," Blue Letter Bible, www.blueletterbible.org/Comm/mhc/Jhn/Jhn_001.cfm?a=998001.

56. Charles Spurgeon, *Lectures to My Students* (Grand Rapids, MI: Baker, 1975), 49, quoted in Sidney Greidanus, "How to Preach Christ from Ecclesiastes," *The Southern Baptist Journal of Theology* 15, no. 3 (Fall 2011): 56–61.
57. Paul R. Van Gorder, "Christ in Ecclesiastes," *The Old Testament Presents . . . Reflections of Christ* (Grand Rapids, MI: RBC Ministries, 1982), www.thebookwurm.com/ref-ecc.htm.
58. *Merriam-Webster,* s.v. "loyal," www.merriam-webster.com/dictionary/loyal.
59. James Orr, ed., "Isaiah, 1–7," *International Standard Bible Encyclopedia,* 1915, www.biblestudytools.com/dictionary/isaiah-1-7/.
60. *Strong's,* s.v. "Beyth Lechem" (H1035), Blue Letter Bible, www.blueletterbible.org/lang/Lexicon/Lexicon.cfm?strongs=H1035&t=KJV.
61. David Guzik, "Study Guide for Micah 5," Blue Letter Bible, www.blueletterbible.org/Comm/guzik_david/StudyGuide2017-Mic/Mic-5.cfm.
62. *Random House Unabridged Dictionary,* s.v. "revival," www.dictionary.com/browse/revival.
63. *English Oxford Living Dictionaries,* s.v. "lamentation," https://en.oxforddictionaries.com/definition/lamentation.
64. *Jon Courson's Application Commentary: Old Testament,* vol. 2, *Psalms–Malachi* (Nashville: Thomas Nelson, 2006), 680.
65. Randall Price, *Rose Guide to the Temple* (Torrance, CA: Rose Publishing, 2012), 135; "The Eastern Entrance to Herod's Temple," Bible History Online, www.bible-history.com/jewishtemple/JEWISH_TEMPLEThe_Golden_Gate.htm.
66. Matthew Henry, "Commentary on Ezra 3," Blue Letter Bible, www.blueletterbible.org/Comm/mhc/Ezr/Ezr_003.cfm?a=406012.
67. *Willmington's Guide to the Bible,* 197.
68. *Strong's,* s.v. "'Ezra'" (H5831), Blue Letter Bible, www.blueletterbible.org/lang/lexicon/lexicon.cfm?strongs=H5831.

69. *Jon Courson's Application Commentary: Old Testament,* vol. 1, *Genesis–Job,* 1242.
70. "Facts About the Bible," King James Bible Dictionary, http://king jamesbibledictionary.com/biblefacts.
71. David Guzik, "Study Guide for Matthew 1," Blue Letter Bible, www.blueletterbible.org/Comm/guzik_david/StudyGuide2017 -Mat/Mat-1.cfm.
72. Apostolon, *Homiletic Outlines,* 37.
73. Matthew Henry, "Commentary on Matthew 17," Blue Letter Bible, www.blueletterbible.org/Comm/mhc/Mat/Mat_017.cfm?a=946024.
74. Howard and Rosenthal, *Feasts of the Lord,* 50–51.
75. *Willmington's Guide to the Bible,* 266.
76. *Willmington's Guide to the Bible,* 266.
77. *Willmington's Guide to the Bible,* 509.
78. Matthew Henry, "Commentary on Luke 24," Blue Letter Bible, www.blueletterbible.org/Comm/mhc/luk/luk_024.cfm.
79. David Alexander and Pat Alexander, eds., *Eerdmans' Handbook to the Bible* (Grand Rapids, MI: Eerdmans, 1973), 631.
80. *Willmington's Guide to the Bible,* 390.
81. Henry H. Halley, *Halley's Bible Handbook: An Abbreviated Bible Commentary* (Grand Rapids, MI: Zondervan, 1965), 657.
82. J. A. Morrison, *Martin Luther: The Great Reformer,* rev. Michael J. McHugh (Arlington Heights, IL: Christian Liberty, 1994), 102.
83. *Strong's,* s.v. "endyō" (G1746), Blue Letter Bible, www.blueletter bible.org/lang/lexicon/lexicon.cfm?Strongs=G1746&t=KJV.
84. *Strong's,* s.v. "lytroō" (G3084), Blue Letter Bible, www.blueletter bible.org/lang/lexicon/lexicon.cfm?Strongs=G3084&t=KJV.
85. Elvina M. Hall, "Jesus Paid It All," Hymnary.org, 1865, public domain, https://hymnary.org/text/i_hear_the_savior_say_thy _strength_indee.
86. Jackie DeShannon, "What the World Needs Now Is Love," by Hal David and Burt Bacharach, *This Is Jackie DeShannon,* copyright © 1965, Imperial Records.

87. *Matthew Henry Study Bible: Revised King James Edition* (Dordrecht, Netherlands: Importantia, 2010), 1857.
88. *Strong's,* s.v. "logos" (G3056), Blue Letter Bible, www.blueletterbible.org/lang/lexicon/lexicon.cfm?Strongs=G3056&t=KJV.
89. *Strong's,* s.v. "martyria" (G3141), Blue Letter Bible, www.blueletterbible.org/lang/lexicon/lexicon.cfm?Strongs=G3141&t=KJV.